HISTORY OF THE LABOR MOVEMENT

IN THE UNITED STATES

VOLUME VI

HISTORY OF
THE LABOR MOVEMENT
IN THE UNITED STATES

VOLUME VI: On the Eve of America's
Entrance into World War I, 1915-1916

BY PHILIP S. FONER

INTERNATIONAL PUBLISHERS, New York

Errata

Dr. John A. DeBrizzi is co-author of
Chapter 4, "The Standard Oil Strike
in Bayonne, New Jersey, 1915-1916."
His name was inadvertently omitted
from the Table of Contents

The authors acknowledge with
thanks the information furnished
by Mr. Francis J. Katusa and by
Dr. Walter F. Robinson.

Copyright © 1982 by International Publishers

This printing, 2010

Library of Congress Cataloging in Publication Data *(Revised)*

Foner, Philip Sheldon, 1910-
  History of the labor movement in the United States.

  Includes bibliographical references.
  CONTENTS: [v. 1] From colonial times to the founding
of the American federation of labor.—v. 2. From the
founding of the American federation of labor to the
emergence of American imperialism.—[etc.]—v. 6. On the
eve of America's entrance into World War I.
  1. Trade-unions—United States—History. 2. Labor
and laboring classes—United States—History. 3. Industrial relations—United States—History.
HD6508.F57   331.88'0973   47-19381
ISBN 0-7178-0602-2 (v. 6)
ISBN 0-7178-0595-6 (pbk. : v. 6)

Manufactured in the United States of America

CONTENTS

HISTORY OF THE LABOR MOVEMENT

IN THE UNITED STATES

VOLUME VI

PREFACE

In the fifth volume of my multivolume *History of the Labor Movement in the United States: The AFL in the Progressive Era, 1910-1915*, I traced the story of American labor's economic and political activities in one of the most crucial eras in its development. The present volume brings the story to the eve of America's entrance into World War I. In the next (or seventh) volume, I will carry the story to the declaration of war by the United States against Germany and the other Central Powers in April, 1917. In the process I will trace the position of the labor and Socialist movements toward U.S. imperialism from the turn of the twentieth century, and toward the events between the outbreak of World War I in August, 1914 and America's entrance almost three years later.

The present volume covers a shorter time span than the previous ones. This has been necessary because most of the movements and labor struggles discussed here have been totally ignored or casually treated in the fourth volume of the Commons-Wisconsin *History of Labor the United States* (1896-1932) by Selig Perlman and Philip Taft. As in the previous volumes, the focus in the present work is on organized movements and resistance, on workers who belonged to or sought to belong to trade unions, and on those who, as in the case of Blacks and women, had to wage a persistent (and often futile) struggle to convince the racist, sexist, and craft-oriented labor leaders that there was a place in the American labor movement for all workers, regardless of skill, race, color, sex, or national origin.

A number of American scholars still cling to the view that unless a work on American labor emphasizes exclusively the new trend in labor historiography associated with the approach of E.P. Thompson in England and Herbert Gutman and David Montgomery in the United States, it is merely a continuation of the Commons-Wisconsin School. A work, in their opinion, to merit the label of "labor history" must focus on community, family, social relations, and cultural traditions. Should it deal with the development of working-class institutions and conflicts.

mainly trade unions and strikes (as does the present volume), it is dismissed as traditional labor history.

All who are interested in the history of the American working class must welcome the valuable information and insights of recent community and industrial studies of the American working class associated with the "new" labor history while, at the same time, regretting the absence of any integrated analysis by the separate studies. But to assume that this is the only significant aspect of our working class history, and that any effort to deal with the development of working class institutions and struggles, through trade unions, strikes, and political action, is no longer relevant—smacks both of ignorance and elitism. In moving beyond what they call "the traditional confines of labor history," not a few of the "new" labor historians have left the working class without any outlets through which they can voice their discontent and change their conditions.

As in the case of the previous volumes, this work could not have been completed without the generous assistance of numerous libraries and historical societies. I am again indebted to the American Federation of Labor, particularly the late Florence Thorne, for permission to use the incoming correspondence of the Federation and the Letter Books of Samuel Gompers. I wish again to thank Dorothy Swanson and her staff at the Tamiment Institute, Elmer Bobst Library, New York University, for kind assistance and cooperation; and the staffs of the Chicago Historical Society, Library of Congress, National Archives, State Historical Society of Wisconsin, Amalgamated Clothing Workers Union, Arthur and Elizabeth Schlesinger Library on the History of Women in America, Radcliffe College; Library of the U.S. Department of Labor, New York State Library, New York Public Library, Free Library of Philadelphia, Bayonne Municipal Library, Bayonne, New Jersey; Youngstown Public Library, Youngstown, Ohio; and the libraries of Columbia University, University of Arizona, University of Pennsylvania, University of Nebraska, University of Pittsburgh, Rutgers University, University of Maryland, Georgetown University, University of Washington, Brown University, Catholic University of America, University of Florida, University of Chicago, and University of Rochester. I also wish to thank the members of the library staff of the Langston Hughes Memorial Library, Lincoln University, Pennsylvania for cooperation and assistance in obtaining materials through interlibrary loan from libraries, historical societies, and other institutions.

PHILIP S. FONER

CHAPTER 1

Henry Ford's Five-Dollar Eight-Hour Day

In the "Age of Industrial Violence," which preceded America's entrance into World War I, during which years labor had to battle endlessly and militantly for every gain in shorter hours, higher wages, and better working conditions, Henry Ford inaugurated a grand experiment in welfare capitalism: on January 5, 1914, he instituted a five-dollar daily wage and the eight-hour day.[1]

WHY THE FIVE-DOLLAR EIGHT-HOUR DAY?

Scholars have long debated over what factors were responsible for these unprecedented industrial innovations—whether humanitarian or fiscal considerations predominated. We need not concern ourselves over deciding whether Ford was self-serving and hypocritical or self-serving and honestly interested in progressive reform. (It is likely that both elements were present.) What we should note is that certain basic factors compelled Henry Ford's voluntary establishment of the five-dollar eight-hour day.

It is certainly no accident that the voluntary adoption of these two major policies occurred shortly after Ford instituted a moving belt assembly line. The new methods and techniques of production, developed from 1910 to 1914, drastically altered the skills necessary for factory operations. Consequently, with the expansion in plant facilities to meet the growing demand for the Model T Ford, thousands of unskilled Southern and Eastern European immigrants swarmed into the Highland Park factory. "By 1914," Stephen Meyer points out, "the Ford Motor Company employed 12,880 workers, and the overwhelming majority (9,109) were foreign-born. The five largest nationality

groups—Poles, Russians, Romanians, Italians and Sicilians, and Aus-
tro-Hungarians—constituted a majority of the workforce and came
from the least industrialized area of Europe."[2]

The second factor to bear in mind is that Ford's Highland Park plant
experienced tremendous problems which interfered with establishing a
stable force between 1910 and 1913. In 1913, Ford hired over 52,000 men
to maintain a complement of 14,000 workers. Six times as many
employees quit as were fired. Absenteeism ran as high as ten percent
daily.[3]

Ford himself offered several explanations for the labor liberalization
of 1914. His most direct linking of such policies with the labor crisis
confronting the company occurred in a statement recalled by Joseph
Galamb, an official in the experimental toolroom. "Mr. Ford," Galamb
reported, "said he would lick the IWW by paying the men the five-dollar
day."[4] The eight-hour day was even more pointedly designed to disarm
the Industrial Workers of the World (IWW) which had led a brief,
unsuccessful strike of 5,000 Studebaker workers seeking eight hours and
had won the shorter day at three Detroit metal wheel factories during the
previous year. Although Melvyn Dubofsky minimizes the Wobbly role
in Detroit in his history of the IWW, and although Allan Nevins'
uncritical biography of Ford finds the connection between fear of the
IWW and the 1914 policies "not supported by real evidence," there can
be little doubt that the IWW, or more exactly, the employers' fear of the
IWW, helped to shape Ford's labor policy.[5] The Wobblies propagan-
dized widely at Ford's factory gates, demanding eight hours and causing
Ford officials to revoke the employees' privilege of eating outside plant
gates in order to insulate them from IWW agitators who were rumored
to be readying a strike at Ford. While the IWW had probably not
organized more than a thirtieth of Detroit's 60,000 auto workers, it had
shown, at Studebaker, a capacity for influencing those who were not
members.[6] Moreover, IWW doctrines of sabotage and slowdowns
spread fear among auto factory owners and the industrially-organized
AFL Carriage, Wagon and Automobile Workers' Union as well as AFL
craft unions were organizing the plants with some success. The employers, who favored Detroit as the location for the auto industry in large part
because of its status as an open shop town, could, as one scholar has
recently put it, "not assume that their antagonists were as weak as they
proved to be." For that reason, Ford's "lick the IWW" stance embodied
also in his statement to a Detroit periodical that there "will be no more
excitement in Detroit's labor circles," following his 1914 innovations,
deserves to be considered a serious motivation for his actions.[7]

In a second and more general explanation of his rationale for instituting the eight-hour day, Ford declared, "We have settled on the eight-hour day, not because eight hours is one third of a day but because it so happens that this is the length of time which we find gives the best service from men, day in and day out."[8] One can argue that there was no solid evidence on which to base such a conclusion, but there certainly is no doubt that in inaugurating three shifts, with only one ten-minute lunch break on each shift, Ford secured optimum use from his machinery. "As a part of low-cost production . . . ," he noted, "one must have big investment machinery and power plants. Expensive tools cannot remain idle. They ought to work 24 hours a day."[9]

Ford and his advisors also believed that efficiency would be served by the eight-hour, five-dollar day in that the new labor policy decreased turnover and absenteeism and increased labor discipline. The distance of the Highland Park plant, an early suburban factory, from working class urban enclaves, helps to account in part for the high turnover and absences. Reducing the length of the working day could partially compensate for this long commute.[10]

More fundamentally, the high absenteeism reflected alienation engendered by a rapid rationalization of production. In 1903, at the Mack Avenue factory, according to Ford, workmen fetched parts and material to one central location and built a car "exactly the same way one builds a house." By 1907, at the Piquette Plant, 45 cars sat in a circle and specialized workers (or work groups) walked from one to the next performing a limited task. That same year, time and motion studies began at Ford and foremen received orders to enforce standards of production based on calculations of engineers armed with stop watches. "If the first man does not come up to that standard," Production Supervisor Max Wollering wrote, "try another. That was Henry's scheme of things."[11]

"SPEED-UP KING"

The tendency toward rationalizing labor and toward calculating production by the minute and second accelerated with the building of the Highland Park plant in 1910. Henry Ford mechanized material delivery systems in the foundry in 1912, and began to produce flywheel magnetos on a moving assembly line in April, 1913. The magneto assembly, formerly done in about 20 minutes by a single skilled mechanic working at a bench, broke down into 29 separate tasks performed by 29 men at the chain-driven pace of 13 minutes 10 seconds per person per assembly.

Within a year, the line had just 14 workers, producing a magneto in just five minutes per person. Efficiency experts juggled the line's speed to give "every second necessary but not a single unnecessary second" to the assemblers.[12] In the fall of 1913, Ford men also pondered how to put assembly functions on a moving line. They knew, in September of that year, that stationary assembly required 12 hours 28 minutes of labor time under ideal conditions. Within six months, that standard was cut to 1 hour and 33 minutes on a moving line. Such dramatic productive advances, calculated to the second, undoubtedly predisposed Ford to reduce hours voluntarily from ten to nine in 1912 and then to eight in 1914.[13]

Ford engineers completely revolutionized automobile making, but their changes also produced serious social consequences. Technology eliminated the multiskilled, relatively autonomous craftsman and replaced him with a de-skilled specialist who performed only one task all day long. In the absence of material incentives of wages and hours, the rationalization of production necessarily brought with it astronomical turnover rates. Immigrant workers referred to the Highland Park plant as the "Home of Corrections" in 1913, and the IWW branded Ford the "Speed-Up King."[14] Upton Sinclair, whose *The Flivver King* is a keen analysis of the manufacture of automobiles at Ford, traced the career of Ford worker Abner Shutt. Sinclair observed that 1914 was

> a far cry from the days when Abner Shutt had travelled to the shed and rolled in two wheels by hand, and sorted out the right spindle-nuts from lofts and screwed them himself. Now he oversaw a group of men whose every motion had been calculated by engineers. The completed wheels, products of an assembly line of their own, came on rows of hooks, and descended to exactly that right height to be lifted off and slid onto the axle. The man who did this did nothing else; another man put on the spindle-nuts and started them by hand; still another finished the job with a wrench.[15]

Liberal policies could insure a work force willing to put up with a speeded-up assembly line and disciplined labor. As Stephen Meyer observes, "the Five Dollar Day . . . was an ingenious profit-sharing scheme to induce Ford workers to alter their attitudes and habits to meet the rigorous requirements of mass production. Under the Ford Profit Sharing Plan, the company divided an unskilled worker's income into two approximately equal parts—his wages and his profits. Each worker received his wages for work done in the factory. But he received his profits, and hence, the Five Dollar Day, only when he met specific standards of productive efficiency and specific standards and conditions of domestic life. The 'work standard' for a particular job and the pace of the assembly line determined the standard of efficiency."[16]

In his book, which is an expansion of this article, Meyer notes that when the Ford Motor Company introduced its Five Dollar profit-sharing plan in 1914, it became "the most famous labor-management reform in the annals of American business." (Stephen Meyer III, *The Five Dollar Day: Labor Management and Social Control in the Ford Motor Company, 1908-1921* [Albany, N.Y., 1981], p. 108.)

Actually, failure to keep up with the "work standard" meant loss of a job and not only loss of the "profits" in the wages. During the first week of the application of the 1914 reform, 1000 workers, mostly Greeks and Serbs, were fired for taking off on a Greek Orthodox religious holiday.* Working at Ford was to be a privilege; conditions of wages and hours, however beneficent, were "a matter for management," a gift and not a right. Dissident employees knew, as the engineers Horace Arnold and Fay Faurote put it in their 1914 study, that "the door to the street is open for any who objects in any way . . . to . . . unquestioning obedience to any directions whatever."[17]

Such division of labor also entailed a division between mental and physical work, or, more precisely, an abandonment of mental work to management. Ford, although he sometimes held that, "the average worker . . . above all . . . wants a job in which he does not have to think," saw repetitive and purely physical work as "terrifying" and tried to compensate for it by encouraging an intellectual life for workers—but only outside the shop. "Man needs leisure to think," he wrote, "and the world needs thinkers," as he experimented with a variety of night and technical schools.[18]

FORD SOCIOLOGICAL DEPARTMENT

The 1914 reforms, as Ford's educational activities suggest, not only compensated for alienated labor, but also sought to develop through leisure a more efficient work force. Italian Communist philosopher Antonio Gramsci, whose commentary on "America and Fordism," is still an indispensable source on Ford, defined Ford's goal as the creation of "a new type of worker and of man," thoroughly Americanized by night classes and utterly committed to morality and family; a worker,

*As justification for these dismissals, which amounted to six percent of the Ford work-force, a Ford official declared that "if these men are to make their home in America they should observe American holidays." (Stephen Meyer, "Adapting the Immigrant to the Line: Americanization in the Ford Factory, 1914-1921," *Journal of Social History* 14 [1980]: 74.)

moreover, who would never need to join a trade union.[19] This effort constituted another rationale on Ford's part for the shorter day and higher wages. Leisure, Ford insisted, would be used by the worker "for the greater happiness of his family," and this orientation toward family, whether voluntary or enforced by the 100 "investigators" of Ford's Sociological Department, was to insure "proper living" among employees. The five-dollar wage was designed as a "family wage" which would function by "not only supplying [the worker's] basic need, but also in giving him a margin of comfort and enabling him to give his boys and girls their opportunity and his wife some pleasure in life."[20] Ford refused to hire married women whose husbands had jobs and discouraged the taking-in of boarders. Profit-sharing, a large part of the five-dollar wage, did not extend to young males without dependents, family men living alone, or men in the process of divorcing.

Functionaries in the Sociological Department, formed immediately after the labor reforms to see that money and time were wisely spent, checked to see whether men were "living unworthily" by drinking excessively, smoking tobacco or defaulting on family obligations.[21] The result, according to Ford, should be that a man "has more leisure to spend with his family. The family life is healthier. Workmen go out of doors, go on picnics, have time to see their children and play with them." For Ford, increased leisure was impossible without supervision, prohibition and a buttressing of family life. With these, it could be a part of the process, to use Ford's mechanical metaphor, of "repairing men like boilers" or, to use Gramsci's language, "to maintain the continuity of physical and muscular nervous energy of the worker."[22]

Efficiency, then, meant both the creation of a stable, disciplined labor force on the job and the reproduction of that work force through family life. Public and private—fiscal and humanitarian—considerations were inseparable. Indeed, John B. Lee, Ford personnel manager and first head of the Sociological Department, recalled that it was not until 1912 that management "began to realize something of the relative value of men," and that it did so after an investigation into declining production in a drop hammer operation revealed that "sickness, indebtedness, and fear and worry over things entirely related to the home had crept in and put a satisfactory human unit entirely out of harmony with the things . . . necessary for production." The company's first response in that case— cutting hours from ten to nine and raising wages fifteen percent and interpreting the problem as one of family life—set the precedents for 1914.[23]

Although it is difficult to judge how much family life, temperance, and education were really benefited by Ford's labor reforms, productive efficiency was served. Labor turnover dropped by ninety percent and absenteeism was at least halved and, according to some figures, plummeted from 10 percent to .3 percent per day. During the first week of the 1914 reforms, 14,000 job-seekers descended on the Highland Park factory in search of now-desirable employment. In departments where no technological or operations changes occurred, eight-hour productivity easily exceeded that formerly accomplished in nine. Ford could report that the five-dollar eight-hour day was "one of the finest cost-cutting moves ever made."[24]

It is significant that Ford was achieving success with his system of "scientific management" precisely when the theories of Frederick W. Taylor, the father of "scientific management," were having less impact. According to Daniel Nelson's definitive work, *Frederick W. Taylor and the Rise of Scientific Management,* Taylor's time and motion studies, and piece work, wage and bonus systems, met with only limited success at the time Ford was achieving great results. Labor rebelled against the "speed-up," and management wanted to avoid trouble. While Taylor was a genius with machines, he lacked any understanding of how to appeal to working people.[25] Ford's five-dollar eight-hour day did appeal.

HOW REPRESENTATIVE WAS HENRY FORD?

Despite its obvious advantages profit-wise, Ford's labor reforms did not spark a broad imitative trend among American industrialists on the eve of the U.S. entrance into World War I. Even in Detroit, where other auto makers faced problems like Ford's, the 1914 reforms met with opposition rather than enthusiasm. As the Socialist Party of Michigan expressed its appreciation in a pamphlet, some among Ford's fellow auto makers branded him a "traitor to his class." Hugh Chalmers, a leading auto entrepreneur, called Ford's step "radical," and chided him for not consulting industry leaders. Only one auto-related company, Timken Axle in Akron, followed the Ford formula of shorter hours and higher wages.[26]

General business reaction was also negative. The *Wall Street Journal* criticized the new policies as an "economic crime" and an intrusion of "Biblical principles . . . where they do not belong." The *New York Times,* then (as now) an excellent barometer of corporate opinion, branded Ford's actions as "distinctly Utopian and against all experience," and sent a reporter to ask Ford if he were a socialist. Pittsburgh's

Industrial World saw the action as part of Ford's "madness for publicity," and the Detroit press predicted that it would spark an epidemic of strikes.[27]*

Actually, an "epidemic of strikes" did occur in the years immediately following the introduction of Henry Ford's five-dollar, eight-hour day. By 1916 the country was gripped by the largest strike wave it had yet experienced. Many were for higher wages as workers sought to catch up with the rising cost of living, and more than 600 strikes for the eight-hour day began on May 1, 1916. Whatever the cause, the number of strikes in 1916 doubled over that of the previous year, which itself was a year marked by many strikes.

Not only were these strikes of unprecedented size but a sharp upsurge of interest in workers' control was manifested in these struggles. Underlying this development was a collection of grievances affecting both the skilled and unskilled. The introduction of a series of managerial rationalizations, including incentive pay programs; the institution of engineering departments, specialized machinery, new methods of cost accounting, time clocks and assembly lines (in short, what was commonly referred to as "Taylorism") undermined the traditional control over production that skilled workers had held by virtue of their knowledge and expertise. Among the largely immigrant unskilled workers, speedups, unemployment, long hours, and low wages drew militant protest. As David Montgomery put it, "the new industrial discipline had promoted a sense of raw injustice among, as well as within, the... ethnic communities."[28]

---

*According to Upton Sinclair, praise for Ford came mainly from "labor and the social uplifters." (*The Flivver King*, New York, 1928, p. 123.) However John R. Commons, the progressive labor historian, called Ford's labor program "just old fashioned industrial autocracy tempered by faith in human nature." ("Henry Ford: Miracle Maker," *Independent* 102 (May, 1920): 161.)

In 1934 Mike Gold, Communist writer, recalled that many progressives believed at one time that Henry Ford's "program of 'high wages and shorter hours,' combined with the most ingenious technique of mass production would abolish poverty and unemployment forever." It was all "a great myth," Gold noted, and "it blew up with a great bang and a nauseating smell during the depression." The Ford Hunger March of March 7, 1932, or the "Ford Hunger Massacre," as it came to be known after four of the unemployed marchers were killed and two dozen wounded by Dearborn police and Ford's service men, "ended all this liberal talk about Henry's benevolence forever." ("Henry Ford's Inferno," in *The Mike Gold Reader*, New York, 1934, pp. 91-92.) For a discussion of the "Ford Hunger Massacre," *see* Alex Baskin, "The Ford Hunger March—1932," *Labor History* 13 (Summer, 1972): 331-60, and Maurice Sugar, *The Ford Hunger March*, Berkeley, Cal., 1980.

CHAPTER 2

An Unusual Strike in the Arizona Copper Mines

On January 22, 1916, the *New Republic* issued an appeal for support of five thousand copper miners on strike in Arizona. In its appeal, the liberal weekly noted: "An entire mining community in eastern Arizona has been on strike for nearly four months. Rather than submit to the terms of employment imposed by three large mining corporations, five thousand copper miners, their wives and children, are enduring deprivation and hunger." A special reason supporting the plea for aid was also noted: "Though the people are in dire need, many of them actually starving, and though more than two-thirds are Mexicans, there has been no disorder. Not a single arrest has been made for violence. The mining towns of Greenlee County have never been more peaceful."[1]

Although *The Outlook* did not share the *New Republic's* viewpoint on most issues, it did endorse the appeal. The journal noted in amazement that "for more than nineteen weeks a strike of copper miners has taken place in Arizona but virtually without violence."[2]

GRIEVANCES OF MEXICAN-AMERICAN COPPER MINERS

In our previous volume, we described the long, bitter, and, in the end, defeated strike led by the Western Federation of Miners in 1913 in the Northern Michigan copper mines operated by the giant Calumet & Hecla corporation.* But two years later there was another strike in the towns of Clifton, Morenci, and Metcalf of Eastern Arizona, in the copper mines operated by the Arizona Copper Company, the Shannon

*See Philip S. Foner, *History of the Labor Movement in the United States*, vol. V, New York, 1980, pp. 196–213.

Copper Company, and the Detroit Copper Company. The three companies employed about five thousand miners, over two-thirds of whom were Mexicans. Of the three, the most important was the Detroit Copper Company, owned by the giant Phelps Dodge & Company, a leading Wall Street corporation.[3]

Regardless of whether they were Mexican nationals who had recently arrived in the Arizona mining camps or Mexicans who had resided in the area a considerable number of years, the Mexican miners were paid "the same 'Mexican wage,' assigned menial tasks with little promise of upward mobility and treated in a distinct manner in comparison with their Anglo counterparts."[4] For a double standard of wages prevailed throughout the Southwest mining districts—a higher wage for Anglos and a lower wage for Mexicans, even though both did precisely the same work.[5] Moreover, Mexicans were paid by a system of "half-pay, half goods" under which a greater part of their wages went for goods at the company store. This resulted in a profit of one hundred to three hundred percent for the mine operators.[5]

Until 1915 the Western Federation of Miners did little to change this situation. On the contrary, the Federation contented itself with referring to Mexicans as either cheap labor and thus a constant threat to union wage standards, or as natural strikebreakers. In either case they were not suitable for membership in the Western Federation of Miners (WFM). Hence the WFM concentrated on unionizing the American Anglo workers employed in the copper mines.

However, so long as the Mexicans were excluded from the union, little real progress could be made. The mine operators simply recruited Mexicans to replace U.S. miners who were sympathetic to the Federation. At the same time the operators extolled the Mexican worker as being "obedient and cheap. . . . His strongest point is his willingness to work for low wages." To be sure, he was also described as being "childlike," "unambitious," "listless," "physically weak," "irregular and indolent." But when the Mexican workers sought to change their conditions and presented grievances to the mine operators, they were discharged and banished from the district. In justification, the *Engineering and Mining Journal* argued that Mexicans possessed "primitive instincts," and were "dangerous when aroused. . . ."[6]

In 1915 George Powell, an organizer for the Western Federation of Miners, broke with the traditional pattern of the union toward Mexican miners and launched an organizing drive in the copper mines of Eastern Arizona, where for years the Mexican miners had been working for a lower wage than was being paid in the other mining sections of the state. Powell pointed out that "in Miami, one of the nearest camps to Clifton,

Morenci, and Metcalf, where the Mexican workers are in the majority, the American miners have a minimum of $3.50 a day underground when copper is selling at 13 cents or less. But in Clifton, Metcalf, and Morenci, the men are working for as low a scale as $1.62 a day even though copper is selling at 18 cents."

But wages was only one of the grievances of the Mexican miners, Powell explained. Others were "the selling of jobs to the Mexican miners, the refusal on the part of the managers to meet committees or to listen to any grievances, raffling off worthless or nearly worthless articles by petty or under bosses, the workers in many cases being compelled to buy chances."[7]

This was not an exaggeration. In the other Arizona copper camps the miners belonged to the Western Federation of Miners, and elected grievance committees which negotiated regularly with the mining companies. In Clifton, Metcalf, and Morenci, they were unorganized, there was no machinery for discussing grievances, and the companies had made it clear for years that they did not consider unions suitable to the needs of Mexicans. For years these workers had been forced to endure the dishonesty and brutality of petty foremen who had sold jobs, forced raffles on them, and in other ways taken advantage of the fact that they were unorganized Mexican-Americans. While the mining companies obeyed the state's eight-hour law, they paid the men for only seven hours and a half, deducting the time required to pass from the collar of the shaft to the working place and back again at the end of the shift. There was also an uncertain leasing system, under which written leases for company houses were either not given, or when given might be cancelled, or rents raised, as soon as miners began to earn more wages.[8]

THE MINERS ORGANIZE

In the summer of 1915, George Powell arrived in Greenlee County to organize the unorganized Mexican-Americans and the small number of white Americans into the Western Federation of Miners. He pointed out that since the outbreak of war in Europe in the summer of 1914, there had been a greater demand for copper and that prices were escalating. So too were prices but wages were stationary, and the miners, he emphasized, received little of the huge profits the companies were reaping from war orders.[9]

The miners responded eagerly by organizing three locals of the Western Federation of Miners, one in each of the mining towns of Clifton, Metcalf, and Morenci. Once organized, the locals served notice on the managers of the three copper companies that they wished to have their committees meet with them to discuss the miners' grievances. The managers of the Arizona Copper Company and the Shannon Copper Company were out of town. The manager of the Detroit Copper Company told the union committee that his company would deal with its employees directly, and that he "must decline to meet a Western Federation of Miners committee." When the other managers returned, they issued similar statements. A journalist who interviewed the managers later reported that they told him frankly: "The men must not be allowed to feel that their organized effort had won them any advantage. One of the companies, Phelps Dodge & Company, operates vast, larger properties elsewhere, and it was important that the tactics of its Clifton employes be discredited lest they be adopted at other mines."[10]

THE MINERS STRIKE

On September 11, 1915, following the refusal of the three companies to meet in conference with representatives of the miners, five thousand workers went on strike. To the companies' astonishment, although the American miners were earning more than the Mexican–Americans and were reported to be "satisfied with their higher wages," they joined in the strike in sympathy with the Mexicans.[11]

A few days later formal demands were made upon the companies. These included a sliding scale of wages equal to those being paid in other parts of the state, abolition of the raffle system and other petty tyrannies of the foremen, written leases with firm rents for company houses, and recognition of the Western Federation of Miners as the strikers' bargaining agent.[12]

THE COMPANIES RESPOND

The companies did not even bother to reply to the demands, confining themselves to charging that the strike was solely the result of "outside agitators." Ironically, Walter Douglas, General Manager of Phelps Dodge & Company, raised the "outside agitator" charge from New York City where the company headquarters was located. "The Western Federation of Miners," he told reporters, "introduced its agitators and organizers into the district, knowing that Mexican workingmen are easily intimidated, and has exercised its arbitrary and despotic methods to bring suffering and loss in a formerly happy and contented community."[13]

Even Arizona papers friendly to the companies could not buy this argument. They noted that the strike was a process of long, slow growth, and that the WFM organizer had merely touched the match.

Others pointed out that the real reason for the strike was indicated by the banners inscribed *"Viva la Union,"* borne by the Mexican-Americans.[14]

After two committees of strikers had been refused a hearing by the managers on the ground that they included Western Federation of Miners representatives, a third committee was appointed which succeeded in getting the companies to a conference on September 26. But the conference did not last long. "It became apparent soon after it started," a mine manager told the press, "that the committee was composed of hand-chosen delegates of the Western Federation of Miners, and under these circumstances, a conference was useless." The managers then issued a joint statement notifying the strikers and the public that the mines and plants "will remain idle indefinitely." The statement continued:

> When it shall appear that conditions in this section warrant it, and the companies are satisfied that the general sentiment of the community and their former employes is unanimously in favor of a resumption of operations on the basis of wages and conditions that have prevailed heretofore in this district, the companies reserve the right to themselves to decide whether or not they will again start up their plants.[15]

But while they closed the mines which had already been shut down by the strike, the managers were making plans to reopen them with strikebreakers. The mining companies established a camp at Duncan, Arizona, several miles distant from the strike district. All former workers, they announced, who did not wish to join the union or to continue on strike, were invited to appear and enjoy free board and lodging at company expense.[16]

COMPANY MANAGERS APPEAL TO GOVERNOR HUNT

Having made arrangements to resume operations in the future with strikebreakers, the three managers boarded a train and fled the stike district to Texas. Before departing they issued a statement asserting that they had been forced to leave for fear of their lives because of the "lawless and desperate Mexican strikers," and appealed to Governor George Wiley Paul Hunt to send the state militia to the strike district to protect lives and property. Newspapers in various parts of Arizona and even outside the state published the statement under the heading, "Mine Managers Flee For Their Lives," and backed up the call for state troops.[17]

In the Colorado Coal strike of 1913-1914, Governor Ammons, at the behest of the Rockefeller interests who controlled the mines, had ordered the state militia to the strike district. This began a bloody process which was climaxed by the tragic "Ludlow Massacre" and the crushing of the strike.* The mining companies and leading Arizona newspapers were confident that the chief executive would follow the Colorado precedent. But Governor Hunt proved to be a different kind of chief executive, in fact one of the most unusual in American history.

A poor boy who had become a prospector, ferry boat operator, writer, rancher, and banker as well as an eight-term territorial legislator, Hunt had presided over the constitutional convention when Arizona became a state in 1912. As the state's first governor, he set out to ally himself with organized labor and progressive elements among the farmers, ranchers, and the middle-class. At the time when a strike seemed imminent in the Clifton–Morenci–Metcalf district, Hunt made a public speech in which he warned that in the event of a strike, the companies should realize, "We are to have no repetition of Colorado here." Hunt also warned workers that he would not countenance any violence on their part. Referring to the notorious "bull pens" of Colorado where strikers had been imprisoned under appalling conditions by the militia, he announced that if any were established in the strike district, he would see to it that both strike agitators who threatened violence and managers who imported strikebreakers and thus incited disorder, would go into them.[18]

Meanwhile, Governor Hunt attempted to achieve a peaceful solution of the dispute through arbitration of the differences between the employers and miners. But every effort in this direction came to nothing, chiefly, Hunt declared, "owing to the seeming unwillingness of the mine managers to make any compromise on every one of the workers' demands."[19]

GOVERNOR HUNT'S UNUSUAL RESPONSE

When the strike began, Governor Hunt immediately sent an agent to the strike district to investigate. General John Harris, Adjutant General in command of the state militia, followed. Both reported that the strikers were orderly, that they asked only for a conference with the managers to discuss their grievances and that these grievances were real. Meanwhile, they also reported, the strikers, having dispersed the companies' guards, had placed pickets in the mines, converters, powerhouses, and smelters to prevent their being operated. Moreover, Sheriff J. C. Cash of Greenlee County, having only four deputies, had appointed several strikers as deputy sheriffs, and had sent them to guard the mine properties. What is more, he had forced the companies to pay their wages as deputies and

*Foner, *History of the Labor Movement in the United States*, vol. V, pp. 196-213.

watchmen. "Thus," Governor Hunt was informed, "these men appeared in two roles—as strikers and as deputy sheriffs." Under this arrangement, there was no need for state troops to be sent to the strike district except for the purpose of standing watch.[20]

Governor Hunt acted on this recommendation. The militia was sent to the strike district, but with instructions to cooperate with the strikers in protecting property. Soon company spokespersons were denouncing the fact that officers of the state militia, "in the pay of the state and stationed in the strike district ostensibly to preserve law and order, are engaged in drilling strikers in military formation and tactics so that they may function efficiently as deputy sheriffs."[21]

Meanwhile, Governor Hunt was becoming concerned by reports that the camp established at Duncan by the companies to receive, lodge and feed anti-union workers was really a center for strikebreakers being recruited from outside Arizona. Hunt sent Adjutant General Harris to investigate. Harris found that carloads of nonunion workers had arrived at Duncan from El Paso, and convinced by this and other evidence he considered conclusive, he reported to Hunt that these men had been imported into Arizona as strikebreakers. Governor Hunt immediately announced that he would not tolerate strikebreaking, and ordered the militia to prevent any strikebreakers from entering the strike district. This order remained in effect throughout the strike.[22]

So unusual, so remarkable was the position he had taken in industrial conflicts on the eve of America's entrance into World War I, that Hunt was flooded with requests from newspapers and magazines to explain his stand. His most detailed response was to *The Survey*. In it he wrote, in part:

> Every one concerned with the strike situation was allowed to understand that the importation of hired strike-breakers or gunmen would not be permitted. In taking this position, I found my justification in the firm conviction that under our present industrial system controversies between employers and employes are virtually inevitable, and that when such unfortunate differences arise, the preservation of life and property acquires importance paramount to all other issues. It was, moreover, my honest belief, as it still is, that no intelligent body of workingmen will voluntarily initiate the certain hardships and risks of striking unless they are first convinced that their grievances are just and their cause is entitled to conscientous consideration by their employers.
>
> It may, in fairness, be conceded, as has been demonstrated time after time in the industrial history of this country, that the importation of strike-breakers by the employers under conditions above described is nothing short of an invitation to violence, and, in fact, almost surely presages bloodshed and other disastrous consequences.

It will, of course, be understood in this connection that when a strike is initiated on a large scale in any mining or manufacturing district a unusual condition is at once created, and cannot always be controlled by narrow adherence to such technical interpretations of law and individual claims of constitutional rights as may ordinarily be successfully upheld. By way of illustration, it may be pointed out that during a serious industrial trouble, the voluntary advent of strike-breakers in a district, even though effected under the guise of exercising constitutional rights, is virtually a precursor of violence endangering the lives and property of everyone residing within the strike zone. In such an emergency, I would be impelled to place the constitutional right of protection guaranteed every law-abiding citizen under our government as being a more important consideration than the upholding of the claim of the strike-breaker to the privilege of seeking employment wherever he pleases.

In brief, during a strike, actualities rather than theoretical contentions for individual liberties, must be successfully dealt with, if violence and bloodshed are to be prevented. . . .[23]

Hunt did not act alone. Sheriff Cash cooperated, and together Governor and Sheriff wrote new pages in American industrial history. When the company managers fled the strike district, Cash wired the authorities at the Texas border that the three were guilty of having "incited to riot" by their departure, the strikers fearing that the mines might never again be opened. He urged that they be brought up on charges, and they were actually brought before a justice of the peace. But they were discharged. The managers then made their way to El Paso, where they established headquarters for the next four months. From El Paso, they issued statements denouncing the strikers for "lawlessness," and it was from El Paso that they arranged for potential strikebreakers to be sent to the camp at Duncan, Arizona. But because of Governor Hunt's order to the state militia to prevent strikebreakers from entering the strike district, they were never used.[24]*

*Shortly after the strike, Walter Douglas, General Manager of Phelps Dodge & Company, argued that the companies had never planned to use "professional strikebreakers," and that the only men at the camp in Duncan were employees who refused to join the union and the strike. The reason the camp was established, he said, was solely to assist such faithful employees. (*New Republic,* March 18, 1916.) Hunt replied: "With reference to the concentration camp maintained by the companies at Duncan, Arizona, I can hardly place credence in Mr. Douglas's assertion that the objects of this camp were purely philanthropic. A national guard officer of Mexican birth, who in the guise of a workman gained admission to the Duncan colony, reported in writing on his return that previous employment by the companies was not a prerequisite for enjoyment of the privileges of the encampment, and that it was understood by the campers that as soon as their number should acquire sufficient proportions, they would enter the strike zone and go to work. The officer reported further that he was not questioned concerning previous employment by the companies." (*Ibid.,* April 15, 1916, p. 293.)

After the managers' departure, Sheriff Cash appointed more strikers as deputies, and had them join the others in guarding the abandoned mining companies' properties. Again, too, the companies had to pay their wages. "Clifton, Morenci and Metcalf have never been more orderly than during these weeks when the strikers have been functioning as deputy sheriffs," one New York reporter wrote to his paper.[25]

STRIKE SETTLED

Under community pressure to reopen the mines, the managers finally agreed to meet a strikers' committee in El Paso, provided they were first given the opportunity to scrutinize a list of the names and select those who were acceptable. The strikers submitted fifteen names, and the managers picked five whom they said were acceptable. The five went to El Paso on October 15, and held a three-day conference. At the end, however, the managers declared that the committee was "so handicapped by Western Federation influences that its efforts were unavailing."[26]

Now the companies tried a new strategy. They began a campaign in the press denouncing Governor Hunt as "a IWW-Wobbly sympathizer" who was misusing his office in the interests of "alien terrorists from Mexico," and called for his immediate recall. Indeed, recall petitions were circulated, but Hunt had gained the support not only of organized labor but of many ranchers, merchants, and farmers. He was able to expose company payment to newspapers for printing items vilifying him. The campaign to recall Hunt fell flat.[27]

While strikebreakers, gunmen, militiamen, sheriffs and their deputies—the usual array of forces relied upon by corporations in their battles with unions—could not be counted on in the Arizona copper strike of 1915 to bring about a settlement favorable to the mining corporations, hunger threatened to accomplish the same result. The Western Federation of Miners had not officially approved the strike, and severely weakened by the defeat in Northern Michigan, was unable to pay out money for strike benefits. Thousands of strikers, with their wives and children, became dependent on credit from local shopkeepers. But as the strike dragged on, these merchants were forced, one by one, to shut up shop and leave the district. This situation, the companies were convinced, would force the strikers, already facing "the pinch of starvation," to capitulate.[28]

They were wrong. Few of the strikers left for Duncan where they were assured ample food and lodgings in return for having abandoned the strike. Governor Hunt issued a proclamation inviting contributions to the relief fund, and he called on the state militia to solicit and distribute necessary supplies to needy families of the strikers. Reporters who had covered many bitter labor struggles were astounded to see militiamen gathering and distributing food and clothing for the strikers' families, and they wrote that "the best of feeling prevails among representatives of law and order and the strikers." What made this especially remarkable, they noted, was that Anglo-American militiamen were assisting Mexican-American strikers.[29]

Strike funds were obtained through voluntary contributions of sympathetic labor unions and individuals in Arizona, and from appeals in other states to aid the strikers. One appeal noted: "The resources of the miners cannot compete with the resources of the companies, and unless we aid them, they will have to capitulate on the corporations' terms—namely, to go back to work and abandon their union before any talks of reform or betterment can be held or even the slightest concession made."[30]

After four months without a serious break in the strikers' ranks, the companies were forced to surrender. The final settlement was produced by two federal mediators sent in to mediate by the U.S. Department of Labor—Hywel Davies and Joseph S. Myers. The settlement, reached on the nineteenth week of the strike, provided for the elimination, as far as possible, of all distinctions between Americans and Mexican-Americans; a minimum wage equal to that paid in the best mining camps of Arizona; a general advance of twenty percent in wages to 80 percent of the workers, and the payment of better wages to skilled workers; the withdrawal of the companies' objections to union representation; the re-employment of former strikers without discrimination, except in a few isolated cases of an unusual nature, the outcome to be settled by arbitration; and the establishment of an arrangement whereby differences between employers and workers would be discussed in conferences at least once a month by representatives of both sides. The first issues to be discussed at such conferences concerned the petty tyrannies of the foremen.[31]

On January 12, 1916, the *Bisbee Review* reported that the strikers had voted unanimously to withdraw from the Western Federation of Miners and to apply to the State Federation of Labor for membership. A major factor in the decision was the unwillingness of the Western Federation either to endorse or fully to support the strike. The State Federation accepted the strikers, and the former locals of the Western Federation of Labor were affiliated with the Arizona State Labor Federation. George Powell, WFM organizer, wished the miners well in their new home. In leaving the district, Powell had words of praise for Governor Hunt and Sheriff Cash:

The workers of these great United States have been given the worst of it by the governors and sheriffs in labor troubles so often and for so long, that now when we get a square deal, we think that we are getting it all, and on the other hand the companies have wholly or in part controlled those officers for so long that when they are told to obey the laws of the state and county or go to the "bull pen," they feel they are getting a rotten deal.

We are proud of our state, our citizens and governor. We are with him in his efforts to enforce the state laws, and in closing we will say, "Bravo George Hunt!" "Bravo Jim Cash!"[32]

AFTER THE STRIKE

When the managers returned to their homes from El Paso after the strike settlement, they were forced to concede that all of the statements they had issued about terrorism and vandalism on the part of the strikers, had been without foundation. Although they had left their homes unlocked and unguarded four months before, not one article had been disturbed. Piles of loose lumber had not been touched although the strikers, the majority penniless and near starvation, had been forced to go into the mountains to cut firewood. During the strike, the workers had been called "incendiaries," but it was now revealed that when a mill began to burn, the strikers sounded the alarm, formed a bucket brigade to fetch water from a neighboring creek, and worked to check the blaze. One striker suffered severe burns in helping put out the fire.[33]

No word of appreciation came from the mining companies. On the contrary, they continued their campaign of vilification of Governor Hunt for coddling "terrorists and arsonists," and began a major campaign to defeat him for re-election.[34] But Hunt had many supporters not only in Arizona but outside the state as well. Mother Jones called him "the greatest governor that the country has ever produced," and stumped Arizona for his re-election.[35*] A number of leading journals hailed him as having shown the way in which strikes could be conducted without bloodshed, namely, by banning strikebreakers and professional gunmen. "The outstanding feature of the copper miners' strike in Arizona is that a strike lasting nineteen weeks and more has been managed without violence," declared *The Outlook*. For this Governor Hunt was responsible, and for this he deserved "national prominence."[36] International prominence, too, for not only was Hunt unusual for

*Facing a well-financed corporation campaign, Hunt was defeated by Thomas Campbell, who won by 30 votes out of 15,000 cast. Hunt contested the result, and the state Supreme Court ultimately gave Hunt the majority of the 30 disputed votes, and Campbell was deposed after serving about half of the two-year term. (Alan V. Johnson, "Governor G.W.P. Hunt and Organized Labor," unpublished M.A. thesis, University of Arizona, 1964, pp. 76-85; James R. Kluger, *The Clifton-Morenci Strike: Labor Difficulty in Arizona, 1915-1916* [Tuscon, 1970], pp. 181-84.)

having prevented corporations from using the state militia in their interests and bringing strikebreakers and gunmen into the district to defeat the strikers, but he had done so when the vast majority of the striking miners were Mexican-Americans, workers who were usually held in contempt by corporations and governors alike.

Hunt gave credit to Sheriff Cash for the unusual stand he had adopted during the strike, but he singled out the labor movement for special praise:

> In virtually every instance the union officials responded to my urgent admonitions against disorderliness, and many went so far as actively to assist in preventing lawlessness. Instead of being cast against organized government and communal peace, the labor unions' influence became an important ally in the discouragement of overt acts. Thus the nature and extent of the union workingmen's co-operation as a factor in one of the most serious industrial troubles that ever arose in the United States may be readily realized, and so far as I am concerned in my official capacity is gratefully acknowledged.[37]

CHAPTER 3

A Steel Strike, a Riot
and an Unusual Sequel

On Saturday morning, December 30, 1915, readers of newspapers all over the United States were shocked to see on their front pages underneath headlines reading, "ALIEN STEEL STRIKERS SET EAST YOUNGSTOWN ON FIRE,"* an account of how a "mob of strikers" in East Youngstown, Ohio, enraged by the fatal shooting of eight strikers and the wounding of twelve others by gunmen hired by the Youngstown Sheet and Tube Company, had suddenly turned themselves loose "to burn and pillage, and destroy," and had not stopped until four complete city blocks, and parts of other blocks had gone up in flames and were utterly destroyed. They also read how the "mob" had burned the property of the Youngstown Sheet and Tube Company, where the strikers had been employed, and that of neighbors and fellow countrymen of the men on strike, that of merchants where they shopped, a bank, and the post office. The story continued with the news that by nine o'clock Friday night, the property damage was estimated at over $300,000 and the blaze was still beyond control. A call had been sent to the Youngstown Fire Department, but the officials refused to send the firemen, saying that they were not assured protection from the "angry mob of strikers." When an earlier attempt had been made to put out fires, "the rioters cut the hose and refused to permit the firemen to check the blaze."[1]

*The headline in the socialist New York *Call* was different. It read: "Shooting Down of Strikers By Private Police Infuriates People." (June 8, 1916.)

"EAST YOUNGSTOWN ARSON"

"What made them do it?" was the question on everyone's lips that December 30th. Many answers were offered. One was that "bloody Friday" had occurred because that Friday was the Austrian New Year. Many steel workers had emigrated from the Austro-Hungarian Empire and had gotten dead drunk on that day. Another was that the violence happened because that day was the Jewish New Year, and a few days before many strikers had seen Israel Zangwill's "The Melting Pot" at the movies.* No explanation was offered to show the connection, but it was assumed that the point being made was that the conception of "The Melting Pot," depicting America as a land which brought various peoples together, offering them a haven and a home, and an opportunity to become something better than they had been by enabling them to throw off their "slave-minded" European heritage and becoming "Americanized," clashed with the reality of life in the steel mills, causing the angry outburst.[2]

In the end, however, most commentators placed the blame for the "East Youngstown Arson" on the fact that it was "in the nature of immigrants from Southeastern Europe to become drunk and act violently." But Chester M. Wright, editor of the New York *Call*, the Socialist daily, who spent days in Youngstown and East Youngstown studying the situation, wrote:

> It never occurs to them that the industrial system might have something to do with it, that hours of work, wages, profits, juggling, speculation, any of the fifty-seven kinds of deviltry that the capitalist system can play might have had something to do with causing men to say to the bosses, "you go to hell, we don't like the way things are going and we're going to strike until we do."[3]

DEVELOPMENTS IN STEEL

Despite all the theories devoted to drunkenness, it soon became evident that the steel industry had almost invited the blind, angry response of its workers that had occurred in East Youngstown, Ohio on December 29, 1915. Not only did the industry, and especially its major corporation, U.S. Steel, aggressively boast of its success in maintaining an open shop, but the whole industry had a long record of lengthening the working day and reducing wages. In the 1880's, Carnegie plants had experimented with the eight-hour day, but, after completion of mecha-

---

*Israel Zangwill (1864-1926), British Jewish novelist and playwright, and Zionist leader. The image of America as a crucible wherein the European nationalities would be transformed into a new race owes its origin to the title and theme of Zangwill's 1908 play, "The Melting Pot," which was transferred to the screen in 1915.

nization, the employers, using the excuse that the hard work had disappeared from most of steel production, turned to much longer shifts. Forcing through the extensions during economic depressions, the employers instituted twelve-hour shifts in much of the industry. This began at the Edgar Thompson Works in 1887, and spread to other plants in different parts of the country during the first decade of the twentieth century. In a period of economic boom, Sunday labor came to be added to the work week, in response, as David Brody puts it, "to the cry for more steel." By 1910, 30 percent of all steelworkers labored on Sunday and the working week, according to figures compiled for Illinois, was seven hours *more* than it had been in 1882. Once every two weeks, workers in many departments put in a 24-hour "long turn."[4]

At its 1909 convention, the AFL passed a resolution calling for "thorough organization of all branches of [the steel] business." Although the AFL did launch a campaign to carry out the resolution, anti-immigrant sentiment, craft organization and craft jealousy plagued its organizing drives in the industry. The AFL approach was hardly the best method for organizing in a mass production industry in which immigrant workers of different nationalities, and especially those from Southeastern Europe, played an ever increasing role; at the same time, mechanization and the change in the division of labor were diluting craft expertise and creating a wide range of semiskilled and unskilled job classifications.

The AFL unions committed only six organizers to the steel effort and had lost enthusiasm for the project when a strike for shorter hours at Bethlehem, Pennsylvania, in 1910 presented new opportunities for changes in steel.[5] At Bethlehem Steel Company, skilled workers had a Saturday half-holiday. But they worked ten hours and twenty-five minutes each of the other six days—sixty-eight hours per week. The less skilled complained of a thirteen-hour, twenty-minute workday. Since 1907, the company had refused to pay time-and-a-half for overtime. On February 3, 1910, some of the skilled mechanics at Bethlehem struck, demanding an end to Sunday work and time-and-a-half for overtime. Shortly thereafter, unskilled laborers and apprentices joined their ranks. With the aid of AFL and International Association of Machinists organizers who enrolled 3,800 members nationally during the strike, the local craft unionists actively pursued unity with the unskilled workers, most of whom were Hungarian immigrants. Not only did many laborers stand by the machinists through much of the 108-day strike, but, more amazingly, the skilled workers refused a separate settlement which ignored the unskilled. Even so, the strike never succeeded in shutting down the entire plant of 8,000 workers, having perhaps 1500 participants at its peak. The promise, in the words of the strike chairman, that "We are going to win. We are to have our nights to ourselves, and the Sundays also," was realized in part. Overtime and Sunday work became optional as a result of the settlement, but wages remained unchanged and so low that long hours remained a necessity.[6]

The unity of skilled and unskilled, of Americans with the immigrants, had already had a precedent in the great strike of workers of the Pressed Steel Car Company at McKees Rocks, led by the IWW, in July, 1909, a strike which ended in favor of the men.* Although the Bethlehem strike was defeated and a summertime ten-hour initiative at McKees Rocks failed, the events of 1909 and 1910 changed labor relations in steel. Reformers, especially the members of the Federal Council of Churches and the Pittsburgh Survey group,** publicized conditions in steel mills relentlessly in the wake of the McKees Rocks and Bethlehem strikes, pointing to the seven-day labor and the twelve-hour day—"the man-killing system," as the New York *World* called it. An article in the January, 1913 issue of *Metropolitan*, depicting the heavy labor in the steel mills, concluded: "Had you thought of doing that for one hour? And then for two . . . and finally for twelve hours? Had you? That is the barbaric twelve-hour day which obtains in the steel industry."[7]

"The entire industry," according to David Brody, "stood implicated." The AFL and the reformers forced a full-scale investigation of the steel corporations by the House of Representatives during which Louis Brandeis testified to the fact that the "terrible conditions of labor are the result of having killed or eliminated from the steel industry unionism. . . . It is a condition of repression, of slavery in the real sense of the word, which is alien to American conditions." The investigation won significant support for requiring the eight-hour day on government-constructed steel. Of course, the welfare of the steel workers was not the only consideration favoring introduction of the eight-hour day. The superintendent of the Judson Manfacturing Company of San

---

*See Philip S. Foner, *History of the Labor Movement in the United States,* New York, 1965, vol. IV, pp. 282-95.

**The Pittsburgh Survey drew its staff from settlement houses, charity organization societies, ethnic organizations, and universities. The staff of the survey formed an assemblage of experts, with Paul U. Kellogg as its director, and John Fitch one of its most important analysts. The Pittsburgh Survey was published first in three special monthly issues of *Charities and the Commons,* beginning January 2, 1909, and then in Paul U. Kellogg, editor, *The Pittsburgh Survey* (six volumes, New York, 1910-1914). For a summary of the work of the Survey with a critical analysis of its backward approach to immigrant workers, which viewed them solely as competitors "who retarded the wages and working conditions of the native," see John F. McClymer, "The Pittsburgh Survey, 1907-1914: Forging an Ideology in the Steel District," *Pennsylvania History* 41 (1974): 169-86.

Francisco, one of fifty-four structural steel companies in that city to switch to the eight-hour day in the summer of 1916 in response to a demand from the structural steel workers' union,* stated that on the eight-hour day, production

> will be increased from fourteen percent, and that overhead expenses, cost of oil, lighting, etc. will be reduced. The men are far more efficient, more willing, more capable of first-class work under the new system. Directly in charge of the work here as I am, I have been in a position to closely observe the new order, and I can safely make this unqualified statement: A worker can and will do more work in eight hours than in twelve.[8]

Perhaps most crucially, the craft structure was beginning to give way in steel. As Brody points out: "The experience of 1909-10 held enormous future importance. The question of union structure was settled. All steelworkers—skilled and unskilled—and every branch of the industry (excluding blast-furnace workers) would be under a single jurisdiction."[9] Established craft organizations (e.g., bricklayers) kept jurisdiction in the mills, but all jobs peculiar to the steel industry were to be under one amalgamated jurisdiction. "Semi-industrial" unionism committed to organizing the ethnic unskilled, had come to steel. When ambitious AFL organizing returned to the mills in 1913, with a goal of union recognition and "the three shift system of eight hours," agitational literature was printed in thirteen languages. In listing the reasons for the abandonment of the organizing campaign in iron and steel in 1904, the AFL organizers assigned to this work gave as a leading cause the fact "that a large number of the workers we approached are foreigners, hardly able to speak or understand the English language, thereby complicating, and, in the end, nullifying our efforts at every point."[10] But McKees Rocks and Bethlehem had proved that immigrant workers could be organized, and one of the most important means of organizing them was to use their own languages.

CONDITIONS IN EAST YOUNGSTOWN

Youngstown and East Youngstown, Ohio, were ripe for the new organizing drive. The Youngstown Sheet and Tube Company had more than 8,000 men on its payroll in East Youngstown. In Youngstown proper the Republic Iron and Steel Company employed about

---

*However, ten structural steel firms rejected the union's demand, and with the aid of a newly-organized Law and Order Committee, began operating an open-shop with scab labor on the old nine-hour day. By December, 1916, these companies were forced to surrender. (Steven C. Levi, "The battle for the eight-hour day in San Francisco," *California History* 57 [1978]:343-53.

6,000 men, and the Carnegie Steel Corporation another 6,000. The plants of all three companies were strung along the Mahoning River, which made its way through the city of Youngstown and the village of East Youngstown. Both Youngstown companies had plants in other parts of the country, and the Carnegie Company was part of the United States Steel Corporation: but Youngstown Sheet and Tube Company, around whose plant the village of East Youngstown had been built, was an independent company, most of whose stockholders lived in Youngstown.[11]

Youngstown, with its suburbs, included about a hundred thousand people. A third of the total population, it was estimated, consisted of foreigners—chiefly Poles, Lithuanians, and Serbs. East Youngstown was not part of the city of Youngstown, but a village with its own government, three or four miles from the "square" which was the heart of Youngstown. The Youngstown Sheet and Tube Company of East Youngstown was the largest plant in the entire district. The company prided itself on its welfare work. President J.A. Campbell instituted a voluntary system of compensation for accidents, and later supported a compulsory state law. The plant was viewed as a model for safety, and its hospital in East Youngstown was considered to be excellently managed.[12]

However, welfare work did not include decent wages for the steel workers, especially the unskilled, the vast majority of whom were immigrants. President Campbell frankly told reporters that the question of living standards and the needs of the workers had nothing to do with wages and should not have anything to do with them, "but wages were and should be met by competitive conditions."[13] With this approach, it is not surprising that wages in the district were hardly sufficient to stave off hunger. In 1910 a government investigation showed that 70.8 percent of the steel workers at Youngstown and East Youngstown were of foreign birth; that only 48 percent of these worked nine months a year or over; that of 330 families investigated the heads of families earned an average of $440 a year, of whom 40 percent earned less than $400 a year, and 14 percent less than $200 per year. Since 1910 wages had advanced 10 percent by the fall of 1915, but the cost of living, according to the United States Bureau of Labor Statistics, had advanced more than 12 percent in the same period—and wages had been totally inadequate in 1910. Poverty was so widespread in the steel districts that in 1913, according to the United States Census, 41 percent of deaths in Youngstown were children under five years of age.[14]

Some of this, of course, was also due to the wretched housing provided immigrant workers. J.M. Hanson, general secretary of Youngstown Charity Organization Society, acknowledged that housing conditions in both Youngstown and East Youngstown for steel workers were abominable, unsanitary to the highest degree, with filth, open garbage, and dry privies abounding. John A. Fitch, who knew steel conditions perhaps better than anyone else in the United States, called housing in the Youngstown area especially terrible:

> I talked with a man who lived with his wife and three children in two rooms, for which he paid $7 a month. The other three rooms of the house were occupied by a family of six who paid $9 a month. The house had running water but no bathroom or toilet. I passed row after row of houses in Youngstown with outdoor privies and with hydrants in the yard. The houses in this section near the Brown–Bonnell plant of the Republic Iron and Steel Company were in bad repair generally, and garbage scattered about spoke eloquently of an inefficient Board of Health. . . .
>
> As East Youngstown is a village of more recent origin, one need not be surprised, perhaps, at lack of sewers and running water. The village has been bonded for a water works system, I was told, and work is soon to begin upon it. But the mud of the unpaved streets of that desolated village—mud nearly hub deep, a clinging, all-pervasive mud that plasters itself on shoes and trouser-legs, distributes itself over sidewalks, up from steps and across thresholds, a tell-tale record of a town's perambulations—seems somehow to be symbolic of the community's civic development and its regard for human values.[15]

There were other symbols. In 1915 East Youngstown had a population of 10,000 of whom 450 were qualified voters. There was no opportunity in the village for a foreigner to learn English. There were, for example, no night schools. The YMCA at Youngstown had made plans to start citizenship classes, but its efforts were abandoned because of lack of funds. East Youngstown had not a single church building nor any church organization of importance. But the state license commissioner's report revealed that there were eighteen saloons in the village in June, 1915. It had grown to twenty-two by the end of the year, but most of them were burned up in the angry outburst of the immigrant steel workers.

There was no organized social work in East Youngstown. The village employed a visiting nurse for a while in 1915, but it was found to be illegal to spend money for such purposes, so the nurse was dismissed.[16]

Perhaps one reason for the absence of churches in a village where the overwhelming number of inhabitants were steel workers was that Sunday work in the mill kept them from attending church services. Moreover, while the standard twelve-hour day prevailed at Youngstown Sheet and Tube Company, there were even men who worked fourteen hours a day.[17]

Hunger and fear of starvation had checked rebellion for years at Youngstown and East Youngstown.* Management was sure that there was nothing to be concerned about. Unionism seemed to be as remote a threat as ever. In short, management in Youngstown and East Youngstown was slow to realize that with the end of the depression of 1913-14 and the rush of new orders stimulated by the war in Europe, at the same time that the cutting off of immigration created a shortage of labor, an entirely new situation had developed. A sense of independence swept the steel mills, and worker unrest began to manifest itself daily. "Workmen of the most docile tendencies have been making demands," John Fitch reported, noting "insignificant little rebellions verging on strikes here and there."[18]

It was in Youngstown and East Youngstown that this situation came to a head. Here workers realized quickly that "at last they could register a protest without facing starvation. All the resentment and bitterness born of years in which excessively long and arduous labor had alternated with shame and humiliation of begging work and bread flamed up in their hearts."[19] In other words, after a period of depression and half time, the steel industry in Ohio, as in other states, had suddenly leaped into a condition of such prosperity that there was a backlog of unfilled orders. In industries supplying munitions, the profits were enormous. In steel, they were soaring, even though management insisted that the prosperity was exaggerated because many of the orders had been contracted for during the depression months at low prices. What is important is that the prevailing view among the steel workers was that the industry was making huge profits, and that they should get some of it.[20]

It was inevitable that such a feeling should emerge. Unskilled steel workers at Youngstown and East Youngstown were earning nineteen and a half cents an hour. They now demanded a wage increase to twenty-five cents an hour and double pay for Sunday work. Management was willing to concede half of the demand, but the men would not agree.

THE STRIKE AND THE RIOT

On December 27, 1915, the laborers employed in the tube plant of the Republic Iron and Steel Company walked out. A few days later the whole department, congested with unfinished work, had to close down.

*In the summer of 1912, *Solidarity*, Eastern organ of the IWW, reported that "the East Youngstown plant of the Youngstown Sheet and Tube Co. is operating at only 65 to 70 percent of capacity." (Aug. 10, 1912.)

Then men began to walk out of other departments. Mostly they were the unskilled laborers, but they constituted the bulk of the labor force in the plants. In a few days the two big plants of the Republic Company were closed down.[21]

The AFL organizers succeeded in unionizing many of the men on strike at the Republic plant, and negotiations began again with the company, this time with the workers represented by union committees.[22] When John J. Granley, district AFL organizer, attempted to hire a hall in East Youngstown to address the workers at Youngstown Sheet and Tube Company, he was prevented from doing so by the company which hired the hall over his head.[23] As a result when the men walked out from the plant in East Youngstown, they did so without any union to represent or influence them.

The strike at the Youngstown Sheet and Tube Company in East Youngstown began on Wednesday, January 5, 1916. As in the Republic mills, it began with the laborers and soon was effective in shutting down the plant. The demands made were the same as those of the Youngstown strikers. Now with the men out in Youngstown and East Youngstown, there were 15,000 workers on strike.[24]

On Friday afternoon, January 7, 1916, a reporter for the Youngstown *Vindicator* came to East Youngstown with a photographer to take pictures and describe a march planned by the strikers. As he wrote that evening, thousands of strikers were on the streets. Many had been drinking, but they were not in an ugly mood. They posed cheerfully for the photographer. Many were massed near a steel bridge leading over a number of railroad tracks to the steel plant—a bridge which was actually the main entrance to the plant. As the property of the Youngstown Sheet and Tube Company, the bridge was being guarded by members of the uniformed police force employed by the company. There were signs of hostility between the guards and the strikers; suddenly, the reporter wrote, one of the guards advanced along the bridge and opened fire at the approaching strikers. The strikers started to run, and when they had reached a safe distance, they stopped. At this particular spot there was a pile of bricks, and when the crowd surged forward again, many of the strikers carried a brick or two. Suddenly a brick was hurled at the twenty-five private guards, whereupon the leader of the group opened fire with his revolver, and his companions, taking this as a signal, poured a volley into the strikers. Twenty of the strikers and two bystanders fell, eight of them fatally wounded.

The crowd then became a wild, angry mob. An amazing destruction and pillage of six square blocks in East Youngstown followed, and did not end until the smoking ruins of an estimated million dollars worth of property remained as a momento of the fierce anger of the strikers. Only with the arrival the next day of 2,000 members of the National Guard, who patrolled the streets with fixed bayonets, was order restored.

EXPLANATIONS FOR THE RIOT

Explanations for the riot, as we have seen, came fast and furious. (The *Outlook,* however, refused to use the word "riot," preferring that it "be called by its true name—private war," that is, a "private war" of armed company guards against unarmed strikers.)[26] In addition to the explanations we have listed above there was the charge that the IWW was responsible for the outbreak. But it was soon disclosed that the only visible evidence of the IWW in the strike districts was the scrawled message upon a dingy window of an unoccupied building in East Youngstown reading: "I.W.W.—Eight Hours—Slaves Unite." In general, both authorities and journalists agreed that there was no evidence to indicate that IWW influence was a factor in the rioting.[27]

Another rumor was that the AFL planned the riot, and had "brought it about by secretly and insidiously preaching violence." This quickly died when it was learned that while the AFL had been active in Youngstown after the men went on strike, it had not even been able to hold a meeting in East Youngstown to appeal to the strikers. Thomas Flynn, AFL organizer in Youngstown, replied to the charge:

> The men who are on strike are not organized into a union and are not affiliated with any union organization.... The American Federation of Labor representatives will have nothing to do with the strikers because of the pillage and burning of innocent people's property. When the Republic Iron and Steel Company's men went out on strike, we went down there and counseled them to do no violence. They followed our advice. When we learned that the Youngstown Sheet and Tube Company's men were threatening trouble, we went out to persuade them not to do any violence, but we could not even obtain a hall in which to talk with them. . . . The American Federation of Labor does not countenance violence in strikes and will have nothing to do with this one from now on.[28]

Still Flynn did not entirely wash his hands of the strike. He issued another statement in which he charged that Wall Street interests were behind the riot, seeking to depress the stock of Youngstown Sheet and Tube Company during negotiations for a proposed merger that would include the Cambria Steel Company of Johnstown, Pennsylvania, and the Lackawanna Steel Company of Buffalo. The riot, by depressing the stock, would enable the promoters of the merger to buy the stock of

A STEEL STRIKE, A RIOT AND AN UNUSUAL SEQUEL   35

Youngstown Sheet and Tube Company at bargain prices. Moreover, Flynn charged, thugs of the worst sort, supplied by detective agencies which specialized in breaking strikes, had been shipped into East Youngstown by the Youngstown Sheet and Tube Company, and that this had been done in the interest of the merger, which, besides it and Cambria and Lackawanna, was to include the Colorado Fuel and Iron Company. "The latter company," Flynn pointed out, "means John D. Rockefeller and brings up strangely familiar remembrances,"[29] such as the "Ludlow Massacre!"

The theory of a conspiracy hatched in Wall Street being responsible for the devastation in East Youngstown received wide publicity. Even the conservative New York *Tribune* gave it some credence while the Socialist New York *Call* devoted columns to the theory under headlines reading: "Wall Street Interests Pay For Youngstown Massacre To Force Steel Merger," and "Buy Riot With Hired Thugs So They Could Get Stock They Wanted."[30] The story that followed was by Chester A. Wright, the *Call's* managing editor, who had been sent to Youngstown to get the facts about what lay behind the riot, "the whole truth about the riot at that place."[31] The *Call* summed up its managing editor's findings as follows:

> Briefly, this is the situation. The shares of the Youngstown Sheet and Tube Company were mostly held locally by some 1,300 comparatively small capitalists. A merger was on foot by which the company was to be consolidated with several others—the Colorado Fuel and Iron Company being one of them. Opposition to the merger scheme was rampant in Youngstown, these 1,300, of course, comprising "the community" and speaking in their name. So the battle lines were set between 1,300 small local capitalists, and an unknown but much smaller number of big ones of the Rockefeller type who wanted the merger, while the others objected to being swallowed.
>
> How to shake the little fellows loose from stock; how to compel them to come into the merger? Then comes the scheme. The labor dispute is the handiest way. The "ignorant foreigners" are on hand, also the low wages—the conditions of the class struggle. Foment this, utilize it, and shake the little fellows down.
>
> So along come the strikebreaker and the gunman; the agent provocateur circulates among the community; whisky and rum ad libitum. Then the gunmen get busy; fire a volley into the "ignorant foreigners." Panic. The torch. Looting. Rioting. Militia called out. Youngstown stock drops fifty points.
>
> And such is the inside story of the Youngstown Riot.[32]

It was a colorful story, but it did not go far. John D. Rockefeller, Jr. issued a statement asserting that the Colorado Fuel and Iron Company was not involved in the proposed merger, and challenging Thomas Flynn who had first raised the charge to give his authority. Flynn admitted that he had no inside knowledge, and offered to send by mail the name of his informant. To this Rockefeller replied that if the name was to be given at all it should be given to the public. At this the Rockefeller involvement was allowed to die, and even the New York *Call* did not raise it again.[33] However, as was already clear in the strike against Standard Oil in Bayonne, New Jersey, which is discussed elsewhere in this volume, the shooting down of strikers by company guards was not something that had ceased to be part of the Rockefeller labor policy.

A more lasting charge against monopoly capitalists was raised by George P. West, formerly an investigator for the Commission for Industrial Relations, who revealed it in the *New Republic* of January 20, 1916. West disclosed that the Republic Iron & Steel Company was ready to give its men a ten percent wage increase and thus nip in the bud a strike that was being planned. But the company felt it incumbent to consult the United States Steel Corporation before doing so. Elbert H. Gary, chairman of the Board of Directors of U.S. Steel, advised against an increase. The Republic plant accordingly remained shut down for two weeks, and the strike spread to the Youngstown Sheet & Tube Company. Thus it was U.S. Steel which set the labor policy for the entire steel industry, including plants of independent companies. This policy, West charged, was responsible for the fatal events of Friday, January 7th, in East Youngstown.[34]

As we shall see, West's charge was based on solid evidence.

The *Iron Trade Review*, one of the two trade papers in the steel industry, noted that the "disgraceful scenes" in East Youngstown on January 7th were enacted by "men of foreign birth," few of whom were citizens, and it suggested that they be deported. "It does not suggest," commented John A. Fitch angrily, "either deportation or any other punishment for those who have made millions of dollars through the labor of men in the East Youngstown plants, but who have been perfectly satisfied to neglect these aliens—who found their presence desirable just as long as they worked and were docile and produced profits."[35]

No deportations took place. But three hundred men were arrested in the two days following the riot, some of whom were immediately released for lack of evidence, but not before the authorities publicized the fact that "almost all of the men arrested could not speak English."[36] A large number, however, were held for the action of the grand jury which had launched an investigation into the events leading up to the riot.

STRIKE RESULTS

Meanwhile, the steel companies made an effort to placate public opinion. President J.A. Campbell of Youngstown Sheet and Tube Company announced that the plant would remain closed for a few days, since operation "would be useless . . . while some of our workers are in the frame of mind they are in now." He had the company gunmen removed from the plant, and promised he would not bring in strike-breakers. At the Republic Iron and Steel Company, the managers made concessions to committees representing newly formed unions.

The strikes were called off on January 11 and 13, 1916, and the men went back to work with the understanding that their wages would be raised about ten percent. Ultimately the great majority of the workers received 22 cents an hour instead of 19½ cents. What they actually earned would depend as before on the length of the working day and the number of days employed. About 50 percent of the workers worked a twelve-hour day. Before the strikes, a day's work was worth $2.34; it would now yield $2.64. A ten-hour day meant $1.95 before the advance; now it would bring $2.20.[37]

"Working in the steel industry twelve hours a day in order to make a living leaves little that makes living worthwhile," commented John A. Fitch. "Strike is Over But Satan Still Reigns Over Industrial Hell," was the way Chester M. Wright put it.[38]

It is worth noting that the increases forced by the strikers in Youngstown spread to the entire steel industry. (In fact, the U.S. Steel Corporation had quickly announced a ten percent increase the moment the Youngstown strikes broke out.) In the midst of a rush of war orders, the industry feared to face the possibility of an upheaval on a scale that might paralyze the entire industry.[39]

THE SEQUEL

The strikes in Youngstown and East Youngstown had a most unusual sequel. The grand jury had been impaneled to determine the responsibility for the deaths and property destruction that had occurred in East Youngstown on January 7th. Contrary to all precedent, this grand jury returned indictments against President J.A. Campbell of the Youngstown Sheet and Tube Company, Elbert H. Gary, chairman of the Board of United States Steel Corporation, and the following companies: Youngstown Sheet and Tube Company, Youngstown Iron and Steel Company, United States Steel Corporation, and the Carnegie Steel Company. All told a total of 113 corporations and officers were indicted. They were charged with violation of the Valentine anti-trust act, an

Ohio law against conspiracy to fix the prices of commodities, against making an unlawful agreement to maintain uniform wage rates, and against conspiring to keep down wages of common laborers.

Maximum punishment under the indictments was one year's imprisonment in the workhouse for each of the sixty-two alleged offenses, and a maximum fine of $5,000 for each offense, or a total of $310,000. The minimum was a $50 fine and six months in the workhouse. According to Prosecuting Attorney A.M. Henderson, efforts would be made in the trial to show that the alleged conspiracy to fix the price of labor by Gary and the steel companies brought about the unrest that resulted in the strike and riot.[40]

The grand jury was unable to find any particular cause for the riot, but its report stated that no evidence appeared to indicate that any foreign government had a hand in it. (This was a reference to the rumor that German and Austrian agents were behind the riot.) It found that members of the Ohio National Guard were employed in the plant of the Youngstown Sheet and Tube Company as guards and that they took ammunition belonging to the state into the plant.

The report charged that the riot was precipitated by acts of the Youngstown Sheet and Tube Company. It severely censured the guards who fired from the Youngstown Sheet and Tube Company bridge, killing eight men and wounding many others, and stated they were not of such a character as to be trusted with the responsibilities that were laid upon them. Concerning the origin of the violence, the report stated:

> While one shot was fired from one of the mob assembled around the gate of the tube company, the shots which precipitated the extreme acts of violence, lawlessness and crime which were committed January 7 were shots fired by the guards of the Youngstown Sheet and Tube Company.

And it continued:

> We find that there is an underlying cause, not only of the strike and of the dissatisfaction prevailing among the men prior to the strike, but of the riot itself, a cause which will shown upon the trial of some of the corporations and individuals against whom charges have been made by the jury.[41]

The grand jury also censured Mayor Cunningham of East Youngstown, six members of the East Youngstown Council, and the police force. Mayor Cunningham and the officials were characterized as "inefficient" and "unworthy to hold office."[42]

"The indictment is an outrage—a travesty," Judge Gary commented in rage. The *New York Times* agreed, declaring that the indictment made the grand jury and the prosecutor of Mahoning County "ridiculous."[43] Samuel Gompers, AFL President, joined the chorus of condemnation, stating that the indictment of the steel companies and Elbert H. Gary on charges of conspiring as a trust to fix the prices of labor was "a menace to organized labor." The Valentine anti-trust law of Ohio, Gompers insisted, was based on the principle that labor is a commodity that can be bought and sold, and he argued: "No principle constitutes a greater menace to the freedom and ultimate well-being of the wage-earners of our country, and our free institutions, than does the principle that labor power of human beings is a commodity or article of commerce."[44] This was the first comment by Gompers on the events in Youngstown and East Youngstown. Evidently the killing of the eight strikers by company guards did not constitute a "menace" to the wage-earners of the country.

There were words of praise for the grand jury action. Frank P. Walsh, former chairman of the Commission on Industrial Relations, called the grand jury indictment and the determination of the prosecuting attorney to carry it into effect "a hopeful sign that a better understanding and more enlightened sense of justice are abroad in the land." Walsh continued:

> Without passing on the guilt or innocence of the defendants, we can be grateful to the Ohio officials for their realization that guilt for the fatal riot did not end with the unfortunate victims of economic exploitation who actually applied the torch, or even with the hired gunmen who fired into the crowd.
>
> Almost without exceptions, such outbreaks as that at Youngstown can be traced to the maintenance of inhumane and un-American industrial conditions and the inevitable effect of such conditions in driving the victims to desperation.
>
> Now, for the first time, the responsibility of those who maintain such conditions has been recognized, and the public prosecutors have not been content with an attempt to put a few workingmen in jail.[45]

The New York *Call*, for whom Walsh wrote his opinion, gave the statement a leading place in its columns, but the *Call* itself was not as impressed by the grand jury indictment and the stand of the public prosecutor. In an editorial entitled "Mysterious Doings at Youngstown," the Socialist daily conceded that it was "certainly...a reversal of the usual form" to find a grand jury placing the responsibility for strikes, rioting and incendiarism "upon anybody but the common laborers," and it was "a still greater wonder for them to load it upon the shoulders of the great Steel Trust and a number of other steel corporations and distinguished individuals connected therewith." Indeed, it was as strange as if Colorado had brought a similar indictment against Rockefeller, Jr. and his managers and executives in that state. However, for all that, the *Call* was confident that nothing would come of the strange and unusual events in Youngstown. There was not "the remotest possibility that Gary and his conferes will ever serve prison terms or be mulcted in fines for their illegal conduct."[46]

Three weeks later, the *Call's* prediction was fulfilled. On March 28, 1916, Judge W. S. Anderson dismissed the indictments upon representations made by counsel for the defendants.[47]

What remained was that the action of the grand jury threw upon the steel companies and their officials the blame for the riot and destruction and removed it from the workers upon whom blame usually is placed. What also remained was the exposure of "inhumane and un-American industrial conditions" in the steel industry. Such conditions, Scott Nearing pointed out in discussing the indictment, were the result of "industrial despotism." And "despotism breeds revolt."[48]

Three years later in the Great Strike of 1919 the revolt came. As for the strike in East Youngstown in 1916, Chester M. Wright summed it up as follows in *The American Labor Year Book:*

> The strike on the whole was one of the most dramatic that the country has known. The complete destruction of so much property, the remarkable solidarity of unorganized workers, and the indictment of company officials as responsible for the result of low wages and unendurable conditions, were features that stamped it as one of most unusual qualities, and worth deep study.[49]

CHAPTER 4

The Standard Oil Strikes in Bayonne, New Jersey, 1915-1916

Dr. John A. DeBrizzi is co-author of this Chapter

Several years ago, in a study of the development of American industrial cities, Herbert Gutman criticized the widely-held view that "from the start, industrialists had the social and political power and prestige to match their economic forces," and that town politics were a reflection of large-scale industrial interests.[1]

GUTMAN'S STATUS-CONFLICT THESIS

Basing his conclusion on a case study of Paterson, New Jersey, Gutman suggests that big business concerns and their employees have been alien elements within the industrial city for some time. Because of the alien nature of big business in the city and the "status resentment" of older community groups—particularly small businessmen and professionals—there developed effective opposition to the large industrialists. So effective was this opposition, argues Gutman, that big businessmen were forced to lobby at the state level where local pressures were felt less strongly.[2] Although his research involved a particular case study, Gutman suggests that his findings enjoy a general applicability. "One or two industries characterized the usual New Jersey industrial city (e.g., Bayonne, Hoboken, Jersey City). . . . Although the social history of such towns has not yet been written, sufficient scattered evidence indicates that the presence of vital clusters of urban working-class subculture, a diversity of attitudes among non-workers toward industrial power, and the unique patterns of protest and politics. . . ."[3] In the end, Gutman maintains that the social and political processes within the cities of industrializing America are best understood from within a status-resentment and conflict perspective rather than from a Marxist-oriented view.

The story of the industrialization process in the municipality of Bayonne, New Jersey suggests that Gutman's status-conflict perspective is inadequate as an explanation for the events which transpired in the city after 1880, and particularly in the two crucial years, 1915 and 1916. Bayonne provides an extremely interesting test for the status-conflict thesis in that its economy changed from an agricultural to an industrial base within the span of a single generation. In addition, the local economy came to be dominated by the giant facilities of the Standard Oil Corporation. Thus, if the status-conflict thesis of Gutman is of general applicability, it should be confirmed in the case of Bayonne.

HOW STANDARD OIL OF NEW JERSEY CONTROLLED BAYONNE

In 1880, Bayonne, located on a peninsula at the southern tip of Hudson County, New Jersey, was still primarily a fishing and agricultural center with a population of over 9,000. During the period 1880 to 1905, the population of the city nearly quadrupled, and overnight Bayonne became an industrial city. By 1881 tax revenues derived from assessments on the Standard and Tidewater Oil companies (the latter a Standard subsidiary) provided almost one-half of the monies expended by the city government. Indeed, as Bayonne's economy shifted toward industry, the livelihood of many old families began to depend, at least in part, upon revenues drawn from Standard Oil.

This dependence was not forgotten when Standard Oil requested that the city grant it permission to lay pipeline necessary for its operation through the community. The first elected Mayor of Bayonne opposed the plan, and the oil company actively campaigned against him for re-election. He was defeated at the polls. The newly-elected Mayor suggested the following to the City Council: "The Standard Oil Company is a large tax payer whose interest we should properly care for when possible, and I trust our citizens and property owners will look at this matter in a liberal and proper light, and further this project."[4]

When Standard Oil called for an addition to the line and expansion of its facilities in 1881, a group of citizens, prominent among whom were members of the old families, petitioned the City Council for favorable action in appreciation of the benefits to Bayonne already derived from the company. The petitioners also cited "the fact that with increased facilities still greater benefits will accrue."[5] The Council acted favorably on the petition.

The Standard Oil-old family coalition in Bayonne is understandable when one realizes that, as Random Noble indicates, in New Jersey "the domination of politics by corporation-machine alliance had reached its full flower. . . ."[6] In April, 1915 Bayonne voted in its first municipal officers under a commission government with Pierre S. Garven, the Standard Oil lawyer, chosen as Mayor.* In August it was announced that Standard Oil property investments in Bayonne would increase by two million dollars. Clearly the atmosphere in Bayonne was judged healthy for business.[7]

During the periods of July 15 to 29, 1915 and October 10 to 20, 1916, Bayonne was the scene of bitter strikes against the Standard Oil Company of New Jersey. Within a span of fifteen months, fourteen workers lost their lives as thousands turned out and demanded enough wages to support their families, and attempted to organize unions. Although the Bayonne strikes remained local, they were typical of those resulting from the type of relationship between big business and its workers in West Virginia, Colorado, and Michigan; typical, too, was the relationship of the Rockefeller interests in the great struggles of the coal miners in the Colorado strikes of 1913-1914.

When the Standard Oil Company initially obtained refining facilities in Bayonne in 1877, it employed twenty persons and produced only six hundred barrels daily. In the forty-year period of 1880 to 1920, however, (the population in Bayonne increased almost eight-fold to over 70,000 people), the refinery became the largest facility in the Standard Oil empire.[8]

Until the early twentieth century, unions did not represent a significant problem for Standard Oil in Bayonne.** However, as the facilities increased in size and more workers were employed, especially foreigners, the company became concerned that it might face an organizational effort to improve working conditions. In 1903 a foreman fired a

*When he interviewed Garven, John Reed was informed "how, during a former term as Mayor, he [Garven] had increased the tax assessment against the Standard Oil Company's property by some $7,000,000. It was after this that the company engaged him as attorney, and now the officials of the Tax Department who make the appraisals of Bayonne property are Mayor Garven's political associates." ("A City of Violence," New York Tribune, Oct. 28, 1916, Magazine Section, pp. 1,6.)

**Herbert G. Gutman has examined the labor policy of the Standard Oil Company during 1874 and 1877, concentrating on its battle with the Coopers' Union as it developed among the barrelmakers in New York, Cleveland, and Pittsburgh. In concluding, he quotes a typical Standard Oil worker who describes himself as a "serf" as he explains his total lack of power under the domination of the giant Standard Oil Company. (Herbert G. Gutman, "La politique Ouvrière de la grande entreprise amèricaine de l'age du clinquant: le cas de la Standard Oil Company," Mouvement Social [France] 108 [1977]: 67-99. The article was written in English and translated into French.)

member of the boilermakers' union and replaced him with a non-union man. Aware that the union had the sympathy of the men and was preparing to demand recognition from the company, Standard Oil fired more workers and hired replacements, among them professional strike-breakers. The union responded with a strike and a picket line around the company's facilities to keep out scabs. The city and county governments quickly dispatched police to the scene in order to protect the strike-breakers. The *Bayonne Herald* complained on July 3, 1903:

> By intimidation and using the county courts as a bludgeon to accomplish its purpose the Standard Oil Company has set about the task of not only quelling the slight disturbance incident to the strike of its boilermakers, but of striking terror into the heart of any person sympathizing with the strikers....

The emerging union in the plant was destroyed, but concerned by the events, Standard Oil introduced a pension plan for its workers and provided benefits beyond those mandated by workmen's compensation laws. Later, Standard extended the pension plan and reduced the length of the work-week from eighty-four to seventy-six hours.[9] But just in case such concessions should not be sufficient to forestall unionism, Bayonne authorities welcomed Pearl L. Bergoff, a notorious supplier of strikebreakers, as a resident. For several years Bergoff had been develop-ing strikebreaking techniques into a refined science, training such spe-cialists as *agents provocateurs,* spies, and undercover men to operate within the unions themselves. Bergoff recruited his strikebreakers and other operatives from notorious gangs of gunmen, dope addicts, and tough criminals from whom he supplied Standard Oil with all the strikebreakers it needed. But this did not interfere with his becoming one of Bayonne's leading citizens. He socialized freely with political and civic figures, and contributed financially to both Republican and Demo-cratic organizations. Mayor Garven appeared frequently with Bergoff at a variety of civic functions.[10]

That Bergoff would continue to be welcome by employers deter-mined to uphold the open shop became clear in April, 1913 when he furnished strikebreakers to Herman Brothers Company, a small capmak-ing firm in Bayonne. Jacob Herman, head of the company, refused to recognize a union of his workers, and he turned to Bergoff for assistance when the men in his factory went on strike. Bergoff quickly complied with the request, and the strikebreakers were escorted to the factory by the local police.

Nearly five hundred strike sympathizers gathered around the cap factory at a mass meeting and parade on May 1, 1913, and support for the strikers was voiced. Later that month, the Bakers' Union, the Hebrew

Benevolent Association, and the Carpenters' Union joined the strikers in petitioning the Mayor for support.[11] But the former attorney for Standard Oil announced that "Bayonne could take care of its interests as regards both employer and employee" without outside interference. While the union represented "outside interference," imported strikebreakers did not. By early August, 1913, the strike was broken, and the open shop continued.[12] Nevertheless, the capmakers' strike had demonstrated sympathy for and solidarity with the strikers among large segments of the working–class community in Bayonne. That solidarity found expression at Standard Oil in 1915.

In keeping with current practice among the leading employers in the mass production industries, Standard Oil mixed the various nationalities in the production departments to prevent solidarity. The vast majority of the workers were foreign-born, and the largest number of immigrants were Poles, with a significant representation of Italians, Russians (including Russian Jews), Irish, and Czechs. Fully thirty percent of the workers could neither read nor write English, and many also could not speak it.[13]

BACKGROUND FOR THE 1915 STRIKE

Standard Oil boasted that since 1903 there had not been any talk of union or strikes at its great Bayonne refinery where five thousand men were employed. This was explained with vague references to pension plans and welfare schemes, all of which proved to be a myth, but when pressed, General Manager George B. Gifford said frankly that it was really because of the company's refusal to deal with any "professional labor man or other outsider." Gifford, moreover, boasted of the "almost navy yard discipline" at the refinery, and justified this on the ground that the "workmen are unable to speak English, and [are] of a class requiring firm treatment, and that large quantities of highly inflammable and explosive liquids are stored at the plant."[14]

But despite the "discipline," dissatisfaction was developing at a rapid pace among the workers at the refinery. Standard Oil paid the "yard laborers," a category that constituted the largest group of workers, only $1.75 for nine hours' work.[15]*

Adjoining the Standard Oil Company's plant was that of International Nickel Company, whose product was converted copper and nickel. It employed thirteen hundred men. Until the summer of 1915,

*Five hundred of the labor force worked in shifts of ten hours during the day and fourteen hours during the night, the men changing shifts once a week and receiving twenty-four hours' rest each seven days. ("The Bayonne Strike," *New Republic*, Aug. 14, 1915, p. 38.)

International Nickel paid its common laborers at the rate of $1.80 for nine hours' work. About July 1st its workers asked for an increase in wages. To aid them in negotiating with the company, they hired Paul C. Supinsky, a Polish lawyer with offices in Bayonne and Jersey City. Superintendent Stanley met Supinsky, and after some discussion, agreed to an increase of ten percent. There was no strike.

Workers at the Standard Oil plant learned that common laborers at the adjoining plant were now receiving 22 cents an hour. Both companies were operating their plants at capacity and exporting heavily to Europe. There seemed no good reason why the Standard Oil Company should pay 19 4/9 cents an hour for the same sort of work that brought International Nickel Company workers 22 cents, especially since the workers knew that the Rockefeller-controlled company could easily afford to provide wage increases from its war profits. In 1914 the earnings of the Standard's Bayonne plant amounted to $332,000. By the next year, the earnings leaped upward to six and one-half million dollars, and earned the plant the description of being "one of the most profitable enterprises in the country."[16]

The growing dissatisfaction at Standard Oil first found expression among the stillcleaners, a group of one hundred men, nearly all Polish workers, whose function was to enter the stills soon after they had been emptied and scrape from the interior walls the tarry substances left from the distilling process. The stillcleaners were paid on a piece-rate basis, and earned about $2.25 a day. They worked in the stills at temperatures ranging from 200 to 300 degrees. To protect their bodies from the intense heat they wore several layers of thick clothing, and swathed their faces with cloths. During a shift of seven hours they drank from ten to fourteen quarts of coffee each, to stimulate perspiration in order to withstand better the intense heat.

A special grievance of the stillcleaners was the treatment they received at the hands of foremen. They complained that the foremen were continuously insulting them, and punished them when they voiced resentment. A common form of punishment was to force the stillcleaner to remain inside the super-heated vats for extended periods of time. It was not uncommon under these circumstances to see workers carried from the vats unconscious. But all complaints to Standard Oil on this issue were simply ignored.[17]

Although International Nickel Company employed no stillcleaners, its operation involved similar arduous work, for which proportionate increases had been granted. The stillcleaners at Standard Oil decided to apply to the management for a similar increase, and for relief from the tyrannical actions of the foremen. They held a meeting and decided to engage Paul Supinsky to draw up their demands. These included a fifteen percent increase in wages and the immediate discharge of a particularly obnoxious foreman. An answer was to be given in twenty-four hours.

The written demands were presented to Superintendent Hennessy by a committee of six stillcleaners. Supinsky accompanied the committee when it presented its demands. Superintendent Hennessy refused to hear the demands, launched into a tirade against the committee chairman for engaging an outside agent, discharged every member of the committee, and issued a statement warning the workers against "outside agitators," declaring that the company would adamantly refuse to deal with any outsider.[18]

On July 15, 1915, all the stillcleaners walked off the job, demanding a fifteen percent wage increase and better treatment by the hated foremen. They were joined by nine hundred coopers who demanded a similar wage increase. On the morning of July 20 the striking stillcleaners and coopers gathered at the gates of the plant to urge other workers to join their strike. By eight o'clock workers from practically every department—firemen, boilermakers, pipefitters, yardmen, and laborers—had turned out and the plant was closed. Five thousand Standard Oil workers were on strike for a fifteen percent wage increase and a working week of 50 hours; and talk began about forming a union representing all the workers. Later, the adjoining Tidewater and Vacuum Oil plants shut down, making a total of 7,000 men on strike.[19]

BACKGROUND FOR ANTI-LABOR VIOLENCE

The position assumed by Standard Oil, or rather by the Rockefeller interests who dominated the company, and the city officials made violence virtually inevitable. A precedent had been established only a few months before: on January 9, 1915 armed guards hired from a Newark, New Jersey detective agency by the Lieby Company and the William & Clark plant of the American Agricultural Fertilizer Chemical Company at Chrome, New Jersey, fired into a gathering of strikers, killing two and wounding eighteen, three of them seriously. One of the dead strikers was found to have six bullets in his body.

The strikers were mainly Polish workers who were protesting a reduction in wages from $2.00 to $1.60 a day. As one of the strikers, who testified later before the United States Commission on Industrial Relations, explained:

> For three years I work all the week and every Saturday too. My wife she take in washing. We have five children. I am a Polak and I don't drink, chew, just smoke a pipe. My name is Antonio Wiater and I work at Liebig's before

the strike. They pay $2. Then the boss say "I pay you 1.60."—then we strike.

Two things were brought to light following the slayings. One was that the strikers who had been fired upon were unarmed. "They simply were butchered," wrote a reporter for the New York *World*. Even the New York *Sun*, never very partial to the workers' side in labor disputes, called the shooting "wanton and outrageous," while the conservative New York *Tribune* viewed it as worse than the "Ludlow battle" in the Colorado coal strike:

> There the miners were armed and organized for resistance.* Here the employees of the fertilizer plants were ready for demonstrations against the strike-breakers, but nothing in the course of the strike went to show that they were armed or organized for resistance to the authorities. When fired on they attempted no violence in return; their sole concern was to get away from the whistling bullets. News accounts of the shocking affair declare that nevertheless the sniping at the fleeing strikers continued for some time. What they (the deputies) did differs no jot from cold-blooded murder.[20]

The other fact brought to light was that the Rockefeller Foundation was the owner of $500,000 worth of stock in the American Agricultural Fertilizer Chemical Company's plant at Chrome where the strike took place. It emerged during the investigation of the unprovoked and wanton shooting of the strikers that "Rockefeller dominated the policy of the plant, and this policy with its resulting violence, bloodshed, and death was singularly in accord with that in force in other Rockefeller-dominated plants. . . ."

Although ten of the 22 gunmen were indicted for first degree murder, and nine were found guilty of manslaughter and sentenced to prison terms (the tenth was acquitted), the use of private gunmen by New Jersey companies continued unabated. As the *Newark Evening News* noted:

> The laws of the State have permitted mercenary private agencies to recruit gunmen squads and battalions and hire them out to carry on war in industrial and other labor troubles. It has permitted the imported gunmen to be judge and executives. . . . Such private detective agencies and strike-breakers should be banished from New Jersey. . . .[21]

STANDARD OIL RESORTS TO VIOLENCE TO BREAK STRIKE

But they were not "banished." On the contrary, Standard Oil made good use of both anti-labor forces to break the strike at its refinery in Bayonne. Pierre Garvey, Mayor of Bayonne and the lawyer retained by

---

*Of course, the women and children killed by the Colorado militiamen in the "Ludlow Massacre" were not armed.

Standard Oil, advised the plant general manager to employ armed guards through the services of Pearl Bergoff. George Gifford, the general manager, accepted the advice and instructed Bergoff to "get 250 men who could swing clubs and you can break that strike. If that's not enough, get 1,200 to 2,000 . . . I want them to march up East 22nd Street and right through the guts of the Polacks."[22]

At first Standard Oil depended on the Bayonne police force. On July 20th, nearly a week after the strike began, the city police responded to the demand of the company that the strikers be prohibited from congregating on streets leading to the plant, and when the police tried to drive the strikers from the public thoroughfares, the workers fought back. On July 21, John Stovanchick, an 18-year-old Polish lad was killed by a policeman's bullet. This enraged the strikers. On the same afternoon, the Standard Oil Company began the importation of five hundred armed guards, supplied by Bergoff Bros. & Waddell, the detective and strikebreaking agency.[23]

The guards were recruited in New York through newspaper advertisements and from among men whose names were registered at the agency's offices. After the strike, Bergoff, the company secretary, admitted that he did not know most of the guards, as he had been forced to act hurriedly. Even his own attorney referred to the guards as "a lot of thugs."[24]

By July 21st, the strike had spread to the plant at the Tidewater Oil Company, next door to Standard Oil. Tidewater's management borrowed a force of armed guards from the Standard plant to supplement its own force, composed of non-striking workers armed with rifles. The strikers gathered in large numbers and threw stones and bricks over the walls and through the gates of the plant. "Several hundred women, wives and daughters of the strikers, took part in the action," reported the *New York Times*. The guards replied with rifle fire. Two strikers were killed and two fatally wounded in the unequal skirmish that followed.[25]

Covering the strike for the New York *Call,* Robert Minor paid tribute to the strikers' courage.* "Rockefeller," he pointed out, "fought the miners brutally in Colorado. Paterson textile workers were courageous. Roosevelt, N.J. saw a fierce battle. Lawrence, Mass. was bitterly fought. But Bayonne, N.J. eclipses them all. The Colorado miners had guns. The West Virginia miners, accustomed to hunting, met the hired army of the coal barons as man to man. Lawrence was a strike of passive resistance largely. In Bayonne the strikers rush the battlements bristling

---

*A leading cartoonist in the United States at the time, Robert Minor sketched a series of moving scenes of the Bayonne strike which were published in the New York *Call.*

The *Literary Digest* of July 31, 1915 carried two pictures dealing with the Bayonne strike. One showed the unarmed strikers being fired at by company guards.

with rifles with their naked hands. Never in the history of the labor movement, especially in the East, has there been such an exhibition of naked courage."[26]

After the slayings, the Standard Oil Company of New Jersey issued a statement from its offices at 26 Broadway which blamed the killings as "due entirely to the action of a few professional agitators who are endeavoring to cause trouble among the employees of the company." As for the company, it had adopted "the course provided by the laws of New Jersey. The proper public authorities of the city of Bayonne, the County of Hudson, and the State of New Jersey have been duly notified and the company has no doubt that the situation will very soon improve."[27] This callous statement so enraged Will Durant that he wrote angrily:

> I am a timid man, much given to counsel against violence except as a last resort. I know that violence itself is not a solution, but only a voice crying out to heaven for a solution. And I hope that this Battle of Bayonne (as, perhaps, our children will call it) can be won without further shedding of blood on either side. But I say now that we should go to Bayonne, line up with the strikers, and fight by their side for the right to picketing and public assembly; that we should organize ourselves in all our strength of numbers; that if violence is used upon us, we should arm ourselves, law or no law, to resist it. . . . For that is what we have come to. There is no longer any other cheek to turn.[28]

Among the men who came to Bayonne were organizers from the International Boilermakers' and Iron Shipbuilders' Union, the Machinists' Union, the Central Labor Union of New Jersey, the Socialist Party, and the Industrial Workers of the World (I.W.W.). Evidently the strikers did not trust the AFL organizers to lead them in a militant struggle against the Rockefeller interests. Frank Tannenbaum, leader of the unemployed movement for the I.W.W., and Jeremiah J. Baly, a young Socialist from Elizabeth, New Jersey, were chosen to lead the strike. Baly was voted chairman of the strike committee.[29]* Immediately, Standard Oil issued a circular to its employes printed in English, Polish, Hungarian and Italian, in which it warned the workers to pay no attention to the efforts of "professional agitators to induce you to make demands for changes in working conditions and wages." "The company is now and always has been," the circular continued, "willing to deal with its employes and consider any complaints they may have, but under no circumstances will it deal with outsiders or consider any ultimatum

*For the role of Frank Tannenbaum in the I.W.W. unemployed movements of 1914, activities which led to his being sent to prison, see Philip S. Foner, *History of the Labor Movement in the United States* vol. 4, *The Industrial Workers of the World, 1905-1917*, New York, 1965, pp. 444-48.

demanding an answer within twenty-four hours." The circular was posted in prominent places about Bayonne and distributed by hand to all strikers in the streets.[30]

ANTI-STRIKE PROPAGANDA

Even before the strike was fully in motion Standard Oil proclaimed that a plant shutdown would cause "a cessation of oil shipment from Bayonne to Europe," thus aiding the Germans. "Much of the oil shipped abroad since the war began is said to have gone to the Allies," the *New York Times* explained. As the strike continued, the charge that the walkout had been inspired by German agents was raised openly. Paul Supinsky, the local lawyer who assisted the strike committee, was accused of being "an agent of the German Emperor."[31]

But Standard Oil did not rely only on the "German issue." The strike leaders were labeled "outside agitators" and "I.W.W. revolutionists." Pointing to the fact that the I.W.W. had been prevented from conducting any meetings in Bayonne in support of the strikers at the Herman Bros. cap factory in 1913, Standard Oil urged a repetition of these events, and the immediate expulsion of Tannenbaum from the city.[32]

As the strike advanced, the local press and even much of the New York press began to portray it as a battle between "Americanism versus Un-Americanism," and of "American versus foreign values."[33] "The strike is all the result of foreign agitators," declared the New York *Sun*. How else explain the fact that "the Bayonne force" of 5,000 men, without any experience in unionism, walked out as a solid mass of workers. "Who fomented the dissatisfaction?"[34]

When the *New York Times,* supporting this position, also asked, "Who fomented the dissatisfaction?" A. S. Martin, describing himself as "One of the Strikers," replied:

> Would it be asking too much of your paper to give a little space to a few of the grievances concerning the Bayonne strike? The "stillcleaners," who were the first to strike, have to enter a still in a temperature anywhere from 135 to 200 degrees, with iron boots on to protect their feet and gas masks to keep from suffocating, and I have several times seen them carrying out one of their comrades overcome. At the time they struck they were paid $2.50 a day, where at one time they were paid $4 and $6 for the same work. Still, they had no intention of going on strike until the Superintendent announced that they were to have their wages reduced 10 per cent.
>
> The barrel factory department was the next to strike, and their grievances are of a like nature. I was in the barrel factory on Friday afternoon, the 16th of July, and also when the first batch of men walked out on Saturday. At 3 P.M. Saturday, July 17, the thermometer registered 116 degrees, and up to that time

three men were overcome by the heat. The day laborer there receives from $1.37 to $1.65 a day, but about half of them are piece workers; still, for a piece worker to make a $2.25 a day, he must work mighty hard. Even at that, their main grievances were the conditions. . . .

The men have to work with hot barrels (so hot, in fact, that they wear leather hand pads so as not to burn their hands), so you can get slight idea of the heat that prevails there. . . . Their demands are reasonable enough, as you can see by the papers, but the Standard Oil is only living up to its past policy of absolute terrorism, as you will notice by their declaration that they don't want the Federal authorities or any one else to butt into their affairs.

The people are mostly of foreign descent, but more than three-fourths are American citizens. As a rule, they are seldom inclined to strike until conditions get intolerable, for a day lost to them means a great deal. . . .[35]

STANDARD OIL REFUSES ARBITRATION

The mention above of "Federal authorities" refers to the fact that on July 23, federal mediators arrived on the scene and met with the strikers' committee. The following day, accepting the suggestion of the federal mediators, the strikers offered to go back to work on Monday, July 26, provided the company would agree to immediate arbitration of the strikers' demands: a fifteen percent increase in wages throughout the plant; a fifty-hour work week; time-and-a-half for overtime thereafter, and agreement by the Standard Oil Company "Not to discharge any of their employes because of their activities in the strike." In response, the only concession made by George B. Hennessy, Superintendent of the Bayonne plant, was that if the men came back to work at once, he would use his personal influence to procure consideration of the demands, and that an answer would be forthcoming no later than "ten days from the day the men return to work."[37]

The strikers rejected the offer, and voted unanimously to remain out. The decision, it must be kept in mind, came at no small sacrifice, for the workers' families were truly suffering as a result of cancellation of credit by local merchants and businessmen, cutting off all food supplies. Despite all this, the strikers maintained a united front, and given the differences in ethnicity and skills which usually divided them, the solidarity was indeed remarkable. The vote taken on July 25 to continue the strike was taken in English, Polish, Hungarian, and Italian. The vote was unanimous in all languages.[36]

Preparing for further attacks on the strikers, the Mayor of Bayonne appealed to the Governor for state militia. But Governor Felder was angered by the refusal of the Standard Oil Company to submit the strikers' demands for arbitration, especially after they had yielded to persuasion from their strike committee to accept the recommendation of the federal mediators. In a telephone conversation with Vice-President Alfred C. Bedford of Standard Oil, Governor Fielder told him that as far as he was concerned, "the company need look for no assistance from him either in the calling out of armed troops or by official influence." In fact, he would do nothing until the company agreed to arbitration.[38]

STRIKEBREAKING ROLE OF SHERIFF KINKHEAD

At this point, Standard Oil decided to rely upon County Sheriff Eugene Kinkhead to help break the strike. Kinkhead played a bizarre role in carrying out this mission. On the one hand, he and his deputies shot at and beat up groups of strikers. But when he brought local priests with him to try to persuade the strikers to return to work, Kinkhead and the priests were set upon and beaten by company guards. Enraged, Kinkhead called in his deputies, placed more than 100 guards under arrest, and forced them to march to jail through a phalanx of cheering strikers. The parade of Standard Oil's guardsmen—who had brutally shot and attacked the strikers—enhanced the sheriff's reputation among the workers, and they hailed Kinkhead as their *Kresniocec* (Godfather).[39]

Kinkhead used his newly-founded reputation among the workers to break the strike. The New York *Call*, the leading supporter of the strikers, was banned from distribution in Bayonne, and its local reporter thrown into jail. Walking into a meeting of the strikers, Kinkhead seized Frank Tannenbaum, the I.W.W. organizer, and after physically pummeling the Wobbly leader, placed him under arrest for inciting a riot. In an interview in the New York *Evening Mail,* Tannenbaum described his experience:

> In the station house I was searched and locked up amidst abuse and curses from the policemen standing by. Three-quarters of an hour later I was taken out and there was the Sheriff in an automobile waiting for me with four other policemen.

Tannenbaum asked Sheriff Kinkhead why he had been arrested, and in reply, he was ordered to take off his glasses. When he refused a policeman took them off, and then Kinkhead struck him several blows:

> That was the beginning of an almost continuous series of blows with the hand, club and blackjack from the Sheriff and police all the way from Bayonne to Jersey City. I cannot repeat the language they used because it is unprintable.[40]

Kinkhead gave Jeremiah Baly, chairman of the strike committee, the same treatment. He was beaten, thrown into an automobile, and arrested on the charge of being both an "outside agitator" and a "German agent," who had started the strike to prevent Standard Oil from "selling their product to the Allies." Baly vainly denied the charge, pointing out that he had been born in Bohemia, that his "sympathies were strongly pro-Allies," and that he had "appealed to all Bohemians to lend their support to Germany's foes so that Bohemia might be freed of Austria's rule." All this was beside the point. Sheriff Kinkhead simply forced Baly out of Bayonne, and threatened him with a long prison term if he dared to return.[41]

When a reporter complained that Kinkhead's beatings, and the arrests of Tannenbaum and Baly were illegal, the Sheriff shot back: "I don't care that there was any law or not. . . . I was there to protect life and preserve the peace, and I'd have killed Baly or Tannenbaum or done anything else if I thought it necessary."[42]

The New York *Call* denounced Kinkhead, "the Kaiser of Bayonne," but Standard Oil was perfectly happy to have a "Kaiser" working for them to break the strike. Indeed, the company empowered Kinkhead to tell the strikers that if they abandoned their strike leaders, followed the Sheriff's advice and returned to work, their demands would be considered. Of course, no written agreement to this effect was made, but the Sheriff was proud to be Standard Oil's leading strikebreaker.[43]

Standard Oil was not the only one to lavish praise on the vigilante-minded New Jersey sheriff. J. E. Roach, special representative and General Organizer of the American Federation of Labor, who went to Bayonne from Washington as the representative of Samuel Gompers, publicly declared to Sheriff Kinkhead:

> I want to compliment you, Mr. Sheriff, for your action. We are fully in accord with you, and your actions up to this time have been fully in accord with the ideas of law-abiding citizens and for the best interest of the country. Your advice to the men to return to work in view of the promises of the company to you to increase their wages and better their working conditions was wise counsel. . . . We have every confidence that the Standard Oil Company will treat with its employes through you, Mr. Sheriff, according to the proposal you have read to them. We highly appreciate your services.[44]

THE STRIKE IS BROKEN

It is incredible that an American Federation of Labor organizer would hail a strikebreaking Sheriff as a spokesperson for the workers at Standard Oil. By the time this statement was made, Kinkhead had demonstrated his true role. When the strikers refused to break ranks and accept his proposal that they return to work—with his assurance that the company would consider their requests once they were back on the job—Kinkhead called the American workmen to a separate meeting in private, and urged them not to allow themselves to be used by "enemies of the United States." He closed his impassioned plea: "If any man not a citizen here is not satisfied with conditions in this country, in God's name let him go back to the other side."[45]

The assembly of native-born workers decided to let the Sheriff work out a deal for them with Standard Oil, and voted to resume work. As news of the break in solidarity reached other strikers, morale sank, and 1500 of them came forward to express readiness to return to the plant and place the outcome in the Sheriff's hands. With the strike committee gone (its members forced to resign by Sheriff Kinkhead) and defections mounting, the workers voted an end to the strike on July 28, 1915. "For the first time in the history of the country," John Fitch commented, "a sheriff, playing a lone hand, had broken a strike." Even the *New York Times* conceded, however, that "Kinkhead's actions in terminating the strike which affected 8,000 men of the Standard, Tidewater, and Vacuum Oil Companies in Bayonne, N.J., left in its wake cries that he was exceeding his authority."[46] None of these cries, however, came from the officials of the American Federation of Labor!

SOME CONCESSIONS TO WORKERS

A few days after the men had returned to work, the Tidewater Oil Company announced an increase of fifteen percent for common laborers and other increases for the more skilled workers or those engaged in more arduous labor. Standard Oil followed this with a wage increase of ten percent for those paid $2.50 a day or less, and a twenty-five cents a day flat increase for those earning above the $2.50 daily wage. In addition, the company reduced the work week from 54 to 48 hours—but mainly for the English-speaking, skilled workers.[47]

At the same time, Standard Oil began firing all members of the strike committee and all strikers who had been most active on the picket line. Moreover, anyone who had dared to talk of the need for a union in the plant was instantly discharged. It was disclosed, moreover, that an informal agreement had been reached between the company and Sheriff Kinkhead under which no complaints would be raised against the dismissal of those "who had opposed law and order."[48] Obviously, anyone who talked union fell into that category.

Having granted some concessions to the strikers and increased the fear of dismissal among those who favored unionism, Standard Oil was confident that it had no further problems to concern it at the Bayonne plant. There was still another reason for Standard Oil's confidence. The 1915 strike had shown that the workers' militancy could be defused by the issue of Americanism. In the event of another strike threat, this technique could be used to split the ranks of the workers soon after the walkout got under way, and was bound to discourage them from attempting another battle with the powerful Rockefeller interests.

In one respect—namely, the value of Americanism in splitting the ranks of the workers—Standard Oil's confidence was proved justified. But it took only a little over a year to shatter the illusion that the breaking of the 1915 strike had ended all determination of workers at the Bayonne Standard Oil plant to achieve a decent way of life.

A NEW WALKOUT

On October 4, 1916, six hundred paraffin workers at the Standard Oil refinery in Bayonne, New Jersey struck for a twenty percent increase in wages. On the following day, thirty-five pickets appeared near the refinery to distribute circulars urging other workers to join the walkout. Instantly the Bayonne chief of police appeared, to announce that all "outsiders" who attempted to address the workers would be arrested on the spot. At a meeting of 1500 striking workers and sympathizers on October 6th, resolutions were adopted declaring that if the demand for a wage increase was not met, a general strike would be called.[49]

On October 7th a strike committee was formed by representatives of workers from the case and can department, the pressmen, yardmen, stillmen, and firemen. The men were mainly foreign-born and the meeting was conducted largely in Polish, Hungarian, and Italian.[50]

SPLIT IN THE RANKS OF STANDARD OIL WORKERS

It was thus obvious in 1916 that the strategy employed by Standard Oil a year before to split the American and foreign-born workers was paying dividends. After conferring with Standard Oil officials, English-speaking craftsmen announced that they would not join a general strike. At a mass meeting of English-speaking workers at Standard Oil, Daniel Boyle, a bricklayer, told the assembly: "I can say for the bricklayers that we have been treated fairly and squarely.... A year ago at the time of the strike the company said that if we would return to work we would be cared for.... Shortly after we returned we were granted a five and ten percent increase in salary. Shortly after this the company voluntarily gave us an eight-hour day.... The present trouble is being fostered by professional agitators, we believe."[51]

The Bayonne *Evening News* reported with hearty satisfaction the stand taken by the English-speaking workers in denouncing the strikers and praising the company. Moreover, it editorialized:

> It is a significant fact that . . . the only men advocating a strike at the present time are of foreign birth, who are not sufficiently acquainted with the English language to attend the meetings where addresses were made in that tongue. . . . It is evident that there will be no general strike at the big Constable Hook plant this time. . . .[52]

STANDARD OIL REJECTS STRIKERS' DEMANDS

Despite the fact that they were abandoned by the English-speaking workers, the foreign-born strikers determined to continue the struggle, and on October 9th, a meeting was held between a committee of nine strikers, representing the men who had walked out, and the superintendent of Standard Oil's Bayonne plant. The committee presented the company with a petition which read:

> Gentlemen—We, your employees of the various departments hereafter named present the following amicable request, feeling reasonably certain that if you consider the conditions under which we are compelled to work,(and) the prices which we are asked to pay for the commodities of life . . . you are bound to realize that our demand is fair and reasonable.
>
> First, we request an increase in wages in all departments, except the still-cleaners, in which wages have been raised and are adequate. . . .
>
> Second, we request an 8-hour day be adopted throughout.
>
> Third, that fairness be exercised in discharging men, and that men will not be discharged without just cause.
>
> Fourth, we request humane treatment at the hands of foremen and superiors, in place of the brutal kicking and punching we now receive without provocation.
>
> Fifth, we request 20 minutes for lunch in the press department.[53]

Hennessy brusquely replied that the company could afford no wage increase and warned that the plant would be shut down if any trouble occurred. On the next day the plant was closed, and 4,600 men were locked out. Hennessy explained that the shut-down was necessary because of the provocative and "unreasonable demands of employees."[54] In the process, of course, even the English-speaking workers were forced out of work.

From the beginning of the battle, the authorities of Bayonne resorted to violence and mob law to break the strike. Once again the Mayor of the city proudly announced that he was the attorney for the Standard Oil company, and that he would approve any action of the police required to break the strike. Superintendent Hennessy issued a statement asserting, "We have absolute faith in the authorities in the city of Bayonne."[55]

POLICE MOB VIOLENCE IN BAYONNE

The faith was amply justified. In the early morning hours of October 10th a squad of police detectives broke into a meeting hall used by the strikers, and arrested and imprisoned a group of workers. At the same time, police, firing weapons and wielding clubs, forced strikers and sympathizers away from the Standard Oil plant into a residential area. The police then marched into the area and forced people off the streets, fired shots into the homes of workers, routed patrons from working-class saloons, and searched houses and individuals at will.[56] As one onlooker reported to an investigator:

> That man Cady [the chief of police] is a bird. . . . He led the bunch of cops in there and put everybody off the street. Nobody dared to say a word, or he got smashed over the head. A fellow was standing in a doorway . . . and Cady laid him out with the butt of his revolver. The man's wife came out to the door and threw her arms around Cady to protect her husband. He just grabbed her and threw her back boldly through the door.[57]

The procedure launched on October 10th became a daily practice. On October 13th, the *New York Times,* under the headline "Bayonne Rioters Held in Check,"* gave an account of the method adopted by the police to break the strike:

> The police, reinforced by 100 special deputies and 30 firemen, had ranged the district where lie the homes of the striking workers of the Standard Oil Company and other plants in the Constable Hook station, herding strikers into their homes, wrecking saloons that had disregarded the order to close, and striving in every way the police knew, to fill the mob with a great fear of organized authority. . . . The little armies marched through streets thronged with strikers. To each they gave the same order, "Get off the street!" and they emphasized it with a flourish of their weapons. At the slightest hesitancy on the part of the crowd the policemen fired. They fired into the air intentionally, but the crowds broke and fled. Even a head at a window brought a shot purposely aimed to miss but to come too close for comfort. "Get in and

*On October 21, 1916, the *New Republic* published an unsigned article entitled "Newspaper Incitement to Violence," angrily accusing the New York press of having so "falsified its headlines as to convey the impression that the local authorities (whom its own strike reports proved "deliberately adopted a policy of intimidation and violence for the purpose of 'breaking the strike,'") were heroically upholding the law against a criminal mob." It cited the above *New York Times* headline as an example, and also such headlines as "Bayonne Rioters Loot Stores" *(Journal);* "New Bayonne Mob Clubbed Out of Captured R.R. Station" *(Mail);* "Bayonne Strikers Apply Torch to Many Buildings" *(Globe);* "Bayonne Strikers Renew Their Threats" *(Evening Post);* "Oil Strikers Begin Looting; Rioting Mobs Hold Bayonne" *(Evening World);* and "Strike Mobs Rout Police, Loot and Burn in Bayonne." The *New Republic* then commented: "Not a single one of these things happened." (p. 285.)

keep in! Keep away from the windows and off the roofs! We'll choose to kill next time!" cried the police.[58]

They did "choose to kill," and eight strikers, were killed by the police, as well as a bride of three weeks, while many strikers were wounded. "Death to Oil Strikers the Order," read the headline in the New York *Evening Telegram* of October 15, 1916. The previous day the strikers had attempted to circulate a handbill which read:

TO THE WORKERS OF STANDARD OIL CO.
Fellow Workers!
The Strike Is On
Wait your committee's decision, be in a peaceable manner, do not congregate on the streets and corners, 4000 workers of Standard Oil Co. of Bayonne are on strike. Be peaceable and maintain order.[59]
STRIKE COMMITTEE.

The police immediately arrested anyone carrying a leaflet and distributors were threatened with guns. Hence the headline in the *Evening Telegram*. The strike committee was forced to withdraw the circulars.[60]

In an effort to persuade the police to adopt a more moderate position, a committee of the strikers went to the municipal building with the proposal that they be permitted to appoint a committee of three hundred "to do patrol duty in the strike section, put down any disorders, to keep the crowds from congregating in front of the plants, and to compel the saloons in that section to remain closed." The police brutally informed the strikers' committee that they had enough machine guns mounted on the roof of the Standard Oil plant to slaughter any strikers who dared even to picket in front of the buildings![61]

Yet every commercial newspaper in New York City gave the impression that it was the strikers and not the police who were practicing and threatening violence. On October 11th, the New York *Globe* carried the following story under the headline, "Bayonne in Grip of a Commune," which began:

Like Paris, in Commune days, when men fought behind street barricades and lawlessness was in the saddle, is the city of Bayonne today.... Behind two barricades a block apart, bristling with paving stones, captured wagons, confiscated ash cans and broken furniture the strikers and the police faced each other at dawn.[62]

In actuality, the only analogy to the Paris Commune was the merciless attitude of the police to the strikers and their readiness to shoot down strikers and their wives, especially if they were foreign-born. The New York *Evening Post* praised this attitude of the police of Bayonne, and called upon police forces in all industrial areas to learn from New Jersey's uniformed vigilantes:

> In dealing with the mobs of Bayonne the police of that city have used stern methods, the actual club and at least the threat of the bullet. Sterner methods yet are justified and are called for unless the disorder has been quelled. . . . Clearing the streets, entering houses forcibly, putting down all opposition by the force of arms are the only means of dealing with riotous mobs that refuse to yield to milder measures.[63]

Representatives of the New York Police Department took the *Evening Post's* advice and visited Bayonne "to get some pointers on fighting strikers." Upon departure, the New York Police Inspector announced that his visit to Bayonne had been "a source of inspiration."[64]

Although the New York commercial press reported the strike in Bayonne as if it were the act of an insurrectionary mob rather than a prime example of police mob rule, the Socialist New York *Call* told the story straight. A. M. Howland, the *Call's* reporter, wrote after a visit to Bayonne:

> I felt last night as though I had just gotten back from the trenches. Only the fellows in the trenches have an incalculably better chance than we had over in Bayonne yesterday afternoon. A trench would have been a most welcome article. Instead, we had to dive for any doorway that was handy, and many of the doorways were locked. Further, we were not always cheerfully admitted to those that were open. It was dangerous to admit strangers to your house over in Bayonne yesterday. Throughout the afternoon there came the sound of volley firing as the police showed no mercy to strikers or mere sympathizers.
>
> Under orders from a Mayor who is the paid attorney of the Standard Oil Company they had shot to kill. And they had killed.[65]

WHAT SHALL BE DONE WITH THESE MURDERERS?

Nothing much was done, but at least Amos Pinchot and Dante Barton of the National Labor Defense Council sent the following telegram to the United States Department of Labor:

> We respectfully urge the Department of Labor to send conciliators or mediators immediately to Bayonne. Something should be done soon to stop the killing and wounding of strikers by policemen, deputies and gunmen in the employ of Standard Oil. Personal investigation warrants this statement. Believe you can do much to avert a reign of terror among thousands of workers who are being terrorized and infuriated by such legalized injustice.[66]

1916 STRIKE IS BROKEN

Some efforts were made to put a stop to the police reign of terror. Despite the general ban on "outsiders," several AFL organizers were able to gain entry into Bayonne and, accompanied by interpreters, mingled among the strikers. Siding with the workers' cause, the AFL organizers instructed a group of special police deputies recruited from the Teamsters' Union either to give up their badges or their union cards.[67]

But this was a mere drop in the bucket, and the violence against the strikers intensified. On October 18th it was announced that Federal mediators from the Department of Labor had arrived in Bayonne. But by the time they entered the city, the English-speaking workers announced that they were starting a back-to-work movement, and under police protection, these workers were escorted into the plant. Bayonne's Director of Public Safety Henry Wilson announced jubilantly: "I've got this strike broken, and we mean to keep it broken."[68]

A meeting between members of the strike committee and the federal mediators was held the following day. Given the steadfast refusal of Standard Oil to negotiate or arbitrate on the workers' demands, the merciless attitude of the police and other authorities in Bayonne toward the strikers, and the disastrous effect of the back-to-work movement sponsored by the English-speaking workers, the federal officials counseled the strike committee to abandon the strike. Demoralized and embittered, the strikers returned to work, defeated, on October 20, 1916. "American Workers Break Oil Strike," was the jubilant headline in the *New York Times*.[69]

ANTI-IMMIGRANT BIAS

It was clear toward the end of the strike that the anti-immigrant bias already stimulated by Standard Oil in 1915 had become even more bitter in the following year and prevented the development of solidarity among the workers. "Threaten Race War in Bayonne Strike," the *New York Times'* headline of October 19 shrieked, and the subheadlines explained: "English-Speaking Workers Declare Readiness to Face Thousands of Foreigners. Police Pledged to Give Aid." The use of the term "Race War" was clarified in an observation by John Fitch who wrote in *Survey:* "As I looked the situation over in Bayonne, it seemed to me that the issue here is primarily one of Americanism. It is tremendously significant that in the language of the street there are two classes of people in Bayonne—'white' men and foreigners."[70]

Bias against immigrant workers was also used to justify the violence and intimidation visited upon the strikers.* As one small businessman in Bayonne put it:

It's [the strike] a case of the ignorant, low-class foreigner making trouble. . . . This is an orderly, prosperous and comfortable town. Those fellows live over by themselves and refuse to become Americans. They live in dirt and filth and hoard their money. . . . This is the first time that I have said a good word for the Standard Oil Company, but I am with them on this deal.[71]

JOHN REED ON THE BAYONNE STRIKES

Noted radical reporter John Reed not only had no "good word" for Standard Oil; he blamed the giant corporation for the outrageous violation of the rights of the workers employed in the refinery and the use of anti-immigrant bias to justify this action. Reed's article, "A City of Violence," illustrated by Boardman Robinson, appeared in the magazine section of the New York *Tribune,* October 30, 1916—too late, unfortunately to be of any aid to the strikers. Reed demonstrated clearly and concisely that the Bayonne police, working on behalf of Standard Oil, were the rioters, and the strikers were the wholesale victims. Reed began:

"Bayonne, N.J., with all its varied industries, is dominated by Standard Oil. The heavy, acrid smoke of the refineries hangs over it like a pall, and to the southward the great tanks, chimneys and buildings of the Standard Oil plant and the works of half a dozen allied corporations—the Tidewater Oil, Texas Oil, Vacuum Oil, Bergen Point Chemical, etc.—loom like a smoking city above the other factories of Constable Hook, and the terrible slums where the workmen live.

As to the these "slums," Reed wrote:

Between Nineteenth Street and Twenty-fifth, and from Avenue E to the tip of Constable Hook, is the dwelling place of these people. They live packed in ramshackle tenements, many of them wooden, in three and four-room flats, for which they pay outrageous rents. Often a man, wife, six children and nine "boarders" will live in three rooms—the "boarders" working in three different shifts, one rising from his filthy pile of rags to go to work just when the other comes in worn out from his shift. There are no sanitary arrangements whatever in most of these places, except a common shed in the back yard; water is procured from a nearby common pump. The best flat I saw in

*The Bayonne *Evening Review* insisted that given the composition of the strikers, the behavior of Standard Oil and the local authorities was necessary: "This condition was created by the unlicensed and unbridled action of perhaps no more than 300 discontented workers, who were doubtless inspired to their activities by a hereditary impulse to wreck and ruin when the restraints of their native environment was changed to the wide freedom in their new homes in America." (Oct. 20, 1916).

the Hook itself had four rooms, a common toilet in the hall, one cold water tap in the parlor—and cost $20 a month.

These driven cattle, unable to speak English, unable even to communicate with each other, forced to the last desperate remedy by hopeless debt and slowly tightening starvation, went on strike. They were forbidden by the police to hold meetings, except to say whether or not they would return to work. Their leaders—such as they were—were not allowed to address them. . .

Reed also emphasized that the strikers got the "Rockefeller treatment":

There is a similarity in all these Rockefeller strikes, which springs from the similarity of Rockefeller industrialism everywhere. In Bayonne, as in Colorado three years ago, I find that the policy of the company has been to keep the great mass of laborers ignorant and disunited and every man's hand against them. Among the unskilled workmen, Americans and English-speaking men have been replaced by Polaks, Slovaks, Lithuanians, Russian Jews, Italians— and their racial and religious antipathies given full play.

Everywhere he went in Bayonne, Reed found the American, English-speaking workers blaming the immigrant workers for the troubles in the plants, an attitude which he regarded as "a tribute to the diplomacy of the Standard Oil Company and the stupidity of the American working class." He found another thing:

For the first time in an American industrial dispute the police officials announced that their object was "to break the strike." And from the first night, when a hundred officers, armed with riot guns and repeating rifles, marched down to the Hook to "demonstrate the futility of striking" to the workmen, the object of the Bayonne city authorities was to drive the strikers back to work "in every way the police knew."[72]*

The strike was broken; eight workers lost their lives, and another twenty-five were seriously injured. Standard Oil of New Jersey became a model for big business on how to use the issue of "Americanism" and radicalism as effective weapons to keep unionism out. As the historians of the Standard Oil Company of New Jersey put it: "The very wording of Jersey's public statements was that employed by other businessmen faced with identical situations in other companies and in other industries."[73]

In the end the workers gained nothing by their strike. Indeed, insult was added to injury when, one month after the end of the strike, an

*The New York *Call* summarized Reed's article, and paid the young reporter the highest compliment by commenting: "Reed could not have been more truthful had he been writing for the Call." (New York *Call,* Oct. 30, 1916.)

industrial parade was held in Bayonne to mark the beginning of a week-long community celebration. Eight AFL craft organizations participated in the affair, but not a single strikers' group was represented.[74] The event symbolized the gulf which Standard Oil had forged between the native and foreign-born and skilled and unskilled workingmen.

Nevertheless, Dante Barton, New York representative of the Committee on Industrial Relations,* warned the American people and American big business to learn some important lessons from the Standard Oil strikes in Bayonne:

> As for the American people:
> Is it not time that the American people should awaken to the essential brutality of millionaires and billionaires running their business on the principle that they cannot and will not pay their hardest-worked workers enough to give them a decent living? Ought we any longer to have business on terms in which it is considered respectable for that sort of treatment to be given to workers? The majority of these Polish workers receive now $2.50 a day, which, with the increased cost of living, does not give them enough for a profitable living.
> And as for big business:
> When these Polish workers have the ambition and the fine qualities to strike against that degraded condition in life, gunmen and special policemen, armed with guns and machine guns, are rushed against them, and the workers are abused because they have manhood and courage.
> This sort of industrial injustice, if it is not cured and overthrown, must necessarily lead to the kind of revolutionary disorder that men like the Rockefellers and Morgans consider so terrible. Men like these are sowing the wind and they will reap the whirlwind.[75]

---

*The Committee on Industrial Relations was organized to continue as a private organization some of the investigative work formerly conducted by the United States Commission on Industrial Relations, and was headed by Frank P. Walsh who had been the Commission chairman.

During the early months of 1916, with a group of progressive friends, Walsh also formed the National Labor Defense Council. The lawyers who were members of the Council were to be available to advise local lawyers in any defense case arising out of a labor struggle where their aid could be useful. (Mariotto Walsh to Frank P. Walsh, January 26, 1916, Frank P. Walsh Papers, New York Public Library.)

CHAPTER 5

The New York City Transit Strike of 1916: the First Phase

In 1916 the major transit companies of New York City and Westchester were faced with the most militant bid for union recognition and improved working conditions that the workers had made in twenty years. Their union, the Amalgamated Association of Street and Electric Railway Employees of America, A.F. of L., ordered a strike on the surface lines in Westchester after management refused to arbitrate. The strike on these lines, owned and operated by the Third Avenue system,* rapidly spread to all the surface lines in Manhattan, Bronx, Queens, and Richmond, shutting down all surface transit in the city of New York, with the exception of Brooklyn, and creating what one historian has called "the era's greatest industrial crisis."[1]

PREVIOUS STRUGGLES OF TRANSIT WORKERS

As far back as the 1880's New York City transit workers complained of their working conditions. "Too Many Hours To Work," read a headline in the *New York Times* of January 1, 1886, and it went on to report that "the drivers have for a long time past complained that they were overworked, being obliged to stand on the front platform in all

*The Third Avenue Railway Company was the center of a group of roads that were generally called the Whitridge System after Frederick W. Whitridge, President of the Third Avenue Railroad. The Third Avenue Railroad Company (the immediate predecessor of the Third Avenue Railway) was founded October 8, 1863. Its original length of route was about eight miles, but from time to time, its route was extended, until it became a veritable network complementing and supplementing the Metropolitan system. By 1906 the company had just about gone into bankruptcy, and two years later, Frederick Wallingford Whitford was appointed receiver.

kinds of weather from 15 to 17 hours a day, and being only allowed a few minutes in which to eat their dinner. They were afraid, however, to demand a reduction of hours of labor, lest the company should discharge those who made the request." Many efforts were made in the subsequent years to end this and other forms of extreme exploitation, but they usually failed. A major effort took place in Brooklyn (then a separate city) in 1895. Five thousand men, employees of the Trolley Railway System of Brooklyn, and organized in the Knights of Labor, struck to raise wages from two dollars for a fourteen-hour day to two dollars and a quarter for a twelve-hour day. The company used the police to protect scabs and beat up strikers, but the Brooklyn police force was not powerful enough to break the strike in view of the great public sympathy for the carmen. As a popular song of the day, "Brooklyn Trollilee" put it:

> Of the trolley strike I now will sing that's caused so much ado.
> And try to show both sides of the facts and story true.
> How, we'll first take the monopolist with all his cars and cash.
> Who'll stand no arbitration, but declares the Knights he'll smash;
> The next we'll take the poor man, working 14 hours they say;
> Who asks only honest wages, two dollars and a quarter a day.
> Judge for yourself—is that too much the rich man to them pay.
> The men who run our trolley cars 14 hours a day?[2]

The company had enough influence, however, to persuade the state government to call in the militia and troops of the 23rd Regiment. The state guards charged the picket lines with fixed bayonets and succeeded in breaking the strike.[3]

This was the last important strike called by the Knights of Labor, but almost a decade later in 1903, the Amalgamated Association of Street and Electric Railway Employees of America, appeared on the scene, and succeeded in gaining some recognition on the Interborough Rapid Transit & Manhattan elevated lines. In 1904, when the subway was opened, the Amalgamated along with the Brotherhood of Locomotive Engineers and the Brotherhood of Locomotive Firemen won an agreement. This collective contract was terminated before it expired, when new demands were made, and rejected by the company.

When the Interborough men struck, at the same time insisting that they were still willing to arbitrate, W.D. Mahon, Amalgamated president, refused to support them, and ordered them back to work. When the men refused, the Amalgamated's national officers publicly repudiated the strike, revoked the charters of the locals, and helped defeat the workers. The union practically disappeared in the New York area.[4]

In 1905 an unsuccessful strike wiped out the remnants of the Amalgamated and the two Brotherhoods from both the subway and elevated lines. In the same year a surface line strike was broken in Yonkers, and later in 1907 another was ended by the company going into receivership. Strikes in 1909 and 1911 were indecisive for the union, but in 1913, the Public Service Commission (PSC) of the Second District, succeeded in bringing both sides together in an agreement underwritten by the PSC, which provided for arbitration of differences between the company and the union. It was the breach of this agreement which precipitated the walkout in 1916.[5]

RAMPANT ANTI-UNIONISM

Electricity as the motive power was rapidly replacing horsepower on the New York transit system. But this changeover did not alter labor–management relations to any extent. Management's determination to run its business without recognition of any trade union remained steadfast.[6] Management, moreover, represented some of the worst enemies of organized labor, men who were pointed to as examples to industry on how to run a company without union interference. Not even the United States Steel Corporation was considered more hostile to organized labor than the great corporations that grew rich upon the nickels of the men, women, and children who used the street cars and subways of New York City. In addition to hostility to organized labor, U.S. Steel and the New York corporations in transit also had in common the fact that both were dominated by the House of Morgan.[7]

In attempting to organize the workers in the New York traction companies, the Amalgamated Association was fighting powerful opponents. The two largest transportation companies, the Interborough Rapid Transit Company (hereafter IRT) and the New York Railways Company (actually under the same management and common ownership) had in 1917 total assets of $230,000,000 and $90,000,000 respectively. August Belmont and Cornelius Vanderbilt, who dominated the Board of Directors of both the IRT and the New York Railways Company, Thomas P. Shonts, President, and Frank Hedley, Vice-President and General Manager, were long-standing enemies of any form of unionism among workers except the company mutual benefit association under the complete control of the corporations. Hedley had behind him the prestige of his victory in the short but bitter subway strike of 1905; he openly declared that he would break any other strike as easily.

The record proved it. The years which followed the 1905 struggle were indeed years of bitter defeat for the workers. Intimidation, suppression, flagrant and unwarranted dismissal, unduly long suspensions characterized these years. The cost of living in this period was steadily rising. Yet until the year 1910 wages of the transit workers remained fixed at the same level. Even then it lagged far behind the increase in living costs.[8]

WORKING CONDITIONS OF TRANSIT LABOR

Commenting on the uprising of the New York transit workers in 1916 after so many past failures at strikes and other attempts to organize, the *New Republic* observed that the revolt "came because the intense dissatisfaction with conditions had provided the cohesive cement of group action. The men had exhausted the possibilities of individual effort. There remained only the power of combination."[9] These conditions were truly abominable. "Working conditions in New York," declared William D. Mahon, Amalgamated president, "are the worst in the world, and that goes for Europe too."[10] New York City's transit workers received lower wages than employees of comparable municipal transportation systems. A listing of scales of wages paid on transit lines of 42 major cities in the United States showed that New York City's pay scale was by far the lowest. The Interborough, for example, employed 634 motormen who received $3.67 per day for 10 hours of work, 7 days a week; 3180 conductors and guards received $2.23 per day for a twelve-hour day, 7 days a week; 710 ticket agents received $2.26 per day, 7 days per week; 883 gatemen received $1.90 per day, twelve hours per day, 7 days per week; 380 station porters received $1.71 per day, twelve hours per day, 7 days per week.[11]

On the Third Avenue line, conductors received a wage averaging 23, 24 and 25 cents an hour depending upon the particular line they worked on. Their average wage was $867.51 per year, or about $16 per week for family men. The motormen averaged 25 and 27 cents an hour or $981.01 per year. And the hours of these workers, as reported to the Public Service Commission, were ten per day, seven days per week, with no holidays, and no vacations.[12]

In the case of New York transit workers the hours of work were longer in actuality than those reported. In 1887 the state legislature passed a law providing that ten hours of labor within twelve consecutive hours should constitute a day's work on street railways. But management simply ignored the law. "Workers," notes James Joseph McGinley, "gave up hope of any solution from government or management when their 1899 strike failed to win even the legal ten-hour day."[13]

New York carmen toiled incessantly long hours. Their basic working day consisted of ten hours of time actually spent in a car run. It frequently took 14 and 15 hours of working time to receive ten hours pay. There was no provision for overtime pay. It was not unusual for a man to spend upwards of 80 hours a week to receive 70 hours of pay. This was so because car runs were frequently not consecutive, or because they were split by a three- or four-hour break.

If a man was brought up on charges of violating some rule, he lost the time spent at the hearing, whether he was found guilty or not. Often a man found guilty was penalized and required to work extra time to make up for his loss of wages. Men were heavily penalized for missing a car run, or for failing to obtain the names of witnesses in case of an accident. Frequently when a car was taken off a run, a motorman or conductor would be put to work flagging or switching, for which he received less pay. Men had to purchase their uniforms at prescribed establishments. Motormen and conductors were usually summoned to answer charges and often they did not know the charge until they appeared. No extra pay was given for instruction on the cars while breaking in a new man, while heavier work on snow plows, sweepers, and scrapers, was paid at the same rate as a regular run.[14]

MANAGEMENT AUTOCRACY

Management's unrelieved autocracy added to the indignity of deplorable working conditions. The IRT's work regulations provided as grounds for dismissal any employee complaint or any failure to discharge exactly and immediately any of an endless list of rules in the regulators' books. As one worker complained: "I wouldn't mind working at the rates as they stand if things were run fairly. But they're not and the only defense we have is to stick together. You can see what chance one man has against the boss and all his spotters and investigators."[15]

But to act together was not easy. The spy system on all the roads, one observer noted, was "as elaborately organized as the Czar's secret police." Any man "talking unionism" was discharged, and the spies sometimes made it their business to lead the conversation in that direction. Any man grumbling at the company's "mutual benefit" welfare system or the company rules was discharged. The whole effect was to rid the roads of any trace of unionism. There were some "brotherhood" men on the IRT from the old steam engine days on the elevated. One by one, and for various reasons, they were discharged. Spies even watched their mail to discover whether they received the brotherhoods' monthly organs.[16]

In place of granting a living wage, the transit companies adopted the newly-created system of "welfare capitalism." Both the IRT and the New York Railway Company instituted sick and death benefits, old age pensions, and as one of its bulletins boasted, it granted passes "to the female head of the households." It also encouraged outdoor sports in summer and balls and entertainments in winter; it maintained at minimum cost, places where the men could read, play games, and "baths." But wages to meet the rising cost of living and even to equal those paid transit workers in other cities, and hours of work less than the 84 often required a week, and the strain imposed by such long hours by metropolitan traffic—such items had no place in New York transit companies' "welfare capitalism."[17]

STRIKE BEGINS IN WESTCHESTER

The conditions that prevailed in the New York transit system in 1916 would have driven any group of workers to revolt. And at five o'clock in the morning of July 22, 1916, the carmen of New York City did revolt.

The strike had its beginnings in the outlying towns of Yonkers, Mount Vernon, and New Rochelle. A small flame of unionism had been kept alive in those cities. Through these locals, the Amalgamated Association—the nation-wide carmen's union—numbering close to 100,000 members working under 250 collective agreements, had kept some influence in the transit systems of the nearby great metropolis. Time and again the Third Avenue company, of which these roads formed a part, had tried to smash the union, but had failed. The union had come out of every struggle in Westchester still alive. After the strike of 1913 it won a promise to arbitrate all differences or, at least, the question of whether they were arbitrable was exacted from President Whitridge.[18]

Since the beginning of 1916, however, Whitridge had sought to break Amalgamated's foothold on the Westchester lines. He had unprecedentedly granted two "voluntary" wage increases in February and June. Meeting with a group of his employees, but not as members of a union, Whitridge on June 15 instituted the second wage increase. This brought wages of motormen and conductors to 25 cents per hour for the first year, 28 cents per hour for the next four years, and 30 cents per hour thereafter. The union was demanding a flat 5 cent hourly increase, which would bring to 30 cents the wage rate of a first-year man, and to 33 cents his rate thereafter. (In other words, the union wanted a man brought to the maximum grade in one year, instead of five.)

As if to punctuate his refusal to meet with the union, Whitridge left for

Europe even though he knew trouble was brewing, since a vote had already been taken to authorize a strike. William Fitzgerald, Amalgamated's general organizer, whose home was in Troy, New York, where he was a car conductor when his union duties were not required, was in charge of the strike operations for the union,* and had already demanded that the issue go to the Public Service Commission for arbitration. He called Whitridge's impervious attitude "a breach of faith" since he was bound by the 1913 truce to arbitrate wage disputes. Whitridge's trip, ostensibly to see his son, who was fighting with the Allied forces in Europe, was really a device to precipitate a strike.[19] As it turned out, the broken pledge and the insolent manner in which Whitridge had ignored the demand of the men for 5 cents more an hour and had sailed for Europe in spite of the workers' request for arbitration, helped create an extremely hostile public sentiment toward his company.

On July 22, 1916 streetcar workers in Yonkers, Mount Vernon, and New Rochelle struck their respective companies—the Yonkers Railroad Company in the first, and the Westchester Electric Railroad Company in the latter two cities. Their walkout in Westchester was remarkably quiet. The reason was that, following the bloody strike of 1907, the Board of Aldermen of Yonkers had passed an anti-scab ordinance requesting that every motorman and conductor must have at least fifteen days' experience upon the streets of that city under a competent instructor. Mount Vernon and New Rochelle, had a similar ordinance. The purpose of the fifteen-day ordinances was to prevent violence during strikes and prolonged stoppage on transit. They were strongly supported by the Amalgamated, and were popular with the people, since business interests suffered from violence and stoppages during strikes, as well as workers going to and from employment. While primarily a measure to eliminate violence from trolley strikes, it was also a safety measure since strikebreakers were generally inexperienced. The number of accidents in previous strikes where they were employed demonstrated this. Violation of the ordinance carried a fine of $150 or 60 days in jail for each infringement.

During the 1913 strike Whitridge demanded that the Yonkers Board of Aldermen rescind the anti-strikebreaking ordinance. They refused, stating that to do so "would authorize President Whitridge to import strikebreakers, and strikebreakers would mean rioting and bloodshed."[20] Whitridge then threatened to test the constitutionality of the measure in court, but the strike was ended before he was able to carry out his threat.

*It is a measure of how ineffective a union the Amalgamated Association was that between 1905 and 1916 it had developed no leader among the carmen either in New York City or Westchester.

Moreover, the effectiveness of the ordinance in preventing violence in Yonkers during the 1913 strike and thereby forcing the company to make important concessions on the issues of hours and wages, influenced Mount Vernon and New Rochelle to enact similar ordinances.[21]

When the Amalgamated struck in Westchester in 1916, the companies returned their cars to the barns, making no effort to run them. Instead, acting on orders given by Whitridge before he sailed for Europe, Leslie Sutherland, Third Avenue Vice-President, sat tight and waited for the cities to act. When Mayor Lennon of Yonkers demanded that the company state why it should not be compelled to run its cars as required under the terms of the franchise, Sutherland replied that the company's hands were tied by the anti-strikebreaking ordinance. Lennon then sent his corporation counsel to Albany to ask the PSC to order the Federal Railroad Company to operate its cars. Such an order would have the effect of setting aside the ordinance.[22]

STRIKE SPREADS TO BRONX

But before the PSC gave its answer, the strike in Westchester had fanned out into the Bronx. Since its formation in 1888, the Amalgamated Association of Street and Electric Railway Employees had been seeking to unionize the conductors and horsecar drivers (later motormen) on the surface lines in New York City, and for William V. Fitzgerald in 1916, the huge metropolis and not Westchester, was the real target. By July 26, Fitzgerald had succeeded in convincing some 1100 Bronx trolley operators to quit work and join the Westchester walkout.[23*]

As the walkout moved into the Bronx, President Mahon of the Amalgamated arrived in New York to establish central headquarters, from which to direct accelerating strike activity. At the same time, Edward A. Maher, Sr., Chief Vice-President and General Manager, took over command of the Third Avenue Company's strategy. Maher immediately informed the Public Service Commission that until it used its power to vacate the 15-day anti-strikebreaking ordinance, "the 100,000 persons in Yonkers, New Rochelle, Mount Vernon and vicinity who were in the habit of riding the cars daily, would be

*Actually, the work of agitation had been going on secretly for some time in the Bronx so that Fitzgerald did not have much convincing to do. The Westchester strikers had many friends on the cars in the upper borough of New York City who were visited and spoken to (mostly in whispers) in the barns, and even leaflets had been distributed among these men urging them to join the walkout in Westchester. (New York *Call*, Aug. 20, 1916.)

The strike in the Bronx was precipitated when Vice-President Maher of the Third Avenue system made a tour of workers' meetings, and had his superintendents take down the numbers of men at the gatherings, who were fired on the spot.

compelled to do without service." Maher received his answer from the Commission the very next day, July 26. Seymour Van Sontvoord, PSC Chairman, refused to issue an order directing the company to run its cars. Sontvoord pointed out that if the Commission did issue such an order, the company would decline to obey it because of the ordinance. Then to enforce its order, the Commission would be compelled to nullify the ordinance, which it was unwilling to do.[24]

On the day preceding the walkout in the Bronx, Maher had herded some 500 strikebreakers into the various barns throughout the borough. The strikebreakers came from the notorious Bergoff agency which brought violence to Philadelphia in the traction strikes of 1909, 1910, and 1913.* Strikebreakers received $5.00 a day which was almost double the pay of a regular employe. Once the strike began in the Bronx, scab-manned cars ran wild in the streets; accidents were so numerous that the police officially announced they could not keep track of them.[25]

At the outset of the strike in the Bronx, circulars were distributed by the workers:

> To the Public! The striking motormen and conductors of Bronx county ask your moral support in their struggle for better working conditions. The company has imported professional strikebreakers to terrorize us and cause disturbances in the county, thereby casting reflections on the peaceful strikers.
>
> Look over the crowds of strikebreakers, and see if you see any good citizens of the Bronx.[26]

Reform Mayor John Purroy Mitchel and his Police Commissioner declared at first that it was not the city's duty to break the strike, and that uniformed policemen would not be placed on the cars. But this lasted exactly one day. On July 29 one policeman was placed on each car making its run.[27] Yet in spite of scabs and police protection of the strikebrakers, few cars ran. Bronx residents trudged to and from the subway and the elevated, supporting the strike by refusing to ride the street cars. Even during the rush hours, only the poorest service was maintained, and by nightfall this was completely abandoned.[28]

STRIKE SPREADS STILL FURTHER

On Saturday afternoon, July 29, Bronx Borough President Matthewson made an attempt at arbitration. It failed when the Mahers, father and son, refused to meet with the union.[29] On that same afternoon a meeting

---

*The Berghoff strikebreaking agency also furnished spies for the traction companies and even had spies working for the companies within the Amalgamated Association. (Edward Levinson, *I Break Strikes: The Technique of Pearl L. Bergoff*, New York, 1935, p. 93.)

of the Third Avenue system was called for the Lyceum at 86th Street and Third Avenue in Manhattan. There, amid scenes of enthusiasm, the strike vote for the Borough of Manhattan was taken, and carried. The resolutions declaring the strike carried unanimously and read:

> Resolved, that we, the employes of the Third Avenue Railway system in the City of New York do hereby join with our fellow workers of New Rochelle, Yonkers, Mt. Vernon and the Bronx, and do hereby declare a suspension of work, such suspension to continue until the company agree to recognize our organization, and grant us the right to deal with it through the accredited committees and officers of our association, and, be it further,
>
> Resolved, That we indorse and declare for the wage demands already announced by our fellow workmen on strike, which are that the company shall establish a rate of wages as follows:
>
> Thirty cents per hour for the first year of service.
>
> Thirty-three cents per hour thereafter; and be it further
>
> Resolved, that we appeal to all of our fellow employes who have not joined us to come with us, and to the public to give us their cooperation and support in this our just contention for our rights as American workmen.

"The strike is on!" said President William D. Mahon of the Amalgamated at the adoption of the resolutions. "They have started it, and we will continue it until they meet us as an organized body."[30]

During the next few days, while the cars were tied up on the Third Avenue system, the organization of the men on the other surface lines in Manhattan and on the cars in Queens and Richmond went on. The corporations controlling these lines prepared for a strike—the New York Railways Company discharged two men who were known to have joined the union. Mayor Mitchel attempted to persuade the Third Avenue officials to submit to arbitration, but he had no more success than had Borough President Mathewson of the Bronx.[31]

On August 3 President Shonts of the New York Railways Company was warned that if he refused to recognize and treat with the chosen union of his employees, his trolley lines would be paralyzed.[32] On Friday evening, August 4, the strike was declared on the lines of the New York Railways Company—the "green system"*—at a meeting at the Lyceum. The strike vote was taken in the presence of representatives from the AFL, the New York State Federation of Labor and the Central Federated Union, who promised moral and financial support, and after Big Jim Larkin, the militant Irish labor leader, spoke to the Irish transit workers and assured them that they would be upholding the real spirit of Ireland by voting to strike.[33]

*The term "Green line" was used for the New York Railways Company because their cars were painted green and white.

That same night the men on the Queens County cars went out, and the next morning the motormen and conductors of the Second Avenue Railroad—the "blue line"—struck without even the formality of a strike vote. In the evening the workers on the Staten Island cars, operated by the Richmond Light, Heat and Power Company, joined the walkout. In all four boroughs—Bronx, Manhattan, Queens, and Richmond—the tie-up was complete. No regular service was maintained.[34]

Meanwhile, the unionization of the men on the Interborough elevated and subway lines and on the Brooklyn Rapid Transit (BRT) went forward steadily. The Brotherhood men on the tubes coming into the city from New Jersey, as well as the power house employees, were contacted and they made it clear they also were ready to go out. It was thus obvious that when the strike call came, it could paralyze the city's main arteries.[35]

The Central Federated Union had already pledged its complete support to the carmen. A committee of thirty from the Federation was on the platform at the Lyceum when the strike vote of the "green car" men was taken. General Organizer Hugh Frayne of the AFL was working closely with the Amalgamated officials, and Federation President Samuel Gompers spent a day in New York City conferring with Mahon of the Amalgamated. AFL local organizer William Collins had cooperated with the carmen since the strike had been called in Westchester, and was to continue rendering assistance in the new walkouts. Local unions, moreover, pledged that no members would ride upon scab-manned cars, and had adopted rules by which members detected in that act, or even found with transfers in their possession would be fined. Circulars were distributed addressed "To the Union Men of New York" which read:

Union men of New York! Brothers!
The street car men have plunged into the fight for decency and liberty—for everything that men fight for against greed and oppression.
It's your fight as well as theirs!
Brothers! It's up to every union man to swing in and help the men on the platforms to come through winners.
No union ever wins for itself alone. If they win, they win for all!
Now what can YOU DO? Much!
You can stay off the cars—as, of course, you will. What union man would put his foot on the step of a fink-run death wagon? He doesn't live.
But there's more that we can do. Every union man can make sure that no member thoughtlessly rides on a struck car. Every union can make dead sure of this by placing a fine on any member that does it. That will be just a sign that nothing is being left to chance, nothing left to forgetfulness. . . .

Organized labor in New York knows how to rally to the support of union men in a time like this!

Organized labor knows what battle looks like and it has yet to shrink from the firing line.

Now that the companies have forced battle upon the workers, the workers rejoice in the fight—AND WE REJOICE WITH THEM! For this fight is going to mean a great victory for a body of fine and loyal men who have been oppressed to the limit of endurance.

The Union forever—with victory![36]

A song entitled, "When We Aid the Street Car Men," expressed the same sentiments:

Now let us give our sympathy and lend a hand to them
Who now fight labor's battles, the organized street car men
May they and we together hold hands and let us say,
"We strike for freedom while we aid those men on strike today."[37]

Soon union pickets and union sympathizers were singing the song and wearing strips of carboard on their hats bearing the legend, "I Walk —I Won't Ride in Scab Cars."

POLICE PROTECTION FOR STRIKEBREAKERS

But, protected by police, some scab cars were moving through the streets of the four boroughs. At the beginning of the strike, the companies demanded that the city assign two uniformed policemen to ride each trolley. Mayor Mitchel at first flatly turned down the request. He was determined, he told reporters, to keep the police department clear of the charge of siding with one side against the other in the conflict. But this seemed not to cover the use of one policeman on a car, and Mitchel offered this protection to the companies.[38]

The companies rejected the offer. One patrolman on a car was insufficient since the rear conductor was increasingly being subjected to "intimidation and violence." To the extent that the city could supply a second patrolman, to that extent would service be increased. In short, "service is a matter of police protection."[39]

This did not at first sit well with New York City's Reform Administration. Deputy Police Commissioner Frank Lord even addressed a strikers' meeting of 2,000 at Lyceum Hall to denounce the request for two policemen for each car, and praised the strikers for refraining from violence. He noted that despite the complaints from company officials, "there had been no real rioting and few outbreaks." Police headquarters confirmed Lord's evaluation, and its own investigation showed that complaints of disorder and intimidation had proved either exaggerated or false.[40]

Nevertheless, Mayor Mitchel again yielded to company pressure, and agreed to have two policemen placed on each trolley. In part, he yielded because the commercial press, cooperating in full with the companies, headlined stories of violence by strikers that bore no resemblance to the reports by the police. A typical headline, in this case, in the *New York Times*, read:

CAR STRIKERS' RAID STOPS BRONX LINES, ARMED YONKERS INVADERS RESORT TO VIOLENCE IN FORCING TRAFFIC SUSPENSION.[41]

With this aid, manufactured out of the whole cloth, the transit companies succeeded in achieving the goal of having two uniformed policemen assigned to ride the trolley cars. (Three thousand policemen were assigned to strike duty.) But even the police conceded that when they arrived on the scene, there was nothing but sporadic outbreaks by strikers and no revolvers found on any of them.[42] In fact, much of their work consisted of preventing angry citizens from attacking the scab drivers who ran their cars wildly through the streets. On July 29th a Bergoff strikebreaker ran over a child. Incensed people of the neighborhood, many women among then, chased him down the street, hurling both missles and epithets at him. The scab was a notorious Bergoff operative who had served time on convictions of grand and petty larceny, and he told the police who saved him from the angered crowd that he had had no experience as a motorman before he began driving the trolley car.[43]

The capitulation of New York's progressive, reform Mayor to the traction companies angered organized labor. The Brooklyn Central Labor Union denounced the city's Police Commissioner for having "complied with the demand to put policemen on the cars manned by strikebreakers at the same time proclaiming his impartiality, and this action has been approved by Mayor Mitchel." The resolution went on to condemn "the action of the city administration in using police upon street cars as an unlawful exercise of the police function in the interest of the street car monopolies."[44]

COMPANY PROPAGANDA

No sooner had the companies succeeded in having the city assign uniformed police to ride the cars than they used this situation to reinforce the impression that the transit companies and "law and order" were synonymous. Despite the hiring of gangsters, despite the fact that collisions and accidents were so numerous as a result of inexperienced scab drivers that passengers risked their lives by riding the cars, the companies kept up a barrage of paid advertisements insisting that they and they alone upheld the principle of "law and order." These full-page advertisements, often quoted in approving editorials in the same papers, emphasized that the strike represented "anarchy," "lawlessness," "outside," "alien," "foreign" interference with otherwise "loyal employees" who were satisfied with their conditions but were forced to strike by "intimidation and threats of violence." Management was not fighting organized labor or the principle of labor unions, other advertisements insisted, but only "labor agitators from other cities" who had come to New York to disturb the "peace and tranquillity of our community." Management was willing to deal with their own employees, but not as members of a trade union or an "outside" organization of any kind. Management was only interested in running its cars and serving the people of New York City and Westchester, and was entitled to police protection for the safety of its passengers and its property.[45]

An indication of the depths to which the companies sank was the attempt to link the Amalgamated Association with the Preparedness Day bombing in San Francisco which occurred July 22, 1916.* Tom Mooney, who was on the Amalgamated payroll as an organizer, was arrested and charged, without a shred of real evidence, with being implicated in the crime. Shonts wired the San Francisco District Attorney, who wired back that Mooney was an accredited agent of W. D. Mahon, President of the Amalgamated. He added that he had evidence that Mooney dynamited an electric tower during a recent strike—but did not mention that Mooney had been twice acquitted of the charge—and that when the strike failed, "the bomb throwing occurred. Mooney's expense account was sent to Mahon." In another report, Fickert added that he did not believe that Mahon had any knowledge of the bomb plot, thus covering himself after having damaged the strike cause in New York City.[46]

ROLE OF THE SOCIALIST NEW YORK CALL

While the commercial press did occasionally criticize the traction companies, the strikers' point of view never found its way into their columns and by playing up the myth of striker violence, the press made it much easier for the companies to present themselves as upholders of "law and order." It was only through the pages of the Socialist New York *Call* that the union and the strikers were able to get their message across to the public. Only the New York *Call*, for example, published William B.

*The story of the Preparedness Day bombing and of the Mooney Case which followed will be discussed in the next volume.

Fitzgerald's answer to the companies' charge that the strike was the work of an "Alien," "outside organization," led by "outsiders." Fitzgerald noted:

> My father spent four years and over as a soldier in the war of the rebellion, fighting to establish the fact that one flag should wave over all the States in this nation, so I leave it to the people of New York City to judge whether I am an alien or not, and I would ask the people to make a comparison with the people that are being brought here now from every State in the Union . . . to take the places of the men of New York. Of the men they are bringing, many of them carry with them prison records from other States.

As to the charge that the Amalgamated Association of Street and Electric Railway Employes being "an alien organization," Fitzgerald answered by pointing out that it was "a part of the American Federation of Labor and has some of the oldest branches in this eastern country." Basically, the transit companies were opposed "to any organization" and not just to the Amalgamated. "They are today paying the lowest wage of any big city in the United States, because of the unorganized condition. They want to maintain that condition, and that is the reason that they are throwing this dust, as it were, in the eyes of the public, to confuse you, that you may help them keep their street railway men in individual slavery."[47]

The commercial press continued to help the companies "throw dust . . . in the eyes of the public," but only the Socialist *Call* published the other side of the story. The *Call* did so even before the strike hit New York City, for when the New York *Evening World* warned Amalgamated organizers to "KEEP OUT" of the metropolis, so that the city, just nearing a settlement of labor difficulties in the garment trade, might enjoy "a little tranquillity just now in business," the *Call* responded: "It is labor's business to determine when to strike. Labor is amply justified in striking whenever it thinks it can gain by striking. . . . To hell with tranquillity; the workers are after justice—and they can't have justice as long as they are robbed."[48]

Once the strike swept through four boroughs, the *Call* carried full reports on its developments and editorials in support of the union. It issued appeals for financial support for the strikers; gave the widest notice to strike meetings, and published advice such as:

> DON'T—
> Ride on the trolley cars of the Bronx, Queens, Manhattan, and Richmond, nor those of Yonkers, Mount Vernon, and New Rochelle. A strike is now in progress. Help the strikers by refusing to patronize cars manned by scabs.

DO—

Ask every motorman and conductor on whose car you ride in Brooklyn, if he belongs to the trolleyman's union. If he says he doesn't ask him why not. Tell him how the union men of Yonkers and other Westchester cities have steadily improved conditions on the whole Third Avenue system.[49]

The Amalgamated, not noted for its pro-Socialist orientation, showed its appreciation at its 1917 convention by answering the *Call's* appeal for funds with a donation of $2000.[50]

TRUCE SETTLEMENT

Although the transit companies clearly had the advantage in the battle to win public support by their almost complete domination of the commercial press, there were weaknesses in their stand which helped overcome this advantage. For one thing, it was clearly contradictory to argue on the one hand that the companies did not oppose labor unions or the principles of organization, but only an "alien organization, with alien interests, working for alien purposes," when the Amalgamated was plainly the organization chosen by their employees. Again, it was contradictory to state that they did not oppose arbitration, and object to treating with the only organization with which arbitration could take place.

The companies received a further blow when the report of the Public Service Commission, signed by Chairman Oscar S. Straus, laid the entire blame for the 1913 strike on Frederick Whitridge, President of the Third Avenue System. It found that there was no dispute, that the men on the Westchester and Yonkers lines "not only were ready to arbitrate the differences between them, but that they asked for the opportunity to arbitrate them." Moreover, the report found that the Board of Directors of the road put the whole matter into Whitridge's hands on June 11, 1916, and two days later, he sailed for Europe. It was obvious, the report continued, that there was an organization drive on prior to the strike and that it was accelerated by the strike. Moreover, the Commission charged that the strike was precipitated by Whitridge's attitude. He had "either intentionally violated the agreement he had made with the men to arbitrate," following the strike, or he had completely forgot about it, but in either case, he was to blame for the initiation of the wave of transit strikes.[51]

The Commission's report helped undermine the transit companies' standing in the public's eyes, and their steadfast refusal to budge was further weakened when on the same day, the Merchants' Association of

New York demanded that in the public interest, the companies meet with the Mayor and their employees' representatives.[52]

In this situation, Mayor Mitchel met with Public Service Commission Chairman Oscar Straus, and both agreed to cooperate in working out a peace settlement. The peace terms had actually already been formulated by Mayor Mitchel prior to this meeting, and reflected what has been called "middle-class Progressivism's basic attitudes toward labor relations and organized labor." This meant that employees have the right to organize and companies have no right to refuse to confer with or to recognize such organizations. But while "the right to organize is a fundamental civil right," the union may not exclude any one from working who refuse to join the organization or to insist upon the closed shop.[53]

On August 6, Mayor Mitchel submitted the peace terms to the union's representatives (W. D. Mahon, Louis Fudiger, union attorney, William B. Fitzgerald, and Hugh Frayne, AFL representative), and to Shonts and his attorney, representing the New York Railways Company, an Interborough subsidiary, but with the understanding that the agreement accepted by the New York Railways would be endorsed by the other companies. Shonts and his attorney had refused to sit with union officials.

The opening provision of the "truce agreement," as it came to be called, read:

> The employees have the legal and moral right to organize, and the company pledges that they will not interfere with the employees in their exercising of these rights to organize, either by intimidation, coercion or discharge, nor shall the employees undertake to interfere with other employees in their exercising of their rights to decline to organize either by intimidation or coercion.

Management also agreed to the election of a committee of its employees and to negotiate with this committee on wages and working conditions. But it was clearly stated that this "shall not be deemed a recognition by the company of the organizations of which they are officers or representatives." Provision was made for arbitration machinery to consider all questions not settled by negotiation. Finally, the strikers agreed to call off the strike and return to work immediately, while all strikers would be restored to their pre-strike status without prejudice.

The agreement (made up of five points) was underwritten by Mayor Mitchel and Chairman Straus. It remained only for both sides to accept the agreement—the companies through their Board of Directors and the union through the local memberships.[54]

The union claimed the agreement to be a victory for the right to organize without interference, and one for the principle of arbitration, a cardinal doctrine of the Amalgamated. (The principle was written into the constitution in the provision that a strike could not be authorized until arbitration had been offered and refused.)[55] But management claimed that it had secured the victory because it was not bound to recognize any trade union. In fact, on the very day following the acceptance of the "truce agreement," Shonts asserted that it was not to the interests of the New York transportation system that his employees should be affiliated with an organization "with interests in other cities and not responsible as we and our employees are to this community."[56]*

Nothing, in short, had happened during the strike or discussions leading up to the "truce agreement" which had altered in the slightest the companies' opposition to the right of their employees to belong to a union of their own choosing. They had thus committed themselves to nothing, and it seems incredible that the Amalgamated officials were willing to accept such an arrangement with companies whose underhand dealings were notorious and of long standing.**

That the agreement left the workers exposed to attack was apparent to anyone who viewed the terms realistically. The New York *Call*, for example, at first greeted the settlement with a sense of euphoria, labelled it as proof that "the day of the union has come," and joined the editor of the New York *World* in congratulating Mayor Mitchel on his "peaceful

---

*In quoting this remark by Shonts, Samuel Waitzman adds the pertinent comment: "This statement was made just after Shonts emerged from a meeting with the board of directors, whose interests ranged from coast to coast, two of them living in Boston, 200 miles away." The directors included "financiers with interests certainly not confined to Westchester and New York City." ("The New York City Transit Strike of 1916," unpublished M. A. thesis, Columbia University, 1952, p. 41.)

**Even more astounding is that the Amalgamated leadership had been willing to accept several revisions President Shonts made in Mayor Mitchel's terms. These included (1) a guarantee by the union not to coerce employees who declined to organize; (2) explicit refusal to recognize any union or "outside" employee organization; (3) a clause granting management absolute control (not subject to arbitration) of employees in all matters relating to efficiency. It was Mayor Mitchel, not Mahon and the other Amalgamated negotiators, who persuaded Shonts to drop his extreme demands. (W. D. Mahon, William B. Fitzgerald, and Louis Fudiger to Mayor John P. Mitchel, August 6, 1916; Theodore P. Shonts to J. P. Mitchel and Oscar Straus, August 6, 1916, John Purroy Mitchel Papers, New York City Mayoralty Office, City Hall.)

Melvyn Dubofsky notes that Mahon "surprisingly accepted" Shonts' revisions, but he has only words of praise for the settlement terms advanced by Mayor Mitchel, and treats them as meriting the highest praise. (*When Workers Organize: New York City in the Progressive Era*, Amherst, Mass., 1968, pp. 135, 136.)

termination of the most serious labor problem that ever concerned New York."[57] But as it studied the terms of the settlement, the *Call* grew alarmed and issued a series of warnings. It warned the transit companies: "If your workers have to strike again to compel you to live up to your word, it will not be good for you and your system." The people of New York would then vote overwhelmingly to place the entire traction system under municipal ownership. "So Mr. Shonts, Mr. Hedley, Mr. Belmont, you had better BE AS HONEST AS YOU CAN!"[58] For the transit workers it had this warning: "A counter attack is coming and unless the men consolidate, they are likely to lose all they have and perhaps more."[59]

As we shall now see, this was no idle warning.

CHAPTER 6

The New York Transit Strike of 1916: the Second Phase

By August 8, 1916 all the companies involved in the strike had signed the "truce agreement" in the form accepted by the New York Railways Company. But just as the union spokespersons were expressing unbounded optimism that the truce gave them the greatest organizing victory in 24 years, the IRT management had already launched a company union movement to head off and undermine any organizing drive by the Amalgamated. Even before the truce had been signed, on August 3, the Interborough management held a mass meeting with 2000 of its employees who were greeted by a white-uniformed company band, and addressed by Shonts and Hedley. At this gathering management announced the formation of the Brotherhood of IRT Employees to maintain management-labor "harmony." The workers were urged to select a committee which was "to serve as the official channel of intercourse between the men and the company officials." At the end of the meeting, 100 employees signed a pledge that they would not join any but the company Brotherhood, and that neither threats nor intimidation would induce them to strike in the future.[1]

Later that same morning a similar meeting of New York Railways Employees was held at which 120 workers were selected to carry a petition to the Mayor informing him that they would join only a company union, and requesting that he afford them protection on their jobs.[2]

THE TRUCE IN PRACTICE

All this occurred before the agreement of August 6th had been signed, and no sooner had the signatures been attached than the IRT management intensified its anti-union activities. Shonts and Hedley set the pace for the rest of the transit companies. They set out deliberately to confront the committee selected by the Amalgamated with one elected under company surveillance. These two committees, it was planned, would then be set to bid against each other, with the company-blessed committee receiving every advantage. As the Shonts–Hedley Plan frankly stated: "we recognize no union . . . we will make conditions so fair and attractive that no man will feel it necessary to go outside the company to attempt to make things different."[3] Interborough set aside two days, August 17 and 18, for elections for members of the company union committee. At company-sponsored meetings, Hedley bluntly told the workers that men who joined a company union rather than the Amalgamated would be especially rewarded.[4]

The Shonts–Hedley Plan was actually nothing more than a replica of the company union established on the Philadelphia Rapid Transit after the bitter strike in 1910.* Its mentor was T. E. Mitten, Vice-President and General Manager who put it across with the aid of Bergoff undercover men. Mitten's brain-child became known as the Keystone Carmen's Union, and it gave birth to an offspring in 1912 on the Milwaukee surface lines. Six years later, another one was born on the New York transit lines.

Despite union protests, management announced that company unions would be established, insisting that "the adjustment of grievances is better left to the employees' own organization without the interposition of any outside body." At meetings with officials of the Amalgamated, management representatives refused to rehire the men who had been fired for activity during the strike, despite the agreement to refrain from such action. They also refused to desist from establishing a company union.[5]

On August 15, a "Committee Representing Employees of the New York Railways," the IRT subsidiary, addressed a letter to President Shonts, pointing to "what we consider a deliberate and flagrant violation of this agreement [entered into between yourself and representatives of the employes] upon the part of the officials of your company." Specific violations were listed: (1) "indiscriminate discharging of men"; (2) interference by the company with the selection of the committees to represent the employees. The committee therefore asked for an immediate conference to settle these differences.[6]

---

*For a discussion of the 1910 strike, which was also a general strike in Philadelphia, and the origin of the company union, see Philip S. Foner, *History of the Labor Movement in the United States*, Vol. 5, New York, 1980, pp. 143-63.

The New York *Call* saw the John D. Rockefeller company union in Colorado as Shonts' model, pointing out that this was "not surprising in view of the fact that 'Rockefeller Ivy' Lee is one of his chief advisers." (Aug. 16, 1916.)

When nothing came of this complaint, Fitzgerald sent a formal protest to Mayor Mitchel charging management with "deliberate and flagrant violation" of the agreement on the same two counts. Since Mitchel, a leading promoter of Preparedness, was at the Plattsburgh Training Camp, nothing could be done. But when the Mayor returned to New York City and met with management and union representatives, the former refused to budge, and insisted on its right to advise its employees that they could join a company union. To the union's chagrin, Mayor Mitchel refused to restrict the company's activities on behalf of a company union. He argued that as long as the employers did not hold out specific financial inducements, "you cannot properly object to the company arguing with the men to join the union. . . . Let us have it clearly understood that both sides have a right to argue, persuade and induce."[7] As Melvyn Dubofsky correctly notes: "Given management's financial resources, its high-powered attorneys, and its nearly unchallenged right to hire and fire, the Mayor's neutrality offered the New York Railways Company free rein to continue its labor-baiting policies."[8] So much for the Amalgamated's faith in Mayor Mitchel.

On August 30 a conference took place between the IRT management and a 23-man negotiating committee representing union men on the IRT subway and elevated lines. The union committee brought with them a list of 24 demands aimed at rectifying the carmen's major grievances—hours, wages, and working conditions. Its wage demands were backed up with a scale of wages paid on transit lines in 42 major cities in the nation, which showed that New York City's scale was the lowest. While the Amalgamated's list of demands did not include a day off for motormen or conductors, it did call for a ten-hour working day to be concluded within 12 consecutive hours; overtime to be paid at the rate of time-and-a-half; that night work was to be concluded within a 12-hour period, but not to be extended beyond 7 a.m. Other demands called for a statement of charges to be handed a man accused of misconduct; that a hearing should include a union representative; that a man should not lose pay for having to answer petty charges; that a man found innocent of alleged violations or charges was to lose no pay; that a man was not to be docked for failing to obtain the names of witnesses; that a motorman's hourly rate was to be paid regardless of what duties he was assigned to; that uniforms were to be purchased in the open market, but conform to the company's specifications of color and style; that a motorman be paid a .35 hourly bonus for instructing; and a .50 hourly bonus for snow-plowing, sweeping or scraping, with an extra man on such a run. Finally, provisions were made for union representatives to carry out their functions in behalf of the employees without loss of position or seniority rights.[9]

These demands reveal how utterly exploited were the workers on the New York transit lines. Yet management's representatives completely ignored the union's demands. Instead, they presented an individual working agreement, or labor contract, which was being circulated among IRT employees. The contract, labeled by the union a master-servant agreement or "yellow-dog contract," forbade the signer from joining any labor organization not recognized by the employer. All workers who signed the individual contract were promised immediate wage increases as their reward for forswearing union organization.[10]

A mass meeting of IRT men was called the following night. When a union spokesperson told some 3000 men what the contract actually meant, they unanimously empowered organizer Fitzgerald to call a strike if the contracts were not withdrawn from circulation.[11]

At a September 5 conference with the IRT local union committee, management rejected the committee's request that the company submit to arbitration the fairness or unfairness of the individual contract. William Fitzgerald replied for the union: "I don't see how we can avoid a strike on the Interborough Rapid Transit Company's lines—subways, elevated, and streetcars."[12]

Actually, the company was anticipating this response and began making plans for another strike. Three thousand strikebreakers were sent to terminal points on subway and elevated lines. Management then posted a notice informing employees who participated in the strike that they would lose benefits of the agreement and all cumulative seniority. Letters were also sent to Mayor Mitchel requesting police protection, and another to Governor Whitman requesting the militia to supplement the police force.[13]

The IRT management was not only ready for the strike, but welcomed it. There was no shortage of strikebreakers since the threatened national railroad walkout had been headed off by the Adamson (eight-hour) Act.* Interborough was in the position to make use of more than 6,000 of these unused "professionals,"—gangsters and thugs who had been collected in and around New York by Bergoff and other strike-breaking agencies. The strike that Interborough wanted, management was convinced, was bound to lead to the destruction of the union.[14]

Basically, the IRT was setting the pattern for the other transit companies. On his return from Europe, Whitridge took over wage negotiations for the Third Avenue System. He claimed the road could not afford to meet the union's demands, unless the city came to its rescue and absorbed some of its costs. But that did not prevent the Board of

*See below pp. 176–83

Directors from declaring its regular quarterly 10 percent dividend. Third Avenue then joined Interborough in discharging strikers and forcing its employees into a company union.[15]

THE SECOND TRANSIT STRIKE BEGINS

At 9:20 P.M., September 6, 1916, at a mass meeting at the Lyceum, the members of Division 731, Amalgamated Street and Electric Railway Employees, voted unanimously to declare a strike on the IRT subway, elevated, and street car lines. The strike vote came in response to the report of a committee which had met with General Manager Hedley at which the IRT Manager had "absolutely refused" to cancel the "master and servant" individual agreements.[16]

When the news of the strike vote was reported to IRT President Shonts, he seemed to be pleased. "All agreements are off," he told reporters. "This is a fight to the finish and we are 100 percent prepared." IRT Attorney James L. Quackenbush added that "if there are enough bluecoasts and brass buttons and night sticks—not revolvers—where they are needed, the strike won't last long."[17]

By the morning of September 7, the second part of the New York City transit strike was on. Although the IRT management offered double pay and 20 percent bonus to all workers who refused to join the strike, over 25 percent of the subway and elevated men walked off their jobs while a majority of the street car men began taking their cars to the barns. Conductors rolled up signs: "No Passengers. On way to the barn!"[18]

New Yorkers were handed leaflets distributed by both sides in the labor dispute. In its appeal "To the Public" the IRT declared:

> Let no one be misled by the charge that the Interborough is trying to crush out unionism.

WE ARE NOT FIGHTING UNIONISM!

The fact was, the statement continued, the company "actually encouraged the formation of a union" among Interborough workers. Nothing, of course, was said about the union being a "company union," but a hint at this was contained in the comment that the IRT believed that "the interests of this company, its employes and the public they serve will be fostered if all relations between the company and its employes were conducted in the light of their common interests, rather than with reference to the interest of outside parties." Then what was the cause of the present strike? It all boiled down to one simple fact:

> The real point underlying the existing difficulties is the determination of the Amalgamated Union to impose itself upon the company, and to supplant

the union of the Interborough employes against the expressed will of the men themselves.

As for the company, all it was doing was "protecting its employes in their right to work and the public in its right to ride as against the efforts of the Amalgamated Association to prevent the doing of these two things."[19]

Since many of the men operating the streetcars, subway, and elevated lines were nearly all professional strikebreakers, who were only able to operate because Mayor Mitchel had placed policemen on every car to protect the scabs, it was certainly stretching the truth considerably to talk of "protecting" the employes of the IRT.

The leaflet distributed by the Amalgamated was entitled, "Why There is A Strike on the New York Car Lines." It went in part:

> Shonts and Hedley want to break the union. They want to control the wages and lives of the men and their families, just as they have done. The men want to be free. They are taxed from seventy-five cents to a dollar a month for Mr. Shonts and Mr. Hedley's "Benevolent Society." They would rather pay that sum to a union of their own. They don't want to pay that much to the company's union to be further "controlled" and subjugated. They don't get anything back if they leave the company and they lose the sick benefits they paid for. In their own union they retain this benefit if they resign or leave.
>
> Shonts and Hedley are only tools. They must enforce the will of the masters. Rockefeller and Morgan want the men subjugated. They want unionism destroyed. They want to control their employes like chattel. . . .
>
> THE MEN ARE NOT STRIKING FOR HIGHER PAY OR SHORTER HOURS. These questions they agreed to arbitrate. They are striking because Shonts and Hedley want to destroy the unions which compelled them to grant the slight increases. They deliberately violated their solemn pact and discharged men who would not quit the union and sign the company's individual agreement. . . .[20]

By September 10 the strike on the IRT had spread to the New York Railways Company and the Third Avenue Transit Company. Despite their existing contracts, the workers on both of these lines struck in sympathy with their fellow workers on the IRT. Moreover, these men understood that if the individual employment agreements prevailed on the IRT, it would only be a short time before they would be the only form of employer-labor relationship on all of the transit lines, and a real union, not a company union, would have no place in New York City's transit industry. So the men on the New York Railways and Third Avenue Lines were striking for themselves as well as for their brothers on the IRT. But the commercial press used the fact that the existing contracts had been broken as a weapon for attacking the transit workers.[21]

As in the first strike only one paper stood behind the strikers—the Socialist New York *Call.* This time, moreover, there were two *Calls* to do the work. On the first day of the second strike, the *Call* announced that there would be a "new paper on the streets this afternoon. It will be the *Evening Call.*" "There is a need for an evening paper supporting the carmen's union," the *Call* explained. "There is need for continuous news. The *Evening Call* will be published as long as the strike requires it. Then it will stop. It will be an emergency paper. The regular editorial staff of the Call has volunteered to work the double trick necessary to handle both papers."[22]

Local New York of the Socialist Party helped distribute the *Call* to the riding public. Moreover, the Socialist Party resolved "to extend to the striking street railway workers . . . the unrestricted use of our halls, speakers and press, and our support in every way possible, and we hereby call upon our members and sympathizers to assist these strikers in which ever way they can, and especially to refrain from riding on cars or trains run by strike breakers. . . ."[23] Responding to this appeal, Socialist Party members helped the striking carmen in a wide variety of ways. On "Sash Day," 5,000 Socialist union young women did picket duty for the striking transit workers wearing the "Don't Be a Scab" sashes. Before the strike was a week old, these sashes were already famous in New York City.[24]

PSC REPORTS

The strike was only eleven hours old when the Public Service Commission intervened, and Chairman Oscar Straus subpoenaed officials of the union and the IRT for a hearing. After six days of hearings the Commission issued a report which was, on the whole, favorable to the union. It found that the IRT was bound by the August 6th agreement to arbitrate its differences with the union, and it concluded that while the agreement had been "violated," it had "not been destroyed by the actions of the parties," and that "the moral obligation to maintain it still continues." The Commission made four recommendations:

(1) That the question whether the distribution of the individual contracts constituted a violation of the agreements be referred to arbitration in the manner provided in the agreement.

(2) That the charge that the company sought to secure acceptance of the individual contracts by fraud, misrepresentation, coercion, or intimidation be referred in the same way.

(3) That the parties proceed with the conferences where they left off, and

that, in order that friction be avoided, they agree upon some impartial person to preside, or if they cannot agree, that they permit the Mayor and the Chairman of the Commission to name such impartial person, to have no authority to decide, but merely to preserve the parties from further misunderstandings and disagreements, and, further, that such conferences be held in public.

(4) That the strike should be declared off immediately.[25]

Shonts immediately turned down the PSC's request that the company arbitrate differences with the union on the ground that he owed allegiance to his loyal employees. He insisted that the PSC had capitulated to the Amalgamated, and he would not let "outsiders come between us and our employees." Moreover, any further conferences with the Amalgamated would only demoralize the discipline of the service with resultant injury to the public.[26]

While the union accepted the Commission's report and agreed to comply with all of its recommendations, provided all employees were returned to their status as of August 29, it rejected the PSC's conclusion that the issue of trade unionism was not involved in the dispute. On the contrary, this was the major issue, and the very fact that the company refused to accede to the Commission's recommendations proved it.[27]

A second PSC report dealing with the Third Avenue Line strike was totally hostile to the union. While the report did concede that the company had acted in a way that provoked the workers, this could not justify their action in striking, especially since the men went on strike after Mayor Mitchel and Chairman Straus had made it clear that such action would constitute "a breach of contract."[28]

The net result of the Commission's reports was to strengthen the transit companies' standing in the community. For the commercial press played down the first report criticizing the IRT, and played up the criticism of the union and the carmen for striking the Third Avenue Line, thereby violating their contract. Since the IRT paid no attention to the PSC recommendations and the Commission did nothing but recommend arbitration, it meant that the strike would be left to work itself out. Meanwhile the companies received full support from the city as they brought in more strikebreakers who received full police protection at taxpayers' expense.

In a bid for public sympathy the Amalgamated sponsored a huge parade of strikers on September 14. It was a march without music, a "silent" parade. Starting at 1 o'clock in the afternoon, thousands of striking employees of the Interborough, the New York Railways Company, the Westchester companies, and the Third Avenue Railroad Company marched from Eighty-sixth Street to Union Square, where a mass meeting was held. The marchers went four abreast carrying banners with such slogans as "Real men need no cages," "Shonts says the public pays. Of course!" "Look over the parade and note the aliens," "This is a strike for the right to live like men," "Watch your step when you ride in scab cars," "The PSC says we are right." An oldtimer with 50 years of service carried the banner, "Do you want men or monkeys to run your cars?" This reference to monkeys was directed at the strikebreaking motormen, whose cars had wire screening placed in front of the windows to protect them from stones, hurled by strikers and sympathizers.

Telegrams of support were read to the gathering in Union Square, and Fitzgerald in his remarks told the cheering crowd that 400,000 unionists in New York City were ready to quit in support of the transit strikers. New York State Federation of Labor President James P. Holland endorsed Fitzgerald's remark. "When you fellows need help," he declared, "remember there are a half a million organized men in this city ready to lay down their tools to help you win your fight for organization."[29]

"Threats of General Strike," was the *New York Times* heading over the report of the speeches by Fitzgerald and Holland.[30]

PREPARATIONS FOR A GENERAL STRIKE

According to figures released by the Police Department, subway and elevated traffic were cut about 45 percent by the fourth day of the strike.[31] Even though it was assumed that this was a conservative estimate, it was clear that it would not be easy to increase the drop in traffic from this point on. With the tremendous assistance the police force was giving the companies by protecting the strikebreakers, with the steady attacks on the union and its members in the commercial press,* with Mayor Mitchel openly siding with the transit companies, and the PSC washing its hands of the dispute after its initial recommendations, there appeared to be no force capable of helping the strikers except organized labor. From the outset the union's leadership sensed that they were in for a long struggle, and that it was bound to be a losing one unless the strikers were able to arouse the rest of the labor movement to the

---

*Dubofsky argues that prior to the violation of the contracts by the strikers of the New York Railways Company and the Third Avenue Line, the strikers enjoyed wide support in the commercial press, that is, apart from the *New York Times*. But this exaggerates the few gestures on the part of the New York commercial papers criticizing the corporation managers. (*See* Dubofsky, *op. cit.*, p. 140.) The New York *Call* found it necessary to issue a special evening edition to present the strikers' side of events even before the workers on the New York Railways Company and the Third Avenue Line joined the walkout.

threat posed by the individual working agreement—the transit companies' "yellow-dog contract"—and the company union movement on the transit lines. In fact, the striking carmen appeared to have believed at the outset of the walkout that if they found themselves unable to halt the wholesale importation of strikebreakers and the unlimited police protection for scabs, the AFL would come to their aid with "a general sympathetic strike of all the trades under its control." "They had been assured by AFL emissaries who practically promised a general strike if the car men found themselves losing, and that the full resources of the national organization were to be ranged on their side in case of need." The *New York Times* so reported after a survey of attitudes among the strikers.[32]

In any event, on the second day of the strike, Amalgamated officials met with leaders of the Central Federated Union, which represented some half a million trade unionists in New York City. The entire meeting was devoted to methods of aiding the carmen. One proposal which produced much applause was advanced by John J. Reilly of the Longshoremen's Union. He declared that his union had discussed a plan of boycotting the "traction trust" by refusing to load coal consigned to the power houses. As a further means of hitting the Morgan interests, "which," Reilly declared, "controlled the transportation system of New York," the union proposed that the men "refuse also to load ammunition and supplies consigned to the Allies."

> That will hit them in two places. We are 35,000 strong and the Central Federated Union has but to say the word for us to take immediate action.

At this meeting, however, all that was done was adoption of a resolution calling upon AFL President Samuel Gompers to come to the city to assume "supreme command of the biggest strike any city has ever experienced."[33] Shonts, however, immediately sensed that the resolution contained the seeds of a general strike, and he issued a public statement expressing doubt that Gompers, "a wise man," would order a city-wide strike, or that he would attempt such a strategy, since there "is also a question of just how much the people of the city will stand." Moreover, he wanted Gompers to understand that the Transit companies were not fighting organized labor, "but only a branch of it," a most irresponsible branch moreover.[34]

Gompers came to New York the following day, and urged all unions to render moral and financial support to the Amalgamated. He labeled the action of the IRT management a lockout, and charged that the companies were trying to "crush out the spirit of organization." To this Shonts made the fantastic reply that actually the company not only favored unions but encouraged the formation of one—a company union. Moreover, "the company went one step further; it not only agreed to a contract with the men collectively, but it asked that the agreement also be submitted to each man individually."[35] What could be more American than a company union and a "yellow dog contract"? Of course, to workers all this was only giving "fancy names for a new method of driving out unions."[36]

Sentiment for a general strike accelerated after the publication on September 17 of a report to the Committee on Industrial Relations on the transit strike in New York City. The report emphasized that the carmen of New York were waging "the greatest fight for trade unionism and industrial freedom" of the era, and waging it, moreover, against "the Morgan and associated financial interests" which were determined to wipe out unionism throughout the land. The report continued:

> From Wall Street has gone forth the order that trades unionism in the city of New York and in the nation must be destroyed. The evidence are multiplying that all the forces in the banking headquarters of New York have drawn together, or are drawing together, in an industrial war on the workers who are seeking to use the opportunities of prosperity to free themselves from industrial servitude.
>
> The challenge was thrown down to labor here by the Interborough and the Morgan interests as a climax to the declaration of war on organized labor in California,* to the increasing efforts of the Steel Trust to beat down the organization of the workers in the Pittsburgh district, in Youngstown and on the Minnesota Mesabi range.** It came in response to the efforts of the National Association of Manufacturers to break up trades unionism, and finally, it was thrown down in the desperate resistance to the great victory for the eight-hour day won by the four railroad brotherhoods.***[37]

After many statements by union leaders, company officials, and city and state government leaders, a number of them contradictory, the Central Federated Union adopted a resolution calling for a general strike on September 22. Since most of the unions planning to join in sympathy with the strikers were working under collective agreements, each of them began issuing statements that if they struck it would be for their own demands, but if their actions would result in aid for the carmen, they would not be sorry.[38]

In an effort to avoid implementation of the CFU resolution, Mayor Mitchel called the Amalgamated and IRT officials to a conference in his office. Shonts consented to meet with Mitchel, but refused to sit with

---

*The reference is to the Mooney case in San Francisco.
**See above, pp. 25–40 and Foner, *History of Labor Movement* 4: 420–26.
***See pp. 184–88.

officials of the Amalgamated, and also made it crystal clear that under no circumstances would management deal with the union.[39]

Instead of condemning management for its refusal to budge from its intransigent position even if necessary to prevent a general strike, Mayor Mitchel read the union leaders a stern lecture:

> Conditions which you yourselves have indicated might follow general sympathetic strikes would be grossly violating of the laws, and would convulse the civilized and orderly life of this community. We wish to make it unmistakably clear to you that to prevent that condition the full civil and military powers conferred by law upon the mayor will be employed. We trust that the sober second thought and better judgment of the men who direct the course and policies of organized labor in this city will lead them to refrain from declaring sympathetic strikes.[40]

Mitchel did more than lecture. He threatened to call out the militia. Meanwhile every available member of the police force was put on strike duty, and Chief Inspector Schmittberger told the transit officials that they might establish night service as soon as they were ready, since the police department was ready to meet any emergency. In other words, the companies were given assurance that the entire police force would be at their service night and day. If there had been any inclination on management's part to negotiate and arbitrate, this ended that. Schmittberger proved he meant what he said by establishing 50 auto patrols, and assigning 100 motorcycle police to tour the city to report where reinforcements should be sent. District Attorney Swann, for his part, stated that he "would prosecute those guilty of disorder under the most drastic laws available." By this he did not mean "disorder" on the part of the gangster-element strikebreakers, but only on the part of strikers.[41]

In addition to these police measures, Mayor Mitchel issued a statement blaming the union for the strike, and, in another statement, with PSC Chairman Straus, he declared once again that the issue of trade unionism was not involved in the dispute between the Amalgamated and the transit companies, only "the integrity of certain contracts entered into."[42] In response Secretary Ernest Bohm of the Central Federated Union issued a statement on behalf of Gompers which read:

> Trade unionists will not surrender their right to organize in this city, and every possible help that the AFL can give will be extended to the Amalgamated ... to maintain this right. This is a fight on the issue of trade unionism, and were the traction companies to win, other employers would resort to the plan of making "master and servant" contracts.[43]

THE GENERAL STRIKE FIASCO

No trade union in New York City walked out on September 22. Instead, late that afternoon, the Greater New York Labor Conference, consisting of ninety union leaders representing the Central Federated Union, the Central Labor Union of Brooklyn, the United Hebrew Trades, and the Building Trades Council, issued a call for a general suspension of work on September 27. (Instead of a general strike, the argument went, a general suspension of work would not entail a breach of existing contracts.) Such a suspension of work was necessary. New York City workers had no choice but to cease working since "no adequate facilities are afforded them. Union men feel that they cannot be true to the cause of organized labor, and still maintain their self-respect as union men if they ride in 'scab' cars. No other means of conveyance is available, so they must stay home."[44]

In a statement to the press, the union leaders charged that the blame for the work stoppage would fall on the city authorities. "The elected government of this city had stepped aside and given way to a government composed of five men. These five men are Theodore P. Shonts, Frank Hedley, James Whitridge, James Quackenbush and Leo C. Bergoff. The wish of these men today is the law of New York City. The police force of the city is at their command. The Mayor, his cabinet and a majority of the Board of Aldermen have ceased to operate to all intents and purposes." At least fifty strikers were arrested each day and given heavy sentences on charges of disorderly conduct.

> Such a condition is almost without parallel. Such a complete abdication of power by the lawfully elected government is unheard of. We call upon the entire city to demand that the elected government be restored to power and this five-man money government of despotism be ousted forever.[45]

Hugh Frayne, AFL representative in New York expressed confidence that the morning of the 27th would see 240,000 striking workers on the avenues of New York. Even this, said the New York *Call*, was an underestimation, and it predicted 800,000 marching "elbow to elbow."

> You can feel the thrill go down the great line. You can see the spring come into the step of men and women you can see eyes alight, heads up! You can see the inspiration of it in the faces of men and women.[46]

The Socialist Party set up a special strike committee to give the general strike all the support the movement could muster, and it made it obligatory upon all Socialist members of unions to go out with their unions.[47]

On the 27th the general strike began. If one were to judge from a resolution adopted by a committee of the Labor Convention, the response was overwhelming.* The resolution hailed "with joy the courageous action of the vast number of workers of the various trades and industries in this city who have this morning laid down their tools and opened the general movement of New York's labor army by calling a suspension of work in sympathetic support of their brothers now on strike against the street car companies."[48] In reality, whether called a general strike or a work suspension, the response was a fiasco. The Joint Labor Committee supervising the general strike, released figures to the press citing 173,000 men and women who were said to have joined the transit strikers. But in actuality only six local unions officially called out their membership in support of the carmen. These included: Brewery Workers (6,000); Paperhangers (1,000); Machinists (4,000); Eccentric Firemen (800); Painters Local 435 (250); Italian Painters Local (450)— a total of 12,500 workers.[49]

On Thursday, September 28, the Building Trades Council of Greater New York comprising some 150,000 men, decided to postpone action for a week. The Teamsters followed suit and other unions decided to emulate the example of the Building Trades and defer participation in the general strike. Since Thursday and Friday, September 28 and 29, were Jewish holidays, the 200,000 Jewish trade unionists remained out, but they were not on strike, and returned to work on Monday. Local 10, the ILGWU garment cutters, was enjoined by injunction from violating its contract by supporting the strike, and capitulated. All the printing trades' unions voted to abide by their contracts and remain at work. The United Hebrew Trades did not answer the strike call, even though its counsel, Morris Hillquit, had voted support of the general strike. Neither did the Tidewater Boatmen nor the International Longshoremen's Association, whose membership had actually authorized the strike.[50]

On October 1st, the Brewery Workers, convinced that they had put themselves out on the limb, returned to work. The following day the Joint Labor Committee acknowledged total failure. "Organized labor," the committee lamely explained, "did want to help the street carmen provided a definite plan had been decided and agreed upon."[51] Only the New York *Call* refused to face the facts. "Why did the general strike movement fail?" it asked editorially, and it answered:

*The committee was composed of Peter J. O'Brien, chairman, Morris Hillquit, secretary, and Melinda Scott, William Holder, Louis Fridiger, James H. Vahey, Hugh Frayne, Ernest Bohm, and William H. Fitzgerald. (New York *Call*, Sept. 28, 1916.)

In the first place, it didn't fail. With serious, purposeful people there is no such thing as fail. Labor doesn't know failure. The men and women who create the world's wealth cannot fail—and they do not fail. The general strike didn't win what it set out to win. But that doesn't mean failure. It simply means that it needed rehearsing before it went into that kind of battle.[52]

The official organ of the Capmakers' Union put it more accurately: "It takes more than vulgar bluff to subdue the thugs of corporation capital."[53]

The commercial press had a field day gleefully proclaiming the death of "the general strike that never was." Or as the New York *American* declared: "Nothing can die until it has first been alive; and the general strike was not even born." Another paper, more severe, termed "the ludicrous bluff of calling the suspension of work by Jewish mechanics and operators during their religious holidays a sympathetic strike . . . the last straw which made the whole thing a farce."[54]

WHY THE GENERAL STRIKE FAILED

Five months after the general strike fiasco a controversy emerged which threw light on the reasons for the failure of the sympathetic strike to get off the ground. Writing in the January, 1917 issue of the *Typographical Journal*, official organ of the International Typographical Union, President Margden G. Scott of the ITU pointed out:

New York Typographical Union did not vote for a sympathetic strike, and no such infamous proposition was ever given serious consideration. The strike order issued over the signature of the Central Federated Union received scant consideration when presented to our subordinate organizations in New York City. Some of them laid the communication on the table. Others put it under the table.

The same treatment, Scott discovered on investigation, was accorded the strike order in other unions. The reason, he also discovered, was that to have complied with the order for a sympathetic strike would have meant "destroying our contracts in New York City," and no "responsible" labor leader would "listen to the invitation to break existing contracts." In short, the transit strikers had been sold a bill of goods which no labor leader was willing to deliver.

Scott then launched into a bitter attack on Samuel Gompers, accusing the AFL President of having failed "to meet the emergency which arose in New York City in September," and even encouraging the forces promoting a general strike, forces which threatened "to destroy labor contracts regardless of the obligations included in them."[55]

Gompers' reply, published in the *New York Times,* reveals further why the general strike never took place. Contrary to what Scott had stated, Gompers claimed he not only had not encouraged the general strike, but had come to New York City for the precise purpose of preventing "a sympathetic strike of the working people . . . in sympathy with the striking street railway men."

> I declared that I would have nothing to do with it and repudiated the entire situation, and declared that it was violative of the fundamental principles of trade unionism and the laws of the American Federation of Labor.

While Gompers did not claim that his stand had resulted "in preventing the general strike being inaugurated," he asked Scott "to draw your own inference. One thing is sure, the general strike did not occur."[56]

At its January, 1917 meeting the Central Federated Union of New York City supported Gompers in his dispute with Scott, and credited the AFL President with having influenced the trade unions of the city to reject the call to join in a general strike in support of the striking transit workers.[57]

It is significant that Gompers did not mention the fact that he had sent a telegram to the Union Square mass meeting of the transit strikers following the "Silent March" on September 14 in which he promised them that "Anything and everything within my power will be freely given to bring about an honorable and advantageous outcome of the heroic defensive struggle now being waged against the heartless traction tyrants, who have no conception of their responsibilities to their oppressed employees or to the public."[58] Nor did Gompers mention the fact that, as we have seen, he had authorized Ernest Bohm of the Central Federated Union, to assure New Yorkers that trade unionists would "not surrender their right to organize" in their city, and that "every possible help that the AFL can give will be extended to the Amalgamated . . . to maintain this right."

In short, Gompers was playing a double game. On the one hand, he was raising the hopes of the transit strikers that the AFL would go all out, even to the point of a general strike, to maintain their right to organize a real union, while he was secretly undermining the movement for a sympathetic strike. It did not seem to matter to Gompers, or for that matter to the other AFL leaders, that the failure to carry through on the promise of a sympathetic strike, after raising the hopes of the transit strikers, broke the back of their struggle.

END OF THE TRANSIT STRIKE

The strike of the transit workers continued, but with declining vigor, all through the fall of 1916, with men, assisted by their wives, daughters, and even mothers, fighting stubbornly. On October 6, the fiery veteran of many labor struggles in the coal fields, Mother Jones, led a group of strikers' wives in a mass demonstration.[59] Gradually, however, with the aid of strikebreakers under police protection, the companies raised the degree of service. Double pay was banned on the lines, though a 20 percent bonus was continued for the month of October. By the third month of the strike, policemen were taken off the trains except for one each on the station platforms, and on surface line trolleys. Despite the continuing number of serious accidents and collisions, due to inexperienced motormen, the companies were permitted to operate their lines with strikebreakers, while the discouraged strikers drifted back on condition that they resign from the Amalgamated and sign oaths guaranteeing to belong only to the company unions.[60]

Christmas of 1916 still found men holding out, but it was clear that the battle was lost. Even then in the fifteenth week of the strike over 1000 remaining stalwarts among the strikers met and voted unanimously to continue the strike. At this time the Amalgamated released its first comprehensive figures on the second half of the strike. It reported that of the 11,331 men who had answered the second strike call, only 1,717 deserted and returned to the struck transit lines. Of the remaining 9,614, approximately 1,600 were still out of work, approximately an equal number left the city to find work elsewhere, while the remainder had already found work in other fields of employment.[61]

Though this report was an admission that serious organized resistance to the transit companies was at an end, the Amalgamated actually never called off the strike. At its 1917 convention, eleven months later, the union did not list a date of termination for the New York Transit strike of 1916.[62]

AFTERMATH

There were endless discussions in the labor, Socialist, and liberal press over the reasons for the failure of the transit strike. Liberal journals generally placed the blame on the Amalgamated and its supporters for having alienated public opinion by arrogant disregard of existing contracts and pushing for a general strike.* Labor and Socialist papers placed

*In his analysis of the causes for the defeat of the strike, Dubofsky puts his entire emphasis upon this theme. (See *Dubofsky, op. cit.*, pp. 141-43.)

the blame on the free and unlimited use of strikebreakers and the open assistance given the corporations by the city and state administrations. Certainly the fact that, as it was disclosed after the strike, the transit companies had spent $3,500,000 for scabs and other thugs to break the strike, lent strength to this argument. But as James Connolly, the Irish patriot and labor leader, explained:

> It was not the scabs, however, who turned the scale against the strikers in favor of the masters. That service to transit capital was performed by good union men with union cards in their pockets. These men were the engineers in the power houses which supplied the electric power to run the cars, and without whom all the scabs combined could not have run a single trip. . . . They were unconsciously being compelled by their false system of organization (craft unions) to betray their struggling brothers.[63]

The same point was made early in the strike by the *Weekly People*, official organ of the Socialist Labor Party:

> We see certain trains upon the elevated lines and subway running. Why are they running? Why are not the firemen and powerhouse men called out? The stationary firemen's union, an AFL organization, whose chief is Timothy Healy, has let its men remain on the job aiding the company to run the trains. What is such an act but an act of scabbing, of treason, to the men on strike.[64]

The narrow AFL craft form of organization, embodied in the transit unions, led inevitably to the "Union Scab," and the "Union Scab" became a powerful weapon of the corporations in defeating the 1916 strike. In an analysis of the declining power of the strike movement, Reverend Bouck White of the Church of Social Revolution noted that organization along craft lines rendered the transit unions unable to grapple with the Wall Street-dominated, highly financed traction corporations. He charged, too, that the failure of the AFL unions to respond to the general strike was a symptom of their narrow craft outlook.[65]

A major cause for the defeat of the transit strike was the Amalgamated's reliance upon arbitration and its faith in the progressive outlook of Mayor Mitchel. The union hailed the August 6th "truce agreement" as an unprecedented victory even though it was clear to most observers that it left the companies in a position to destroy the union piecemeal. Fitzgerald conceded the fundamental weakness of the union's approach when he told a public gathering on September 17 that the second strike was called to preserve the victory won in the first walkout.[66] A queer victory indeed! In the second strike, Mayor Mitchel showed his true colors, but signs of this were already present during the first walkout. In the second strike, the powerful traction companies were well prepared to crush the union, and only a united power of organized labor could withstand the power of monopoly capital, aided by the city and state governments. But that united power of labor was never forthcoming.

The New York transit workers certainly demonstrated that they did not lack fighting spirit. But fighting spirit was not enough, and they paid a terrible price for the narrow outlook of the union with which they were associated. The defeat of the 1916 strike tied the transit workers to company unionism and miserable working conditions. As late as 1934, 35,000 transit workers in New York City were still compulsory members of company unions. In order to obtain a job with any of the transit companies—the IRT, BMT, Third Avenue Line, Yonkers Railroad, Fifth Avenue Coach and New York City Omnibus Corporation, as well as the other smaller lines—a worker had to join the company union.

In May, 1934, 2,000 leaflets were distributed to the New York transit workers announcing the formation of the Transport Workers Union, Independent. It was an industrial union, and it marked the opening of a new and decisive stage in the history of unionism among the transit workers.[67]

CHAPTER 7

New Unionism in
the Garment Industry

The era of the general strike in the garment trade came to an end with the 1913 uprising of the white-goods workers.* When the members of the Women's Trade Union League (WTUL) of New York looked back over the period from late 1909 to early 1913, they were able to see definite impressive gains. More New York City workingwomen belonged to unions than ever before, and tens of thousands of them were covered by written agreements.

To many League members, however, this was not enough. Despite the increasingly important role played by the sixty thousand woman members in the trades that had been virtually unorganized only three years earlier, the unions to which they belonged were still dominated by men, and these WTUL members felt that as long as such domination continued, the women would remain "powerless in their unions just as they were powerless in their shops."[1]

UPHEAVAL IN THE GARMENT UNIONS

During 1914, the long-standing discontent among rank-and-file workers with the leadership of the garment industry unions triggered a general upheaval that left the International Ladies' Garment Workers' Union (ILGWU) with new national officers and the United Garment Workers torn asunder. Union women, although just recently organized, stood in the forefront of these developments, expressing their grievances, demanding internal reforms and a greater role in the functioning of

*For a discussion of this strike, *see* Philip S. Foner, *History of the Labor Movement in the United States*, New York, 1980, Volume 5, pp. 256-57.

the unions, and participating actively in the events that ultimately provided them with a greater share in the organizations they had helped to create.

It did not take long for workers in the women's garment trade to realize that union leaders who relied solely on the machinery of the Protocol* and the good will of the employers to establish permanent industrial peace were not likely to build strong organizations. As early as February, 1912, workers in the trade complained openly that the Protocol, by forbidding the use of the strike, had tied their hands and had paralyzed union action in their behalf. But ILGWU leader John Dyche opposed the demands of the rank and file for greater control over working conditions, and when strikes were called against Protocol violations, he broke them by sending non-union members to replace those who refused to return to work. Dyche was proud of maintaining "a spirit of cooperation between the Union and the [Employers'] Association," but the rank and file regarded this "cooperation" as useless in the face of continued employer violations of the Protocol.[2]

While support for Dyche's ouster from office was mounting among all garment workers, women members were especially angered by the fact that under his administration, men continued to dominate the official positions within the ILGWU. By 1914, women constituted over 50 percent of the international's membership, but there were only eighteen women delegates at the biennial convention held that year. Nine of these represented White Goods Workers' Union, Local No. 62. Local No. 25, the waistmakers' local, already the largest women's local in the nation, sent nine male delegates and three women to the convention. With a few exceptions, men held all union offices and executive board positions and staffed the protocol, grievance, and arbitration machinery as well. In addition, the great majority of the international's organizers were men.[3]

*Despite important gains won in the "Protocol of Peace," as the agreement ending the strike of 60,000 cloakmakers in 1910 was called, the settlement was a disappointment to many strikers, a large number of whom disapproved of it. One reason was that instead of the closed shop, there was "the preferential union shop." Furthermore, unlike the usual collective bargaining agreement, the Protocol had no time limit; it could run indefinitely but could be terminated by either side at will. As a concession, the manufacturers agreed to exert preference only as between one union man and another; non-union labor could only be hired when union help was unobtainable. The agreement also compelled employers to declare their belief in the union and in the ideal that all "who desire its benefits should share its burdens." But to many rank-and-file workers, this was still only the "scab shop with honey," and they disapproved, too, of the no-strike clause and the provision for compulsory arbitration. (For the 1910 cloakmakers' strike and the full terms of the "Protocol of Peace," see Foner, History of the Labor Movement, 5: 241-46.)

For evidence of workers' discontent with the Protocol, see also Elizabeth Israels Perry, "Industrial Reform in New York City: Belle Moskowitz and the Protocol of Peace, 1913-1916," Labor History 23 (Winter, 1982): 30.

Women garment workers did not just sit by in the face of this situation. Pauline Newman, who had just assumed important responsibilities on the Joint Sanitary Board staff, insisted that the ILGWU could not grow unless women were given additional leadership tasks. She argued that "girls are apt to have more confidence in a woman than a man" and that the failure of the union's leadership to understand this elementary truth was seriously limiting its influence. In August, 1914, Constance Denmark, editor of the women's section of the *Ladies' Garment Worker*, expressed this view even more strongly when she complained:

> It is certainly not normal if thousands of girls, many of them possessing active minds and intelligence, should have to be thrown upon the leadership of a comparatively small number of men. What is worse, the girls are numerically the backbone of the union.[4]

The mounting anger over the operation of the Protocol and the increasing resentment of women members combined to present a serious challenge to the supremacy of the leaders who controlled the ILGWU. In June, 1914, the delegates to the union's convention swept Dyche and his cronies out of office and replaced them with a radical slate of officers headed by Benjamin Schlesinger as president. Women garment workers hailed the convention's action and looked forward hopefully to a leadership that would encourage the presence of more women in executive positions and as delegates to the 1916 convention.[5]

A few weeks later, the leaders of the United Garment Workers (UGW) of America faced a similar challenge. As we have seen in our previous volume, two factions in the UGW vied for power.* Lager and Rickert, the union's top leaders, were enthusiastic advocates of Samuel Gompers' "pure and simple trade unionism." They ran the union on business principles and carried this concept so far that they made a private business of selling the union label, even to firms that operated with non-union workers and ran their shops and factories as they pleased. Frowning upon strikes and depending on the union label for their bargaining strength, the UGW leaders placed their main reliance on workers who lived in small communities and worked in large factories manufacturing overalls. A large section of their supporters were born in the United States.

The other faction of the UGW was made up of tailors and operators who worked in the large urban shops. A great majority of these workers were of immigrant origin, most frequently Yiddish-speaking Eastern Europeans. The U.S.-born workers in the small communities felt that

*See ibid., pp. 260-64.

they had little in common with the workers in the urban centers, and the UGW leaders took advantage of this alienation by repeatedly directing sneering remarks at the non-English-speaking tailors in the big cities. Moreover, when the tailors in these big cities struck, the leaders refused to acknowledge their strikes as legitimate. Then, when the workers refused to abandon the struggle, the UGW leaders invariably sabotaged the strike by arranging a secret settlement.

The tailors in the UGW called for a new unionism that would combine industrial unionism, class consciousness, and socialism. While they wanted to change the entire structure of society, they also understood the need for waging the struggle for such immediate demands as higher wages, shorter hours, and better working conditions. They bitterly resented the corrupt class-collaborationist policies of the national and local officials, and they were enraged by the irresponsible use of the label by these officials and by their intimate relationship with the manufacturers. Above all, they resented the fact that a minority of the membership—the overalls makers—were being used by the autocratic leaders as a means of maintaining their domination of the union.[6]

In 1914, thirteen New York locals in the coat-making trade formed the United Brotherhood of Tailors. The New York tailors and related workers in Chicago, Baltimore, and Rochester now represented a clear majority of the total UGW membership, sufficient to control the approaching biennial convention and wrest the leadership from the conservative leaders. Rickert and Lager, however, were determined to remain in power regardless of the will of the majority of the membership. They therefore scheduled the convention to be held in Nashville, Tennessee, a site far removed from any of the large urban centers and a city administered by officials sympathetic to the UGW leaders. A few weeks before the convention, the union's auditor announced that a number of locals in New York and Chicago had fallen into financial arrears and were therefore ineligible to send delegates to the convention.[7]

Nevertheless, when the convention opened, the New York tailors had a full complement of 107 of the 350 delegates present. They distributed a leaflet appealing for their right to be seated. Rickert, however, brushed this and other attempts to compromise the difference between the two groups aside. Not a single delegate from New York received credentials.[8]

The convention finally split apart when the tailors from New York, Chicago, Baltimore, and Rochester—authorized and unauthorized delegates alike—left the convention hall and regrouped at their hotel. In the meetings that followed the rupture, the bolters declared themselves the properly convened union's legislative body and elected new international officers. Sidney Hillman, then serving in New York as clerk for the Cloak and Suit Protocol, was elected president.

At the AFL convention in November, 1914, delegates appeared from both factions of the United Garment Workers, each claiming to represent the union. The fact that the anti-Rickert forces represented the great majority of the men's clothing workers was ignored by the AFL's Credentials Committee, which seated Rickert and his followers on the ground that they were the regularly and officially elected delegates of the union. Gompers promptly sent a circular to all locals of the United Garment Workers informing them that Rickert was the only president of the union and that the organization he headed was the sole *bona fide* union of men's clothing workers affiliated with the AFL.[9]

At a special convention held by the insurgents in New York from December 26-28, 1914, a new organization of men's clothing workers was formed. Having lost in court the right to use the old union's name, the insurgents called themselves the "Amalgamated Clothing Workers of America," with Sidney Hillman of Chicago as president and Joseph Schlossberg of New York as general secretary. The union at the time represented forty thousand workers in the United States and Canada.[10]

WOMEN OF THE AMALGAMATED

The creation of a new garment union dedicated to progressive principles offered a ray of hope to all workers in the trade, and especially to those who believed that women deserved to play a more prominent role in the labor movement.[11] It did not take long to demonstrate that this hope was justified. During the first trying months of the new union's existence, three dynamic women assumed significant positions. In Chicago, Bessie Abramowitz, who was instrumental in the founding of the Amalgamated Clothing Workers, continued as an important adviser and confidante of the union's leaders. At the first national convention of the new union in December, 1914, she was chosen secretary-treasurer of District Council No. 6. She also served on the Board of Arbitration which dealt with grievances between the union and Hart, Schaffner & Marx. In addition, Abramowitz lobbied and campaigned for passage of an eight-hour law for the women of Illinois.[12]

In Rochester, New York, Selma Goldblatt worked tirelessly for the new union. As recording secretary of UGW Local No. 235, she had attended the Nashville convention, had joined the secessionists, and continued in her office after her local had aligned itself with the new union. She was a leading figure in the Amalgamated and one of its most capable administrators.[13]

One of the most remarkable women in the new union was Dorothy Jacobs, the dynamic president of Baltimore's Buttonhole Makers Union, Local No. 170. She was born in 1894 in Latvia and had moved with her family to Baltimore at the age of thirteen. She took a job as a hand buttonhole sewer on men's coats, where she worked ten hours a day and earned $2 a week. She soon began to agitate among her fellow workers, insisting that they join her in forming a union. Before she was fourteen, she had been labeled a troublemaker and had been fired from several jobs. Late in 1908, the women in her shop organized a union which affiliated with the UGW as Local 170. Jacobs, then all of fourteen, was its first president. In 1912, she led the hand buttonholers in a successful strike, and by 1914, not only were all of Baltimore's women hand buttonhole makers organized, but they decided to unionize the male machine buttonholers as well. They formed committees to visit the homes of the unorganized men, whom they found totally ignorant of union principles and hostile to women organizers. After months of work, led and organized by Dorothy Jacobs, they succeeded in organizing the men in the larger factories so that 65 percent of the machine buttonholers belonged to the union.[14]

When the UGW split, Jacobs led her local into the ranks of the Amalgamated. She represented Local 170 at the first Amalgamated convention, where she introduced a resolution on behalf of the Buttonhole Makers' Union of Baltimore, calling for the assignment of a woman organizer to that city.

The convention passed the resolution, but, as was too often the case with unions of that era, the Amalgamated did nothing to implement it. However, Jacobs did not stop agitating for greater attention to the organization of women. Soon after the convention, she was elected to represent her local on the Amalgamated's Baltimore Joint Board. From that position, she spoke out on the importance of taking special measures to encourage women to join and participate in the union. She became the most outspoken champion of women's rights within the garment unions.

STRUGGLES OF THE AMALGAMATED

During 1915 and 1916, the Amalgamated Clothing Workers struggled for its life against the unrelenting opposition of both the manufacturers and the AFL. When the United Hebrew Trades in New York City, reflecting the general sentiment of Jewish labor, recognized locals of the Amalgamated, that organization was singled out as a major target in the AFL's campaign against the new union. In March, 1915, the Central Federated Union of New York and Vicinity—the AFL's central labor council—suspended the United Hebrew Trades (UHT) from membership and ordered every international union with locals represented in it to instruct those locals to withdraw their delegates. The UHT, however, refused to retreat, declaring that it did not intend to "give up on a question of thousands of workmen who are struggling against a parasitic clique."[15] Its attitude infuriated Gompers. At a UHT meeting on May 10, he warned the organization to expel the Amalgamated's delegates or face the wrath of the AFL, which had already determined that the United Garment Workers must be upheld.[16]

The anti-UHT campaign reached its climax at the 1915 AFL convention, when the Executive Council reported that the UHT, in harboring the Amalgamated locals, was "injurious to the solidarity or progress of the trade union movement of New York City" and directed Gompers to have all AFL-affiliated unions resign from the United Hebrew Trades. Rather than see the UHT destroyed by the AFL because of its support for the new garment workers' union, the Amalgamated's New York Joint Board decided to remove its locals from membership in the Jewish organization.[17]

Nevertheless, the war against the Amalgamated by the AFL and its affiliates continued. Each year, at AFL conventions from 1916 through 1918, the ILGWU regularly introduced resolutions designed to restore peace in the men's clothing industry through recognition of the Amalgamated as the actual representative of the largest number of clothing workers in the trade, but on each occasion, the AFL Executive Council rejected the proposal.[18] After 1917, the Amalgamated did not attend another AFL convention until 1933, when it was finally accepted into the federation's fold.*

Even while they were battling against the AFL leadership, the members of the Amalgamated were busy extending the union into unorganized segments of the industry. In early 1915, the Amalgamated

*At its 1916 convention, the AFL awarded jurisdiction in the millinery industry to the United Hatters of North America and ordered the United Cloth Hat and Cap Makers' Union, which had organized the millinery trade, to surrender these workers. Following the Amalgamated's lead, the Cap Makers' Union refused to bow before the ultimatum. Then, when the 1917 AFL convention ordered it to comply with the federation's decision or stand suspended, the union walked out of the federation. It operated outside the fold of the AFL until 1934, when the Cap Makers and the United Hatters merged. Before the Cap Makers had organized the millinery workers, who were mainly young immigrant women, the United Hatters, whose membership was restricted to males, showed no interest in organizing the milliners. (Donald N. Robinson, *Spotlight on a Union: The Story of the United Hatters, Cap and Millinery Workers' Union*, New York, 1948, pp. 200-04; *The Headgear Worker* 2 [February, 1917]: 9-12; *ibid.* 3 [January-February, 1918]: 9-12; *ibid.* 3 [January, 1919]: 83-84, 110.)

wrested control of the New York unions from the UGW. It also gained a strong position in Baltimore and Boston and initiated drives in Philadelphia, Cincinnati, Cleveland, and St. Louis.[19]

In 1915, the Amalgamated leaders decided to stage an all-out campaign in Chicago, where a strong manufacturers' association had devised an extremely effective program of blacklisting. Only one-fourth of Chicago's forty thousand men's clothing workers belonged to the Amalgamated, nearly all of whose members worked at Hart, Schaffner & Marx. The organizing campaign during the spring and summer of 1915 was highlighted by mass meetings, a giant May Day parade, and agitational speeches in several foreign languages. In mid-September, union leaders presented a list of nine demands to the Chicago manufacturers. Instead of responding to the union's demands, the employers called on the Chicago police to provide additional protection for their factories.[20]

By September 29, between 20,000 and 25,000 men and women had walked out on strike. Strike leaders divided the strike area into four districts, each with its own headquarters, meeting hall, relief committee, and designated leader. Bessie Abramowitz headed one of the four districts and was called in to assist the others. The police responded in classic Chicago style, escorting strikebreakers through the picket lines by brute force. Riding through the picket lines on horseback, they arrested the strikers—men and women alike—at the slightest provocation, jamming fifteen to twenty of them into patrol wagons designed to hold less than ten. By the end of the day, many women bore bruises inflicted by the officers' clubs.[21]

As the press publicized the attacks on the picket lines and the arrests of female strikers, society women, settlement house workers, and other concerned citizens came to the aid of the beleaguered strikers. They joined the picket lines, marched in union parades, distributed circulars, raised money for the strikers, and campaigned to bring about arbitration of the strike. When a number of these upper- and middle-class citizens were arrested, newspaper protests and demands for an investigation of police brutality mounted. The mayor refused to order such an investigation, but members of the City Council launched one of their own of the working and sanitary conditions in the city's sweatshops and clothing factories. A number of women workers appeared at the hearings to testify to the oppressive treatment that had caused the strike.[22]

Still nothing could persuade the manufacturers to arbitrate. As the strike dragged on into October and November, the labor agitator and organizer *par excellence*, Mother Jones, then in her eighties but with her energy and zeal undiminished by her incarceration and labors in a long series of miners' strikes,* rushed to the scene to add her voice to the calls for arbitration. Once again the manufacturers held firm, and in a dramatic gesture, Mother Jones called on Secretary of Labor William B. Wilson, a former leader of the United Mine Workers, to enter the strike. "Send at once to investigate the clothing strike," she wired. "It is fierce, girls getting 8 cents an hour as slaves. Signed Mother." Secretary Wilson replied that he already had an observer on the scene but did not feel it was wise to interfere while the City Council committee was conducting its investigation. Mother Jones then led a parade of women strikers and sympathizers through the streets of Chicago, hoping to dramatize the strikers' cause and bring additional pressure to bear on the manufacturers. As usual, she came under attack from the conservative press as an "outside agitator" who was stirring up the peaceful, law-abiding clothing workers of Chicago. The strikers, however, appreciated Jones's assistance, since both the Chicago Federation of Labor and the Women's Trade Union League were prevented, because of their affiliation to the AFL, from offering concrete aid to the strikers.[23]**

By early December, the strike appeared to be lost. Strikers had begun to abandon the picket line and drift back to work. Even though a number of the women strikers urged continuation of the struggle, offering to do double duty on the picket lines to take the places of those who had left, Hillman and his strike leaders decided to end the strike. Only after the strike appeared doomed did Samuel Gompers speak out, voicing his hope that the strikers would achieve victory.[24]

In early 1916, Amalgamated members launched strikes in a number of other cities, including Boston, Philadelphia, and Baltimore. Everywhere young women were among the leading activists in the strikes, and in Baltimore they practically ran the walkout in the city's three leading men's clothing establishments. The union had called the strike in order to gain control of Baltimore's men's clothing market and to drive out the UGW, with its pro-employer policies. Once again, the police brutally arrested hundreds of young women, many of whom remained in jail for some time because they were unable to raise the money for the excessive bail. Once out of jail, they went back to the picket lines.[25]

---

*As a result of her break with John Mitchell, president of the United Mine Workers, whom she came to regard as a collaborator with big business in general and with the mine owners in particular, Jones's efforts were directed for a number of years to workers other than miners. When Mitchell resigned as UMW president in 1908, Jones renewed her efforts on behalf of miners. For her work in the bitter struggles in West Virginia and Colorado in 1912-1914, see Foner, *History of the Labor Movement* 5: 184-190, 203-15, and Philip S. Foner, ed., *Mother Jones Speaks: Speeches, Articles, Interviews, Testimony before Congressional Committees and Letters* (New York, 1982).
**For further discussion of the League, see below, pp. 123-42.

The women of Baltimore's Hand Buttonhole Workers Union had maintained a strong organization for years, successfully resisting repeated efforts by the manufacturers to weaken their union and cut wages. Following the local's somewhat limited success in organizing the male machine buttonholers, the women went on to organize women in other branches of the men's clothing industry. In one of the largest factories, the young women unionists gave up their lunch hours to visit different floors of the factory, spreading the message of unionism to their unorganized sisters.[26]

As in Baltimore, in the strikes in Boston, Philadelphia, and soon afterwards in St. Louis and Chicago, both the press and the Amalgamated organizers noted the devotion and spirit displayed by the female pickets. Clearly, women were demonstrating again and again their enthusiastic and constructive participation in union activities. It was equally clear, however, that old prejudices die hard. The male leaders of the Amalgamated Clothing Workers were still unwilling to actively recruit women members. Amalgamated women organizers worked tirelessly among women workers, but they received little cooperation from male organizers. Dorothy Jacobs, president of the Hand Buttonhole Workers' Union and most active in the organizing effort, complained to Hillman: "It seems that the men are not awakened as yet to the importance of organizing the women and lose sight of the fact that women are the majority in the industry."[27]

A PROGRESSIVE WOMEN'S PROGRAM

Jacobs, Bessie Abramowitz, and Selma Goldblatt launched a campaign to compel the men to recognize the fact that the union could not survive without the full cooperation of the women. They insisted that the Amalgamated undertake a campaign to recruit women, and, once they were enrolled, to sustain their interest. At the 1916 biennial convention, the demands began to pay off. This time, when the Baltimore delegation requested a woman organizer, the convention concurred. Then New York's delegation, headed by the Bellanca brothers, demanded a special women's department, and Dorothy Jacobs supported the proposal with an eloquent appeal for greater emphasis on organizing women. Then four women delegates introduced a resolution pointing out that, as the number of women workers in the clothing industry increased, the future of unionism in the industry demanded that women become a part of the organized labor movement. The women delegates asked the convention to instruct the incoming General Executive Board to make a special effort to organize women workers, to assign a special woman organizer, and to issue special literature for women.[28]

When the convention adopted this wide-ranging resolution, the women members of the Amalgamated believed that a new day had dawned for them. They soon discovered, however, that most men in the union continued to oppose any increase in the role of women in the organization. Dorothy Jacobs was elected to a position on the General Executive Board, but the opposition she encountered, sometimes taking the form of open and outright hostility, did not disappear even after she took her seat.[29] It was not until October, 1916, months after the convention, that the board did anything to implement the convention's instructions about women workers. It called on local unions to organize women's clubs and other organizations designed to promote the organization of women in the industry and to educate those already organized. It also notified local union officials that it planned to send a woman organizer out on tour periodically. In addition, it suggested that the locals enlist the aid of women belonging to organizations friendly to labor in arranging meetings, lectures, and entertainments for women. In order to sustain the interest of women members, the board directed the locals to conduct frequent meetings of an educational nature.[30] This was the most far-reaching position yet adopted by any international union to deal with the organization and retention of women workers.

Fortunately, in a number of cities, the position of the General Executive Board did not remain confined to paper. In Baltimore, the chairwomen of the individual shops decided that they needed a special "girls' local" where women could discuss their special problems and new women members could be familiarized with the union's special activities. Women who joined the "girls' local" would retain their membership in the original shop local. In early December, 1916, the women working in Baltimore's Sonneborn factory elected the chairperson of Local 170 to represent them on the union's Trade Board—the first woman to hold this important position.[31]

In Chicago, Amalgamated women organized the Girls' Civic and Educational Club, which met weekly at Hull House. Members planned their meetings with specific training needs in mind. They presented their lessons and drills in parliamentary law and procedure in order to prepare themselves for participation in union meetings. Other programs included discussions of specific social problems and lectures on industrial and personal hygiene.[32]

Thus, by 1917, the women of the Amalgamated Clothing Workers of America, by dint of their tremendous contributions during organizing campaigns and strikes and by their incessant demands, had persuaded the male union leadership that unless it abandoned the unionism-as-usual approach to women workers, the Amalgamated would never succeed in its bitter struggles against the employers and the AFL. The Amalgamated's convention had yielded to the pressure of the women workers and had adopted a broad program designed to encourage women to join the union and to take an active and meaningful part in its affairs. Thereupon, the women of the Amalgamated, with the support of the union's General Executive Board, had begun to apply this historic resolution where it counted—among the women workers themselves, organized and unorganized alike.[33]

On June 22, 1917, *Advance,* the official Amalgamated organ, began publication of a page devoted to women's issues, and announced it with the following statement:

> Women have not only a special opportunity in the labor movement, but they can make to it a contribution of their own. They can bring to it qualities which, as a mere man's movement, it often lacks—imagination, devotion, inspiration. If working girls are once aroused to the wide and deep significance and beauty of the struggle of laboring mankind to free itself from oppression, they become the devoted and inspired priestesses of that movement. They have much to get and much to give, not only as workers, but as women. . . .
>
> The Woman's Page thinks too of a woman's sphere, but the sphere of the woman of the future and not of the past, the sphere of the woman who is interested in something more than clothes and cooking, a sphere of the woman who claims the whole world for her province, but seeks an opportunity to see that world in her own light, and to build it according to her own ideals.*

WOMEN OF THE ILGWU

During the years between 1915 and 1917, the women of the International Ladies' Garment Workers' Union also began to assume a more important role within the union. Early in 1915, President Benjamin Schlesinger appointed Rose Schneiderman as a full-time ILGWU organizer. She was sent to Chicago, where she offered invaluable assistance in the first successful strike of that city's women garment workers. A number of women glovemakers employed at the non-union

*Reprinting this statement, Mari Jo Buhle refers to it as "couched in sentiment clearly drawn from old traditions of the women's movement," an observation that will probably puzzle many of her readers. (Mari Jo Buhle, *Women and American Socialism 1870-1920* [Urbana, Illinois, 1981], p. 204.)

Herzog company walked out on strike and presented their grievances and a list of demands to their employer. Herzog refused to negotiate; instead, he called on the police to provide protection for strikebreakers. Police in patrol wagons promptly arrested both strikers and their friends and sympathizers. But the police brutality against the tiny group of strikers so enraged the women who had remained at work (and who also had complained of the low $6 and $7 weekly wages for a 60-hour week), that soon all seven hundred workers were out on strike. ILGWU Local No. 59 offered the services of Fannia Cohn to help the strikers; the Chicago Joint Board of the ILGWU, the International Glove Workers' Union, and the Women's Trade Union League all contributed both members for the Strike Committee and aid to the strikers. On August 22, 1915, Herzog accepted the workers' demands, recognized the union, and agreed to the establishment of a price commission. The workers won a 50-hour week, a half holiday on Saturday, a wage increase, and the abandonment of both fines and charges for materials. The teen-age strikers were jubilant, and the ranks of Local 59 swelled to nearly one thousand members.

The success of the Herzog workers encouraged a group of women in the kimono and white-goods branches of the industry to carry through a successful strike. They organized the Chicago White Goods Workers' Union, and two years later, the waistmakers and the white-goods workers merged to form Local No. 100.[34]

The ILGWU national office then called Schneiderman to Philadelphia, where she worked with Pauline Newman to build a new organization among the shirtwaist makers from the nucleus that had remained from the drive of 1909–1913. Newman had been hired as an organizer for the Philadelphia chapter of the Women's Trade Union League in 1910. She was a Lithuanian Jew who had come to New York as a child and had worked in the garment factories from the time she was twelve years old. She became an ardent socialist, for, as she later explained in an interview:

> You see around you the poverty and misery and you know from your own experience the conditions you work and live under, and *if you have any brains at all*, it doesn't take long for you to realize that this is the place where you belong, that the Party offers some hope, some change, and you want to be a part of it in making the change. You become active, and you learn to value people who know more than you do. . . . That's how my own career began. As soon as I was old enough, I joined the SP and traveled for the SP, not only in our own state but in many other states, and in between jobs that's what I did until I become officially an organizer for the ILGWU, and even then I used to

be "loaned" to the SP on occasions. . . . I think we all had the same vision, that we, the society, the people, all people, would have a chance to live in decency. We had a vision that justice and freedom and everything else we deserved would be there under socialism.[35]

By the time Rose Schneiderman arrived in Philadelphia, Pauline Newman had accomplished a small miracle. When she first came to the City of Brotherly Love in 1910, only one shirtwaist factory was organized. She left the city several years later with not only the shirtwaist industry well unionized, but with thousands of other workingwomen organized as well. One of her greatest triumphs was the service she held in the Labor Lyceum in 1911, at which three thousand Philadelphia workingwomen met in sorrow and anger to memorialize the women who had died in the Triangle Shirtwaist fire in New York City.

In June, 1911, Newman began to enter the garment factories of Philadelphia, where she argued with foremen who were cutting piecework rates. She told the women that they could not get higher wages unless they joined the union. In this way, she was "able to convert most of the employees in the shop to union membership." Those garment workers who had joined the union and gained a higher wage scale brought other women workers to the meetings that Newman called in the office of the Women's Trade Union League (WTUL).

Newman's achievements were especially remarkable in view of the fact that she received little cooperation from the male union leaders. In fact, they discouraged women from visiting the WTUL office. Frequently an AFL male organizer would "totally ignore the girls when they came in and continue to smoke his cigar behind his newspaper or would talk to them in an insulting way so they would leave the headquarters." When Melinda Scott, who was organizing for the WTUL, approached the Philadelphia AFL Central Labor Committee to discuss a plan for the establishment of a chapter in Philadelphia and for the use of the organization as a base for organizing women workers, "the men refused to allow her to speak."

Still, the ILGWU national office was more sympathetic, and with the aid of Rose Schneiderman, Newman continued the work of organizing the shirtwaist makers. They were later joined by the newly appointed national WTUL organizer, Mary Anders, and new locals were established in February, 1916 after a brief strike that was characterized by the all too familiar clashes between the strikers and the police, the union and the manufacturers agreed to a settlement.[36]

By 1916, the ILGWU had eight women organizers in the field.

President Schlesinger summoned Rose Schneiderman to New York for a long-term assignment to help the city's petticoat workers organize. Mabel Craig had unionized the waistmakers in northern New Jersey in a year-long campaign during late 1915 and early 1916. Pauline Newman, in addition to her work in Philadelphia, had traveled to upstate New York and Worcester, Massachusetts, organizing corset makers. Fannia Cohn had become a full-time organizer in Chicago, working to amalgamate the city's locals into a single, unified body. Juliet Stuart Poyntz visited Philadelphia to assist the American Branch of Local No. 15, while another young woman worked with the immigrant women of that local.[37]

N.Y. CLOAKMAKERS STRIKE OF 1916

The year 1916 also witnessed the bitter lockout and strike of New York cloakmakers, which led to the scrapping of the Protocol of Peace. While there were other grievances, such as the employers' practice of ridding the shops of the most militant trade unionists, the interpretation of the preferential union shop was the key issue in the dispute. When the employers' association refused to submit the issue to arbitration and unilaterally broke the conciliation agreement, the union proclaimed a general strike in the New York cloak trade on May 3 in order to prevent association employers from subcontracting their work to independent shops. Some sixty thousand union members provided their union's reply to the employers' lockout.[38]

The struggle of 1916 lasted for fourteen weeks and was notable for the outstanding solidarity of the strikers, who were assisted financially by the United Hebrew Trades, the Amalgamated Clothing Workers, the Workmen's Circle, the Furriers' Union, the Cloth Hat and Cap Makers' Union, the Central Federated Union, the AFL Executive Council, the Citizens' Committee for the Locked-out Cloak and Suit Makers, and the Women's Trade Union League. The latter organization raised over $30,000, which it spent on services to the strikers and their families. The ILGWU itself spent more than $627,000 on the walkout, much of it raised by sympathetic unions and organizations.[39] In the face of the workers' militancy, the union labor solidarity, and the support of the public, including even that of newspapers traditionally hostile to organized labor, the manufacturers were compelled to agree to negotiate with the union officials. Pressure brought by Mayor John Purroy Mitchel and President Woodrow Wilson, who authorized the Secretary of Labor to intervene, helped to force the manufacturers to agree to negotiate a settlement with the union.[40]

The collective agreement of August 4, 1916, which ended the lockout and strike, also ended the Protocol in the cloak trade. By its terms, the manufacturers were granted the absolute right to "hire and fire," while the workers were free to strike if they could not peacefully obtain redress from their employers. The new agreement, which had a two-year limit, also gave the workers a wage increase, reduced hours, union recognition, and preference in employment.[41]

Thus, the Era of the Protocol in the ladies' garment industry of New York City came to an end. The workers had regained the right to strike and the ability to place reliance on their own organization rather than on outside boards. The so-called harmony of interests of labor and capital had proved to be an illusion. The 1916 convention of the ILGWU proclaimed that the union was "capable of taking care of the workers' interests without the benevolent protection of the employers."[42]

The 1916 convention also established a permanent Educational Committee, which was charged, in part, with the development of programs to instruct women workers in the benefits of unionism, to train new leaders, and to broaden the intellectual horizons of young women workers. The convention empowered the committee to plan with the representatives of other AFL unions for the establishment of a workers' college where union members could train for leadership positions. The committee selected Juliet Stuart Poyntz as educational director and Fannia Cohn as its secretary.[43]

Even while the ILGWU was adopting broad social programs to involve its female membership, even while militant women garment workers were entering the union as organizers, contract negotiators, and directors of education, and even while women's ideas were beginning to reshape the union, men continued to dominate the official leadership positions. By 1917, women constituted over 50 percent of the international's claimed membership, but only one woman—Fannia Cohn—sat on the international's General Executive Board during the 1916-1918 term.[44]

THE FUR WORKERS FORGE AHEAD

Although it was smaller than either the ILGWU or the Amalgamated Clothing Workers, the International Fur Workers' Union also underwent considerable growth during the years from 1914 to 1916. In part this was because the union organized more shops in which women constituted a majority of the workers. The muff workers of New York City—young women who were employed in typical sweatshops located in attics, cellars, and basements—were organized. After a series of strikes, all the shops employing these women were forced to sign agreements that included a 49-hour week, ten paid holidays, a union shop,* and a wage increase of $2 a week.[45]

In Chicago, St. Paul, Montreal, and Toronto, women operators and finishers were organized and chartered in separate locals. Their agreements with employers established the union shop, seven paid legal holidays, time-and-a-half for overtime, and a reduction in the working hours. In Toronto, the local of women workers, none of whom had ever before belonged to a union, proved to be so militant that they forced the employers to grant the fur workers a 44-hour week, double time plus one-half for holiday work, and a wage increase of 25 percent.[46]

The greatest victory of the fur workers was the organization of the largest fur dressing and dyeing plant in the industry—A. Hollander & Sons in Newark, New Jersey. More than seven hundred workers were employed in this shop, two hundred of them women. The wages were low, averaging $6 to $10 a week for men, while the women workers, often hired to replace the men, worked for even less. An atmosphere of fear pervaded the plant, with instant discharge for any workers who dared to complain or even talk of a union.

Nevertheless, on April 6, 1915, the entire plant walked out. From the beginning, it was a bitter struggle, Hollander refused to even discuss union recognition, and on this issue, the workers were adamant. From the very outset, the firm imported scabs and hired gangsters to smash the picket lines. The police did their part by arresting workers who fought back against the thugs. On April 16, Morris Rubin and Abraham Novick, two of the most militant strikers, where shot and killed in cold blood by gunmen. The mourning strikers vowed not to return to the plant until the strike was won, and they kept their oath. The contract, which ran until December 1, 1917, provided for an increase of $3 a week for skilled workers, $2 for unskilled workers, and $1.50 for apprentices. The workweek was cut to fifty hours, with a half-day on Saturday. Overtime was paid at time and one-half. And the union was recognized, with any new workers hired compelled to join the union after two weeks.

The ending of the strike was celebrated by a parade through the streets of Newark. The victorious strikers marched behind brass bands and flags, proudly carrying aloft a huge banner that read: "THROUGH

*A union shop and a closed shop differ in that the latter requires all workers to be members of the union, while the former requires that they either be members or agree to join within a specified time after being hired.

STRUGGLE TO VICTORY. WE RETURN TO WORK AS UNION MEN AND WOMEN."[47]

By 1916, the International Fur Workers' Union had chartered twenty-seven locals and had greatly increased its membership. Agreements with significant gains had been signed in almost every organized fur center. Women fur workers had been in the lead in these achievements, and the first issue of the union's journal, *The Fur Worker*, on November 2, 1916, paid special tribute to these women, declaring: "In the great strike of 1912* and in the organizing efforts in New York, Chicago, St. Paul, Toronto, Montreal, and Newark, victories gained for our union simply would have been impossible but for the militancy, heroism, and self-sacrifice of the women furriers." But women fur workers, who now made up an important part of the membership, played even less of a role in the union's leadership than in the ILGWU. During the years 1913 to 1917, not one woman sat on the International Fur Workers' Union's General Executive Board.[48]

ON WORDS AND DEEDS

The ILGWU, the Amalgamated Clothing Workers, and the International Fur Workers' Union symbolized the new unionism in the garment industry. All three had been founded by trade unionists from the Socialist Party, and all three proclaimed in their constitutions that their aim was to organize workers industrially into class-conscious organizations and to create a form of society in which workers would receive the full value of their product. The new unionism encouraged a sense of solidarity that was absent in the craft-oriented unions. It challenged the principles of business unionism, which continued to dominate the AFL craft unions and, instead, held aloft a spirit of idealism.

The new unions raised no barriers to the enrollment of women members, and they offered a variety of educational, cultural, and social programs for workingwomen, which were unheard of in the old-line unions. Women members saw their wages increase and their hours of work lessen. But in at least one respect, the organizations that came to epitomize the new unionism were similar to the old-line craft unions: they were male-dominated. Women were permitted to exercise a greater role and influence on the lower levels than they did in the established craft unions, but men still monopolized all union offices, and male chauvinism expressed itself in a variety of other ways. When women were appointed organizers, the male leaders often made their lives miserable by being unwilling to trust them in critical situations. Often,

*For a discussion of the 1912 strike, *see* Foner, *History of the Labor Movement* 5:251-55.

when these women were about to enter into a strike, the leaders of the international would send men in to manage the strike, thus making clear their lack of confidence in the ability of the women to do the job effectively. Protests from women organizers, including even threats of resignation, fell on deaf ears.[49]*

UNIONS AND GANGSTERS

Unfortunately, the garment industry unions also developed a tendency to employ gangsters—first against the thugs hired by the employers, and later against the workers who dared to challenge the union leadership. As the *Literary Digest* noted as early as May, 1915, "even women did not escape this lawless punishment administered by gangsters employed by union leaders."[50]

This scandalous practice went hand in hand with the failure to enforce agreements won by the workers' militant strikes. When workers complained, they were threatened with violence. This was especially true in the New York fur trade. The agreement required the bosses to improve sanitary conditions, but in the hands of Isidore Cohen, the Socialist leader of the New York Joint Board, it became a worthless scrap of paper. In 1915, the New York Department of Health conducted an investigation of the fur industry. It found so many violations of sanitary laws that it came to the conclusion that the life of every fur worker was in grave danger. The Department of Industrial Hygiene recommended sweeping changes in shop conditions, and called upon the union to cooperate in forcing the employers to carry out these proposals. But Cohen refused to cooperate on the ground that doing so would place too

*Rose Schneiderman was so furious over the tendency of President Schlesinger and other ILGWU leaders to deprive her of command in a crucial situation that she often turned in her resignation, only to withdraw it in the interests of the women workers she was seeking to organize. Finally, she could stand it no longer. In a letter of December 1, 1916, in which she spoke for many women organizers in both the old- and new-line unions—including those who held on despite rebuffs from male leaders—she sent in her resignation, which read:

"Dear Sir and Brother: I herewith tender to you my resignation as Organizer of the International Union.

"My abrupt severance of relations with the International, if it requires any explanation, is I judge very logical in the light of the attitude taken towards my work by the powers that be. . . . For the last few months I have found myself working in an atmosphere of distrust which, to say the least, is not conducive to putting forth one's best efforts." (Rose Schneiderman, with Lucy Goldwaithe, *All for One,* New York, 1967, pp. 128-30; Rose Schneiderman to Benjamin Schlesinger, December 1, 1916, copy in Rose Schneiderman Papers, Tamiment Institute Library, New York University). After her resignation, Schneiderman concentrated on work for the Women's Trade Union League. *See* below, pp. 130, 132, 139, 189.

much of a burden on the employers. In vain, Dr. Louis L. Harris, chief of the Department, protested that "we pointed out dangers that severely and gravely menaced the health of the workers in your trade. Up to the present there has been no active cooperation between your organization and the Department of Health."[51]*

From the beginning, the fur workers' union was plagued by gangsterism. The owners of the fur shops hired gangsters to keep out the union, and the union either hired others or developed its own talent. Faced with rising opposition from a membership infuriated by the failure to enforce the agreements, Isidore Cohen used gangsters to terrorize the fur workers. Moreover, he defended the use of strong-arm methods by the union against its own members in the *Jewish Daily Forward* on the ground that Jewish workers tended to be undisciplined complainers and had to be kept in line by such methods.[52]

It required the utmost courage for a worker to criticize the policies of the union leadership. Women fur workers found to their dismay that employers paid them less for the same work that men did, despite the fact that contracts provided for equal pay. When they demanded that the union enforce the agreement on this issue, they were answered by strong-arm methods. Instead of relying upon the workers for support, the Cohen administration had to depend on its strong-arm men. Elections became a formality. When the administration was unable to get the votes of the workers, it simply stole the election.[53]

In 1916, Cohen was replaced by a reform administration, but the techniques he had developed were to be revived in the fur workers' union and were to infect other needle trades' unions as well. However, a "progressive" element had already emerged in these unions that was to combat these policies. A conflict had begun to surface in the needle trades' unions that was to grow in intensity in the years that lay ahead.

---

*The fur workers were not the only ones in the needle trades who suffered health hazards. The Commission on Industrial Relations reported in 1916: "A recent study by the United States Public Health Service of the health conditions of the workers engaged in the garment industry in New York City reveals the fact that the garment workers as a class exhibit a large number of defects and diseases. The specialists who have made a thorough medical examination of representative groups of garment workers report that only about 2 percent can be considered free from defects. In searching for the cause of the prevalence of tuberculosis among garment workers, the investigators for the United States government showed that in their effort to provide for those dependent upon them, the workers are likely to reduce their personal expenditures for necessities to the minimum, and in this way, diminished resistance to the disease through insufficient diet and inadequate clothing. In addition to this, the necessity for earning the greatest possible wage in order to tide over the dull season would, especially in the case of piece workers, lead to unusual exertions, diminishing vital resistance and predisposing them to tuberculosis infection." (Quoted in *Seattle Union Record*, June 24, 1916.)

CHAPTER 8

The Women's Trade Union League on the Eve of World War I

Long have we lived apart,
  Women alone;
Each with an empty heart,
  Women alone;
Now we begin to see
How to live safe and free,
No more on earth shall be
  Women alone.

Now we have learned the truth,
  Union is power;
Weak and strong, age and youth,
  Union is power;
On to the end we go,
Stronger our League must grow,
We can win justice so,
  Union is power.

For the right pay for us,
  We stand as one;
For the short day for us,
  We stand as one;
Loyal and brave and strong,
Helping the world along,
For the end to every wrong,
  We stand as one![1]

A GLOOMY PICTURE

Year after year, members of the Women's Trade Union League enthusiastically sang this song, written by Charlotte Perkins Gilman; but from the evidence disclosed by nationwide investigations, it was clear that despite over a decade of league activity,the gains of women workers were limited to those in the clothing industry. Yet even there, thousands of women still toiled at substandard wages under deplorable conditions. The conditions of women in most other industries remained much as they had been in 1903, when the league was founded.* The same was largely true of union membership among women workers. The dramatic victories in the garment industry from 1909 to 1913 had obscured the fact that women's strikes in a number of trades between 1910 and 1913 had failed, and that in most industries union membership for women remained largely the same as it had been ten years earlier. In September, 1913, about 72,000 women belonged to New York City labor unions, over 63,000 of them in the garment and textile trades. Of the approximately 9,000 others, about 4,000 belonged to unions in the tobacco, printing, and bookbinding industries (a figure that had remained fairly stable since the start of the twentieth century); 3,000 women belonged to the musician's and theatrical unions; while the remaining women unionists were scattered in small, isolated organizations in the service occupations and marginal industries.[2]

The national figures confirmed this gloomy picture. Among the slightly more than 8 million women gainfully employed in 1910, the facts about trade union membership were as follows: (1) of the 2,407 women employed in the liquor and beverage industries, from 20 to 30 percent were organized; (2) of the 333,000 employed in the clothing, printing, and bookbinding industries, from 10 to 15 percent were organized; (3) of the 145,870 employed in leather and in cigar and tobacco factories, from 5 to 10 percent were organized; (4) of the 415,000 employed in the lumber, furniture, and textile industries, from 1 to 5 percent were organized, and (5) of the remaining 7,100,000 less than 1 percent were organized. Apart from the increase in the percentage organized in the garment trades, the figures were much the same five years later, in 1915.[3]

*For the origins and formation of the Women's Trade Union League, see Philip S. Foner, *Women and the American Labor Movement: From Colonial Times to the Eve of World War I,* New York, 1979, pp. 290-302; Foner, *History of Labor Movement 3:* For the history of the League from its founding to the eve of World War I, see Foner, *Women and the American Labor Movement,* 303-46 and Foner, *History of Labor Movement 5:* 228-48, 253-61.

GOMPERS' EXPLANATION

Samuel Gompers attributed the small percentage of women unionists to the refusal of women workers to join men in a concerted drive to improve standards in the industries in which they were employed. "False standards, false pride, [and] misunderstandings," he declared, "have held many back from facing real conditions and facts and employing remedies" to improve their working conditions. Because women first began working for wages outside the home on a makeshift, temporary basis, Gompers continued, they never regarded their employment as a vital or permanent part of their lives and showed no interest in joining unions to improve their working conditions. They tolerated wretchedly unsanitary surroundings and endless hours of work in order to "help out" on a short-term basis. When employers discovered that women would work for lower wages, they eagerly hired them. For all the efforts of the trade unions to defeat these employers' programs, they had come up against a tradition of outright opposition or indifference to unionism on the part of women workers. Conditions such as existed in the industries of the United States for women workers would continue as long as they continued to reject the remedies men had devised for their self-help. Rich women who offered their time and money to help working women, he went on, could produce worthwhile results, but "permanent true betterment of the lives of the working women can be secured when these women achieve it by their own efforts."[4]

Women Trade Union League members must have bristled at Gompers' patronizing comment that rich women could help, particularly after their achievements during the great uprisings in the garment trades between 1909 and 1913. They were also shocked by the fact that even after the uprising of the militant garment women, Gompers still mouthed the time-worn stereotypes about workingwomen. Government reports had exploded several of the myths to which Gompers still clung. Most women were not working for "pin money"; they depended on their wages to sustain their households. While it was true that for many young women matrimony presented the only escape from "ruthless" exploitation, a large number were forced to return to the labor market even after marriage merely to maintain a subsistence living.[5]

THE LEAGUE, THE IWW, AND THE AFL

Not a few league members, in fact, were rapidly becoming infuriated by the AFL national leaders' attitude toward women and more and more convinced that the league's ability to meet the needs of workingwomen was being hampered by its ties with the federation. The Lawrence textile strike of 1912 (which we have discussed at length in a previous volume)* played a particularly significant role in opening league members' eyes to the limitations of the AFL . It will be recalled that the IWW had taken over the leadership early in the strike after the AFL's United Textile Workers, led by John Golden, had demonstrated its unwillingness to organize unskilled immigrants. In fact, when Golden came to Lawrence at the request of the city officials "to assist in quelling the strike," he counseled the Women's Trade Union League to stay out of Lawrence. Nevertheless, as Sue Ainsley Clark, president of the Boston League, later recalled, the strike was a "magnificent uprising of oppressed, unskilled foreign workers. Our strike committee had many members who did not endorse IWW principles but were enthusiastic [about the] strikers."6

Finally, in response to the Boston league's petitions, Golden allowed the branch to open a relief center in Lawrence to collect food and clothing. Meanwhile, the UTW was working to split the skilled workers off from the unskilled. Once Golden had achieved a settlement that the small number of strikers who were newly organized into UTW craft unions voted to accept, he ordered the league to restrict its relief only to those workers to pledged to go back to work. When workers who insisted on continuing to strike went to the Boston league's relief station for assistance, they were told that they could not receive help unless they agreed to return to work. In other words, league members found themselves involved in a strikebreaking operation and some of them were appalled. Still, unwilling to antagonize the UTW-AFL leadership, the league withdrew from Lawrence except for Mary Kenney O'Sullivan, the first woman hired by the AFL as an organizer, and one of the original founders of the Women's Trade Union League, who continued to aid the IWW strikers. Later, the angry O'Sullivan publicly castigated Golden and the UTW and criticized the league for its subservience. She pointed out correctly that at Lawrence, the American Federation of Labor came to be looked upon by the strikers as "almost as dangerous to their success as the forces of the employers themselves." She not only unequivocally condemned the actions of the UTW, but fully supported the IWW strike committee:**

*See Philip S. Foner, *History of the Labor Movement*, vol. IV: *The I.W.W., 1905-1917*, New York, 1965, pp. 306-350.
**O'Sullivan was also critical of social workers in Boston who did not go to Lawrence, but, relying on the testimony of John Golden, fought the strikers from the outset. (Mary Kenney O'Sullivan, "The Labor War at Lawrence," *Survey* 28 (April 1912): 73-74. *See also* Theresa Corcoran, S.C., "Vidda Scudder and the Lawrence Textile Strike," *Essex Institute Historical Collections* 115 [July 1979]: 193-94.)

The sub-committee of the Lawrence strikers which conducted the negotiations that ended in a victory for all the textile workers of New England, is the most unselfish strike committee I have known. With two exceptions, its members are skilled workers in the Lawrence mills. It was at the suggestion of these skilled workers that the lowest paid, unskilled workers received the largest advance in wages and the highest paid skilled workers received the smallest.[7]*

The league's actions in Lawrence also disgusted Elizabeth Glendower Evans, a rich woman who was the financial mainstay of the Boston league. She went up to Lawrence to see the strike committee in action, and realized that the WTUL relief station was "a travesty and a fake. It simply filled me with despair for our League as a live thing at all, that our secretary and Mrs. Conboy, vice-president and organizer, had been there continuously for weeks and had muddled along as remote from the real conditions, so it seems to me, as if they had been in Alaska." Mrs. Evans thereupon resigned from the Boston WTUL expressing the opinion that its affiliation with the AFL had doomed it to inconsequence:

The A.F. of L. in Massachusetts and perhaps pretty generally is narrow and selfish and is losing its hold. Its strict craft organization is not adapted to the assimilation of the unskilled foreign races. Perhaps it has got to be smashed, or purged, or reorganized. Just at present, I don't see where a person in my postition can lend a hand. And I don't see how a League linked strictly to the disintegrating A.F. of L. can become real.[8]

Although it was clear that this was an exaggeration, and that the AFL was not "disintegrating," and although the Lawrence strike was settled favorably, the strikebreaking role of the UTW leadership and the Boston league's acquiescence to it created a major controversy within the WTUL. The seriousness of the split was disclosed in an analysis Sue Ainsley Clark made for Margaret Dreier Robins, president of the National Women's Trade Union League:

Certain members of the Boston League believed that its course was the only one open to it since it was affiliated with the A.F. of L. and aimed to

*On March 12, 1912, the negotiating committee for the Lawrence strikers came back from their meeting with the textile employers with an offer of 25 percent increases for lowest-paid workers, with a decreasing of increases for higher-paid workers. The premium system was not abolished, but all workers would now get time and a quarter for overtime work, and the companies promised no discrimination against strikers. On March 14 twenty thousand strikers voted unanimously to accept the offer, and go back to work. The outcome of the Lawrence strike was more than a local victory. By April 1, about 275,000 textile workers in New England had received wage increases as an indirect result of the Lawrence strike.

propagate the principles of craft unionism endorsed by that organization.* Certain others believe that we might have cooperated with the strike committee from the first, as individuals, though they realize the restraints imposed by the A.F. of L. affiliation. Still others think that our part has been a disgraceful one in this great struggle. Others regard the success of the Lawrence strike, through I.W.W. methods, as an object lesson by which the League—and the A.F. of L.—must profit in order to play a vital part in the rapidly moving evolution of the labor movement today.

Clark herself believed that many in power in the AFL had revealed themselves as "selfish, reactionary and remote from the struggle for bread and liberty of the unskilled workers." The danger to the AFL was the one "immemorially confronted by organizations in church and government when creed and consideration of safety obscure the original spirit and aim." The league must not become rigid, she maintained; "we must be free to aid in the struggle of the workers wherever and whenever we find the 'fight on.'" The crucial question now confronting the league could be summed up easily: "Are we, the Women's Trade Union League, to ally ourselves with the 'stand-patters' of the Labor Movement, or are we to hold ourselves ready to aid the insurgents—those who are freely fighting the fight of the exploited, the oppressed, and the weak among the workers?"[9]

Important league leaders and many rank-and-file members struggled to find an answer to the question. A visit to Lawrence during the strike had persuaded Helen Marot that the league must now concentrate its energies on finding new ways to reach unskilled workers. She was convinced that "we have reached a crisis when the organization of the unskilled worker has become the all-important question of the labor movement." But how to achieve the organization of the unorganized, unskilled workers without breaking away from the AFL? Marot recommended that the league petition the national craft unions for financial contributions to help support the league in its work of organizing unskilled women.[10]

In Chicago, Mary E. McDowell, a league leader, had reached a similar conclusion. Emphasizing that the AFL had much to learn from Lawrence if it seriously wished to unionize women workers, she conducted an intensive campaign, shortly after the strike ended, to convince AFL leaders all over the country to apply the lessons of the struggle. To Homer D. Call, secretary-treasurer of the Amalgamated Meat Cutters & Butcher Workmen, McDowell wrote:

*In one sense, Clark's statement is not accurate; the W.T.U.L. never formally affiliated with the AFL.

I was east and have talked with several thoughtful women who have been in Lawrence and have investigated the conditions before and during and after the strike. I am greatly impressed with what they told me. These people said to me that ["Big Bill"] Haywood had a *method* of organizing the foreigners in a great industry where there was little skill and much specialization that was most wise and successful, and would have to be applied to such industries as Packing and Steel. . . . We dare not ignore the one fact that they (the I.W.W.) have a *method* that will have to be used by the A.F. of L. or harm will come to the unions.

McDowell urged Call to try to persuade Gompers and other AFL leaders to begin organizing the mass-production industries, using the IWW's "method" of industrial unionism, employing militant organizers who spoke the languages of the foreign-born workers, and using women to organize the women workers in these industries. "Mr. Gompers must not be afraid of even *socialists* if they are intelligent trade unionists and see the danger of letting the I.W.W. get ahead." To another AFL leader, McDowell wrote:

It will be a great waste of time and energy if the A.F. of L. misses the point that has been so terribly emphasized in Lawrence, Mass. . . . In such industries as steel, meat, textile, and harvesters, etc., Industrial Unionism of a constructive type is surely the need of this moment. The A.F. of L. will lose out unless it wakes up and adds to the I. W.W.'s clever method, that of permanent and constructive organization.[11]

When the league's Executive Board met in April, 1912, the events and lessons of Lawrence were the main subjects of discussion. Several members defended the IWW, saying that organization had handled the strike in a "splendid way," and questioned the value of the WTUL's alliance with a reactionary AFL. Since the organization of the vast majority of women workers could not be achieved through craft unionism, with its emphasis on organizing only the skilled workers, why cling to an organization that would never abandon this outmoded method of unionization? This view, however, was vigorously challenged by Margaret Dreier Robins, who assumed the League presidency after 1907.

A year earlier, Robins had written angrily to Leonora O'Reilly that AFL leaders' "arrogance and contempt of the working women" made her boil. She admitted that male supremacy, "stand-pat" craft unionism, an unwillingness to organize any but skilled craftsmen, and the conviction that the task or organizing female and foreign-born workers was virtually impossible were too deeply ingrained in AFL thinking to be eradicated.[12] Still, at the 1912 Executive Board meeting, Robins argued that the league must retain its close relationship with the AFL and even expressed displeasure at the fact that the Boston league had gone into Lawrence without consulting the national board.[13]

Robins put down the brief rebellion, and, on the basis that there was no alternative, the Executive Board reaffirmed its ties with the Federation as being in the interests of female workers. In return, Gompers promised the league $150 monthly toward the cost of its organizational work among women. The AFL Executive Council rewarded the league for its loyalty by authorizing payment of this sum, which was used to organize glove workers. Agnes Nestor, secretary of the Glove Workers' Union, assumed the duties of national organizer.[14]

The funds, however, were too limited to permit much organizing, and Robins wrote to Gompers the following spring, reaffirming the league's loyalty to the AFL and asking for the continuation of Federation assistance, by which the good relations between the two organizations would continue, "helping to create a mutual understanding so necessary to concerted action."[15] Although Marot and McDowell had insisted on the need for industrial unionism in organizing women workers, they and other league leaders adopted a scrupulously careful posture, believing that any rupture with the AFL would destroy the league's very reason for being. In the end, after much soul-searching, league leaders came to the conclusion that the league should concentrate on the organization of skilled, American-born women along traditional craft union lines.[16]

Furthermore, aware that Gompers was ardently antisocialist, and convinced that radical political and ideological affiliations could have only adverse effects on their organization's position within the AFL, league leaders requested members not to combine league work with Socialist Party activities. When Rose Schneiderman continued to include socialist principles in her league-sponsored speeches, members of the Executive Board suggested that she resign.[17]

In January, 1914, the AFL Executive Council approved the league's request for the continuation of its appropriation, but instructed Gompers to keep a tighter control over its spending. Gompers promptly requested a personal interview with Robins, accompanied by Agnes Nestor and Alice Henry, and informed them of the Executive Council's requirement that the league prepare periodic reports explaining how they used the Federation's donation. The league women accepted the decision, but privately they expressed their anger over the attempt to monitor their activities.[18]

The league leaders also privately conceded that there was little they could do to alter the humiliating situation they were now being forced to accept. But though the league sorely needed the AFL's financial subsidy, new branches in Denver, Los Angeles, and Philadelphia were joining the older ones in New York, Boston, St. Louis, Baltimore, and Kansas City. Moreover, the league's School for Active Workers in the Labor Movement, which opened in Chicago in January, 1914, with one student, had developed a unique course of training for leadership in women's trade union organization. Three categories of students were to be accepted into the school; those whom the league asked to leave their trades to train as organizers; those sent by their own unions or central labor bodies to improve their effectiveness in working for the organization; and those who came on their own initiative and responsibility. After four months of academic work, there were eight months of field work, which included the theory and practice of organizing, attendance at meetings of unions and the AFL, conferences with men and women leaders, analysis of trade agreements, and instruction in suffrage and civic duties.[19]*

EMERGENCE OF THE WOMAN ORGANIZER

When the W.T.U.L. was founded, there was no such thing as a career as a woman labor organizer. Women who organized unions did so because they felt they had a mission to help their exploited sisters. When Mary Kenney O'Sullivan made the decision to stop being a bookbinder and became an organizer, it was because "someone must go from shop to shop and find out who the workers were that were willing to work for better conditions. I must be that someone." She worked as an organizer for many years while supporting herself in her trade; out of a long life as an organizer, she was paid to do organizing work for only five months.** Leonora O'Reilly did organizing for the United Garment Workers in the late 1890s for no pay. In 1908 she was enabled to become a full-time organizer by the gift of an annuity from Margaret Dreier Robins. This was a personal gift.***

The next generation of workingwomen activists found it possible to become paid organizers. They included Louisa Mittelstadt and Myrtle

---

*The academic work included courses in English, public speaking, the study and analysis of judicial decisions affecting labor injunctions, boycotts, etc., economic history, the history of organized labor, elementary economics, and modern radicalism. Some of the courses were taken at the Chicago School of Civics and Philanthropy and the University of Chicago. The field work was under the supervision of Agnes Nestor or Mary Anderson. Later, an extensive correspondence program was begun, and similar training was sponsored by leagues in Philadelphia and Boston. (Philip S. Foner, *Women and the American Labor Movement*, 477.)

**For Mary Kenney's work as an organizer for the AFL, *see* Foner, *History of the Labor Movement* 2: pp. 193-4; Foner. *Women and the American Labor Movement*, pp. 226-36.

***For the organizing work of Leonora O'Reilly, *see* Foner, *Women and the American Labor Movement*, pp. 220-26, 254-60.

Whitehead of the Brewery Workers; Rose Schneiderman, Pauline New-
man, and Fannia Cohn of the ILGWU; Josephine Casey of the Elevated
Railway Clerks; Agnes Nestor of the Glove Workers; Melinda Scott of
the Hat Trimmers; Elizabeth Mahoney of the Hotel and Restaurant
Employees; Nellie Quick of the Bindery Workers; Mary Anderson,
Emma Stephagen, Mary McEnery, and Mary Haney of the Boot and
Shoe Workers; Hilda Svenson of the Commercial Telegraphers; and
Alice Bean and Mabel Gillespie of the Bookkeepers, Stenographers and
Accountants. Most of them moved up to paid full-time organizing
positions from rank-and-file work. But more and more of them were
becoming paid organizers as a result of having graduated from the
WTUL school and the experience they got as organizers-in-training.[20]

The local leagues also trained women to be organizers and developed
educational programs in unionizing workingwomen. The New York
League used its English-language classes to teach the principles of trade
unionism. It published a reading primer, *New World Lessons for Old
World People,* by Violet Pike, which contained lessions like:

> I go to work at eight o'clock
> I work until six o'clock.
> I have only one-half hour for lunch.
> I work overtime in the busy season.
> I do not get extra pay for overtime work.
> I earn eight dollars a week in the busy season.
> I earn three or four dollars a week in the slow season.
> I have no work at all for three months.
> I pay for my needles and thread.
> I pay for my electric power.
> My trade is a bad trade.

In the series' next lesson, entitled "A Trade with a Union," the
conditions are entirely different:

> I met a friend yesterday.
> She works at a good trade.
> She goes home at five o'clock.
> She goes home at twelve o'clock on Saturday.
> She has one hour for lunch every day.
> She earns twelve dollars a week.
> Sometimes she works overtime in the busy season.
> She gets extra pay for overtime.
> She belongs to the Union in her trade.[21]

The Women's Trade Union League made little effort to organize
Black women or to campaign to lower the barriers against them in both

industry and the trade unions. The reason is not difficult to discover. The league's association with and dependence on the blatantly racist AFL made such efforts practically impossible.[22]

The league's dependence on the AFL was heightened by the fact that it lacked a steady source of income and was, therefore forced to solicit gifts and contributions from rich friends, men's unions, and the AFL. To compound these difficulties, a number of rich allies, including Mrs. Walter Weyl, who annually donated $1,000 to the New York League, experienced financial losses that precluded continuing their bequests. Even Margaret Robins found it necessary to reduce her support for the league's monthly periodical, *Life and Labor,* which ran at an annual deficit. An ominous foreboding of impending bankruptcy darkened the national secretary's report after Robins, who had financed the national league almost singlehandedly, also announced cutback of her contributions.[23]

While yielding to the AFL's conservatism temporarily eased the league's financial problem, relations between the two organizations deteriorated as a result of conflicts over a number of issues, some of a transitory nature, others more fundamental.[24] A deep conflict surfaced as it became clear that the AFL and the league held diametrically opposite views on the desirability of social legislation for women workers. This had not been an issue in the early years of the league's history, because the organization concentrated on unionization and even insisted that legislation would prove of little value if the women workers had no unions to enforce it.

THE MINIMUM WAGE

However, beginning in 1909, the league made the eight-hour day and a minimum wage for women key demands, and increasingly after 1913 it concentrated its time and energy on securing such legislation. On the issue of an eight-hour day, the league did not come into conflict with the AFL, for the Federation continued to support special hours legislation for women. But the AFL, and many of its affiliated unions, were unequivocally opposed to legislation establishing a minimum wage.

The concept of the minimum wage had spread rapidly in the English-speaking world. New Zealand and Australia, during the 1890s, were the first to enact minimum-wage statutes. Then in 1910 England adopted the Australian model. Traveling in Europe two years earlier, Florence Kelley had learned of the minimum-wage idea from Beatrice Webb, and, on her return to the United States, she got the National Consumers'

League, which she headed, to publicize the new reform. Meanwhile, Mary Dewson in Massachusetts was aiding the cause by investigating wage standards in that state, and the Factory Investigating Commission in New York was advancing it further with its own investigation and disclosures.[24*]

Both the National Association of Manufacturers (NAM) and the American Federation of Labor refused to join the campaign for minimum wage laws for women workers. To the NAM it was simply "fantastic and grotesque legislation," which was nothing less than "pure socialism."[25] The AFL, on the other hand, argued that "government paternalism" might discourage union organizing among women; that once women were guaranteed a minimum wage, men would demand the same, and all labor would then come within the grip of the state; and that any minimum wage would soon become the maximum for many workers. Gompers, the leading AFL opponent of such legislation, stressed that "attempts of the government to establish wages at which workmen may work, according to the teachings of history, will result in a long era of industrial slavery." Such laws, he predicted, would paralyze American labor and constitute an "infringement of personal liberty." He reminded the WTUL that the problems of men and women workers were identical: "Women work in industry side by side with men. Their relations to industry and their relations to employers contain no elements different from those of men's relations." Gompers and other AFL spokesmen were quick to point out to the league that they favored statutory limitations on women's working hours, for women needed special protection because they were weaker and more vulnerable than men. But they did not need a minimum-wage law, for "once the state is allowed to fix a minimum rate, the state would also take the right to compel men or women to work at that rate."[26]

It therefore came as a shock, as well as a source of considerable anger to Gompers and other AFL leaders, when they learned that, despite opposition from the AFL and a number of state federations of labor and leading international unions affiliated with the Federation,[**] the Na-

---

* For the conditions exposed by the Factory Investigating Commission, *see* Foner, *History of Labor Movement* 3:, and Foner, *Women and the American Labor Movement:* 459-63.

** Not all AFL unions, however, opposed minimum-wage legislation for women. In New York and California, organized labor disapproved of minimum-wage statutes, echoing the AFL argument that it was an unwarranted government paternalism, but trade unionists in the state of Washington "worked hard and closely with reformist women's clubs to obtain a wage statute." Moreover, labor advocates of minimum-wage laws eventually persuaded both the Brooklyn Central Labor Union and the New York State Federation of Labor to campaign for the legislation.

tional Women's Trade Union League and the local leagues had endorsed minimum wage legislation—although not without a good deal of internal conflict—and had joined the National Consumers' League and the American Association for Labor Legislation in agitating for minimum wage laws. Workingwomen, the league argued, deserved a "living wage," an income that would "allow a young woman to rent a small heated room and pay for sufficient nourishing food, purchase decent clothes, and have a little left over, not much, for candy and other pleasures." Such legislation, it maintained, would generate better living conditions, greater efficiency, and "a more prosperous buying public." And, the league argued, the humanizing touch of the minimum wage might well "make outright socialism undesirable and unnecessary."[27]

THE LEAGUE AND WOMAN SUFFRAGE

Along with the other organizations in the field, the league's activity was effective. Between 1913 and 1923, fourteen state legislatures wrote a specific minimum wage into law.* The league felt its contribution had helped considerably to justify its existence. It was therefore inevitable that as the league's emphasis shifted from unionization to protective legislation, the battle for woman suffrage began to assume greater and greater importance in the WTUL's program. To be sure, the early leaders and members of the league had come to it already committed to the principles of woman suffrage; the first national convention in 1907 included "full citizenship" as one plank of its six-point platform, and in 1908 a Suffrage Department had been established within the league. Nevertheless, before 1909 the struggle for the vote was a peripheral issue, and many league members at first did not even see any connection between the fight for the ballot and the realities confronting workingwomen. Simply having the right to vote would not, after all, shorten working hours, raise wages, or provide decent, safe working conditions. Workingmen had had the vote for decades, yet the industrial conditions

*However, not all the laws were effective. Some legislatures wrote a specific minimum wage into the statutes, but they did not provide for any administrative agency to enforce it. Massachusetts enacted the weakest statute. It established a commission, which was instructed to arrive at a wage that would not "threaten to interfere either with the general financial prosperity of the trade or with the 'reasonable profits' of an individual employer." Furthermore, it could only recommend the wage to employers, and they could accept or reject it. If an employer refused to pay the recommended wage, the commision would add his name to a list of recalcitrants published in the state newspapers. Thus, Massachusetts, the most highly industrialized state, with the largest number of employed women, made it easy for many employers to ignore the minimum wage. (Dorothy W. Douglas, "American Minimum Wage Laws at Work," *American Economic Review* 9 [Spring, 1919]: 701–38.)

of vast numbers of male workers had not basically improved. To the degree that men had better conditions, shorter hours, and higher wages, they had achieved these things not because they could vote but because they had organized into effective trade unions. Since women were oppressed by the same industrial conditions that oppressed men, they, too, could only solve their problems the way men had. As one champion of placing priority on unionization put it to Leonora O'Reilly: "Woman suffrage is beginning at the other end. What the women need is *economic* emancipation, and, Sister, dear, how they need it! And they can't get it without organization."[28]

The anti-suffrage forces in the WTUL were reinforced by the class bias of the early twentieth-century movement. While Susan B. Anthony continued to emphasize the need for establishing close links with the labor movement and workingmen,* the rich matrons who now dominated the suffrage organizations made few attempts to appeal to women workers, and suffragist propaganda frequently included arguments that were bound to alienate many workingmen and women. The suffragists had actually abandoned the traditional demand for suffrage as a universal democratic right and had begun to seek allies among middle-and-upper class men by arguing that granting the vote to women of these classes would offset the votes of the lower classes. There were exceptions to this attitude, especially in some of the highly industrialized states of the Northeast. In Connecticut, for example, Socialist and labor activist Ella Reeve Bloor (later known as "Mother" Bloor when she became a leading figure in the Communist Party) was engaged by local suffragists to organize workingwomen into suffrage clubs. But the more common viewpoint of suffragists of this era was expressed by the National American Woman Suffrage Association (NAWSA), the major suffrage organization in the United States, in a resolution of 1903 advocating educational qualifications that would have had the effect of restricting the suffrage and would thus have prevented many immigrants and other poor people from voting. What is more, the NAWSA refused to endorse the labor movement. Even during the high point of women's union activities—the 1909 waistmakers' strike—NAWSA issued a statement declaring that the Association "neither stands for labor organization nor against it."[29]

And yet, it will be recalled from the discussion in our previous volume,** many prominent suffragists did support the strikers. These

*For earlier relations between Susan B. Anthony and the trade union movement, *see* Foner, *History of Labor Movement* 1, pp. 385–87.
**See Foner, *History of the Labor Movement* 5: pp. 234–37.

women became convinced that the success of their movement depended on their ability to win the workers to their cause. To promote suffrage among trade union members. Anna Howard Shaw, president of the NAWSA, hired the league's Rose Schneiderman to help in the 1912 Ohio suffrage campaign. Schneiderman was delighted to accept the assignment, but she first told Shaw that she was "a socialist and trade unionist who looked upon the ballot as a tool in the hands of working women with which, through legislation, they could correct the terrible conditions existing in industry." Unfortunately, Schneiderman was the only workingwoman used in the suffrage campaign, and she alone could not overcome the opposition of the Cincinnati and Dayton central labor unions, which refused to endorse women's suffrage. Two years later, Margaret Dreier Robins wrote to Leonora O'Reilly: "You know one of the biggest reasons for the defeat of suffrage in Ohio was the inability of the suffragists to reach the mass of the working men. Roschen, our Roschen, was practically the only trade unionist they had."[30] Roschen was, of course, Rose Schneiderman.

The league advanced the woman suffrage cause by working for it actively within its own organization and in coalition with NAWSA groups. Moreover, the WTUL encouraged the formation of independent wage-earners suffrage leagues as a way of bringing female workers into active involvement in the suffrage movement. It also devoted considerable energy to working with trade union men to gain their active support to the suffrage cause. In fact, the league's chief organizers began to devote their attention to full-time suffrage agitation. In New York, Rose Schneiderman, Pauline Newman, Leonora O'Reilly, Mary Dreier, Ida Rauh, and Mary Beard made numerous suffrage speeches. The league also hired Margaret (Maggie) Hinchey, a laundry worker, and Clara Lemlich, famous for her role in the 1909 waistmakers' strike,* as suffrage organizers. Most of the league activists worked with Mary Beard in the Industrial Section of the Woman's Suffrage Party (the local organization of the NAWSA). Early in 1912 Mary Beard wrote to Leonora O'Reilly: "I sent Clara [Lemlich] to call upon our suffrage leaders in several distinctly male labor unions to see what they had done toward getting hold of working women, whether they had any meeting rooms where we might hold a meeting and whether they could give us names of girls." Unfortunately, the women who ran the Industrial Section were not prepared for so radical a firebrand as Clara Lemlich, and it was not long before Beard was complaining to O'Reilly that "she can't

*See Foner, *History of Labor Movement* 5: 231.

swing the job."[31] So she was discarded, even though she had proved herself capable of "swinging" a strike of thirty thousand women workers!

On July 12, 1913, the *New York Times*, in a report of a meeting of suffragists on the Bowery, referred to

the Billy Sunday of the suffragists—Maggie Hinchey, who represents working women.* Maggie is big and sisterly and, above all, human in a good, strong way. When Maggie got up to speak, the Bowery succumbed to a man.

"Brothers," began Maggie, rolling her r's with a good Irish brogue. As she went on her audience alternately wiped its tears and shook with laughter, and when she said at the close, "And now you know what you are going to do on Nov. 2 (on the referendum on woman suffrage), every hand went up to say yes, they would vote for the women. . . . The suffragists are canvassing the Bowery and are getting comparatively favorable results.**

The Woman's Suffrage Party sent Maggie Hinchey to Rochester, where she organized a delegation of six hundred workingwomen to call on President Woodrow Wilson in February, 1914, and ask him for the vote. While there, she also did some street-corner speaking: "I spoke outside of three factories at noon hour and when I got through the men took off their hats and said, 'Hurray, votes for women.'"

Still, like other working-class radicals of the WTUL, Hinchey found it difficult to work with the middle- and upper-class women of the suffrage movement. Too often, their paternalistic attitude, to say nothing of their contempt for workers, and especially immigrant workers, came to the fore. "I feel as I have butted in where I was not wanted," Hinchey wrote to Leonora O'Reilly.[32]

For the sake of their working-class sisters, however, they carried on—speaking and emphasizing that while all women deserved the vote on the basis of equal justice, female workers especially needed it. Workingwomen needed the vote to develop confidence in themselves and to win the respect of both working-class men and employers, and as a tool that would give them some degree of control over their miserable working conditions. Without the vote female workers faced tremendous

---

*Billy Sunday, a flamboyant fundamentalist evangelist often addressed working-class audiences, but his message was quite different from that of Maggie Hinchey. While Hinchey sought to organize exploited workers, especially women workers into trade unions, Billy Sunday made common cause with business against the labor unions. Billy Sunday told his audiences of Protestant workers that they should work hard, live clean. and pray to Jesus for the life to come. A number of his revival campaigns, including a crusade after World War I among striking West Virginia coal miners, were paid for by industrial tycoons like John D. Rockefeller, Jr.

**It was not until 1917, however, that New York women got the vote.

handicaps in their efforts to get the legislation they needed. Rose Schneiderman emphasized this last argument at a mass meeting at Cooper Union organized by the New York Wage Earners' League for Suffrage* in 1912:

> I did some work last year for the 54-hour bill, and I can tell you how conscious our Senators and Assemblymen are when a disfranchised citizen tries to convince them of the necessity of shorter hours for working women.
>
> During the hearing at Albany, our learned Senators listened to the opposition very carefully. . . . But when the Committee who spoke for the working women came to plead for the bill, there was only one Senator left in the room—he was the chairman—he couldn't very well get out. . . . Mind you, we were pleading for a shorter work week for working women. We had evidence to show that physical exhaustion leads to moral exhaustion, and the physical and moral exhaustion of women will lead to the deterioration of the human species. What did these men care? We were voteless working women—no matter what we felt or thought, we could not come back at them.[33]

Thus, in the view of the WTUL, suffrage now became the essential precondition for the unionization of workingwomen. Once they were able to vote, women would automatically gain the independence and confidence that male organizers often insisted they lacked. It would also help them in strikes. The NWTUL concluded a 1915 suffrage resolution with the observation that women were "heavily handicapped" during strikes because they lacked the vote. "Out of our experience in time of strikes," the resolution stated, "we have witnessed the close alliance of politics and police activity and police court justice."[34] In short, suffrage would abolish the sweatshop, raise women's wages, reduce their working hours, and help them unionize. "Behind suffrage," Leonora O'Reilly wrote to the Electrical Workers' Union, "is the demand for equal pay for equal work. Women workers would cease to be a threat to union men's wage scales once they gained the vote."[35]

The trend toward concentration on the battle for the vote intensified after the report of the United States Commission on Industrial Relations

---

*The Wage Earners' League was established in 1911, with WTUL encouragement, to persuade workingmen to agitate for the ballot as an "industrial necessity." Both organizations shared the same headquarters in New York, with the WTUL providing financial support and leadership. Leonora O'Reilly served on the WTUL's suffrage committee, and presided over the Wage Earners' League. O'Reilly helped to set up suffrage committees of workingwomen in Baltimore, Albany, Pittsburgh, New Jersey, Pennsylvania, and Delaware (*See* collection of pamphlets on the Wage Earners' League in Leonora O'Reilly Papers, Arthur and Elizabeth Schlesinger Library on the History of Women in America, Radcliffe College.)

in 1915. The commission charged that the "labor problems of 6,000,000 women workers lie not merely in their relations with employers, but in their relations with men's unions." Given the hostility of most male unionists, the commission declared, it was not surprising that such relief as women workers had obtained from exploitation and abuse had come "through agitation and legislation." At the same time, however, "their disfranchisement" limited the extent of this solution. Therefore, the granting of equal political rights to women workers was "one of the means by which women in industry may obtain living wages."[36]

The criticism of men's unions and the emphasis on legislation and suffrage was, of course, hailed by most women's groups, including the Women's Trade Union League. But Gompers, while endorsing the commission's observation that women in industry menaced "the wage and salary standards of men," asserted heatedly that "workers are not bugs to be examined under the lenses of a microscope in a sociological slumming tour."[37]

Before public audiences, state legislatures, and congressional committees, league speakers argued that the right of suffrage was needed to improve women's working conditions. They also attacked the position of the National Association Opposed to Woman's Suffrage (a women's organization) that giving workingwomen the vote would increase the number of illiterate, uninformed, undesirable voters. Another women's organization opposed by the league was the Limited Suffrage Movement, which sought to enfranchise only English-speaking white women. Mary Kenney O'Sullivan claimed that women who endorsed these racist, anti-suffragist arguments should be classed with scabs and strikebreakers as enemies of the people. A National Women's Trade Union League convention described these opponents of the suffrage as "women of leisure who, by accident of birth, have led sheltered and protected lives" and accused them of "selfishly obstructing the efforts of organized women to obtain full citizenship."[38]

STRAINED RELATIONS BETWEEN LEAGUE AND AFL

In the years from 1915 to 1917 the Women's Trade Union League placed twenty organizers in the field. While they did some unionization work, the main activity of these organizers was devoted to protective legislation and woman suffrage. Despite the AFL's continued support for suffrage as a means of improving the bargaining position of female workers—despite the publication of articles favoring woman suffrage in the *American Federationist*—despite convention resolutions in its favor and appeals to state legislatures for support, the AFL was still uneasy over the trend in the WTUL. In 1915 Gompers asked Leonora O'Reilly to write an article urging men to support proposed constitutional amendments for woman suffrage in four Eastern states, and he even outlined the text for her. But at the same time, he cautioned the league that it was traveling down a dangerous road by concentrating so heavily on legislation and suffrage. Working conditions, he declared at a league convention, were not sex problems but human ones, and "industrial freedom must be fought for in the industrial field." Ballots could never replace the trade union, he cautioned, for votes could not solve industrial problems.[39]

By this time, however, WTUL leaders were not paying much attention to the AFL and its representatives; indeed, its advocacy of the ballot as the main means of improving women's working conditions came about precisely because of the disillusionment of these female leaders with the AFL. After a sharp encounter with male trade unionists at the New York State Federation of Labor convention in the summer of 1915, Leonora O'Reilly wrote to Mary Dreier Robins:

> Now, don't drop dead, but this is my last labor convention. Also my hands are off the Trade Union job in New York. I shall leave for the movement's good. My mind is made up. . . . Trade Unions are necessary. They must be worked for in season and out. Women must be organized better than men are organized. The powers that be in the labor movement of New York State do not and will not recognize an outside body's right to help with the work. Worse than that, they attribute their own shortcomings to the outside body's disinterestedness. They use its work to influence personal animosity or worse and they cover up their own crookedness. The crookedness will sooner become known to the rank and file when the outside body is not there as a scapegoat. By keeping in the struggle, we shall hinder more than help the rank and file from getting real light as to who it is that is playing foul in the game. . . .[40]

The truth is that the Women's Trade Union League was caught in a dilemma. The league had linked its fate with that of the AFL; it had acknowledged the superiority of industrial unionism over craft unionism in organizing the great mass of women workers but had turned its back on the IWW, the chief proponent of this type of unionism. For fear of antagonizing AFL leaders, it had refrained from playing any role in the "new unionism" that was emerging in the garment trades. When the AFL refused to abandon its traditional attitudes toward women workers and change its method of organizing to meet their needs, the league was left isolated.*

*Relations between several of the League and AFL leaders were further strained during the presidential campaign of 1916 when Margaret Robins, president of the National Woman's Trade Union League, traveled across the country with other women suffragists on the "Hughes special," which crossed the United States in support of Charles Evans Hughes, the Republican Party presidential candidate. Since the AFL endorsed and supported Woodrow Wilson for re-election, Federation leaders were furious at Robins' action, charging her with "allying herself with the 'millionaire special'," and using the woman suffrage issue as a "subterfuge." In Los Angeles Robins was denied the right to speak before trade unionists at the Labor Temple. (*Los Angeles Times*, Oct. 19, 20, 1916.) For further discussion of the election of 1916, *see* pp. 222-31.

CHAPTER 9

An Eight-Hour Day for the Railroad Brotherhoods, I: Nine Months of Fruitless Negotiations

The first issue relating to the railroads that confronted the "New Freedom" administration of Woodrow Wilson dealt with the revision of the Erdman Act, passed by Congress and signed by President William McKinley on June 1, 1898.

THE ERDMAN ACT

The Erdman Act provided for two principal functions of the federal government: (1) mediation and conciliation, upon the request of either party, by the chairman of the Interstate Commerce Commission and the Commissioner of Labor, and (2) voluntary arbitration by an *ad hoc* three-man board, two members of which were chosen by labor and management, and the third member chosen by these two. The Erdman Act applied only to the operating personnel of interstate railroads— engineers, firemen, conductors, and trainmen. Courts of equity were to enforce awards for one year, but no injunctions were to be issued to compel any employee to work against his will. Section 10 of the Act prohibited both the blacklist and the "yellow dog" contract. No employer could require, as a condition for employment, that a railroad worker not be a member of a trade union, nor could he be discharged solely because of his membership in one. Finally, no employer could conspire with another carrier to prevent a worker from obtaining gainful employment.[1]

Section 10 of the Act enraged the railroads. They wanted a free hand in hiring and firing in order to weaken and ultimately destroy the Railroad Brotherhoods.* In 1907, they had received support in achieving their aim when the Supreme Court, in *U.S. v. Adair,* upheld the U.S. District Court's ruling holding Section 10 unconstitutional on the ground that legislation prohibiting a carrier from firing an employee because of union membership was not a legitimate federal regulation of interstate commerce.[2]

Even Richard B. Olney, who had broken the Pullman Strike while he was Attorney General under President Grover Cleveland,** criticized the *Adair* decision. "It is archaic—it is a long step back, into the past," he commented, "to conceive of and deal with the relations between the employer in such industries and employees as if the parties were individuals."[3]

Despite the court decision, which constituted a bitter blow to railway labor, the Erdman Act remained only on paper until 1906; the services provided by the Act were never used because the carriers refused to participate in any mediation attempts. In that year, however, a new era was begun when, for the first time, a railroad requested mediation. Between 1906 and 1913, mediation was requested by one or both parties in some sixty disputes. Most of these were settled through mediation, but a few required arbitration.[4]

Thus it appeared that the operation of the Erdman Act had justified the intention of its framers, but this was only on the surface. The carriers had come to believe that a three-member arbitration board was too small, since the third member of the board, representing the public, assumed all the responsibility and usually decided the issue in dispute by "splitting the difference" between the parties. What the railroads now wanted was a larger, permanent board with the power to compel arbitration and enforce its awards. Before 1906, the carriers had scorned both mediation and arbitration. Now, however, as the Brotherhoods grew in strength and began to talk of uniting for strike action, the railroads wanted to force mediation and arbitration on them. Of course, the Brotherhoods found arbitration less appealing for the same reasons, although they still favored mediation.[5]***

Dissatisfaction with the Erdman Act approached a climax in 1912

---

*These were the Brotherhood of Locomotive Engineers, Brotherhood of Locomotive Firemen and Enginemen, Brotherhood of Railroad Trainmen, and Order of Railway Conductors.

**See Philip S. Foner, *History of the Labor Movement in the United States,* New York, 1955, Vol 2, pp 266-68.

***Arbitration usually applied to the plan of referring the settlement of differences or disputes between employers and workers to an "impartial" agency, public or private, with when neither the Brotherhood of Locomotive Engineers nor the carriers were willing to submit their dispute to arbitration under the Act. As a result, an extra-legal seven-man arbitration board was set up to decide the matter. The Brotherhoods, and in fact the entire labor movement, were extremely unhappy with the award when it was made public in January, 1913, for, in an *obiter dictum*, the award suggested compulsory arbitration with wages tied to rates.[6] A few weeks later, when two other Brotherhoods became involved in a dispute with the eastern roads, the Brotherhoods refused to agree to another seven-man board, and the carriers refused to arbitrate under the terms of the Erdman Act. However, since the Brotherhoods were not yet ready to renounce all arbitration, they agreed with the carriers that arbitration would be possible if the Erdman Act were amended in a manner that would be mutually satisfactory.[7]

THE NEWLANDS ACT

Both the Brotherhoods and the carriers wanted, as one of the principal amendments to the Erdman Act, the creation of a permanent independent mediation board. What neither wanted was that the newly-created Department of Labor supervise the mediation of railway disputes. The Brotherhoods were jealous of the AFL's influence in the Department—William B. Wilson, Secretary of Labor under President Wilson, and the first head of the Department of Labor when it was made a cabinet post, had originally been an official of the United Mine Workers, an AFL affiliate. The carriers, in this instance, fully supported the Brotherhoods out of fear of the Department of Labor's friendliness to organized labor.[8]

On the other hand, Secretary William B. Wilson strongly felt that railroad mediation belonged in his department, even if within a separate bureau. As a long-time official of an industrial union which organized skilled and unskilled workers in the mines, he also opposed the legislation the Brotherhoods and carriers wanted passed by Congress because it would exclude non-operating railroad workers from its jurisdiction. Under heavy pressure from the AFL to have the non-operating unions,

powers to conduct an independent investigation of the matter, and to hand down a "neutral" decision or award. Arbitration may be either voluntary or compulsory. The award may or may not be binding on the contending parties, according to the terms under which the dispute was submitted to arbitration.
Mediation refers to the intervention of some "outside" impartial person or body, with a view to promoting the settlement of a dispute by mutual agreement between the contending parties. In arbitration, on the other hand, the dispute is taken out of the control of the contending parties, and settled by a third party, who acts as a judge on the merits of the case.

several of which were affiliated with the Federation, included in the bill, Wilson held steadfast to his position for several weeks. He even succeeded in having a bill incorporating his ideas approved by the Judiciary Committee. When the Brotherhoods, traditionally indifferent to the non-operating crafts, threatened to strike unless the new law complied with their demands, and when they were supported in their stand by Ralph M. Easley and Seth Low of the National Civic Federation,* a conference was arranged with President Wilson at which all the interested parties would be present. In the end, in order to avoid a strike by the Brotherhoods, Secretary Wilson capitulated, and the President agreed to support the bill substantially in the form desired by the Brotherhoods and the carriers.[9]

On July 15, 1913, Congress passed the Newlands Act providing for an independent three-member board—the United States Board of Mediation and Conciliation. The board could offer its services on its own initiative without waiting for a request from the parties. The Act also provided for arbitration by a board with as many as six, but not fewer than three members. Thus, just as in the Erdman Act, mediation, conciliation, and arbitration remained the principal solutions to labor disputes on the railroads for the operating crafts. The method of selecting arbiters remained the same as under the Erdman Act. Each side was to choose one (or two) members and they in turn would choose the third (or fifth and sixth) members.[10]

Secretary of Labor Wilson had been defeated in his effort to include the non-operating railway crafts because of the combined opposition of the Brotherhoods and the carriers. However, he did secure acceptance of his proposal that a provision allowing the courts to interpret and enforce arbitration awards be omitted from the Act.**

It is generally agreed among students of railway labor that President Wilson's intervention, which led to the passage of the Newlands Act, prevented a strike by the Brotherhoods.[11] Within a year, however, the President again intervened to prevent still another Brotherhood strike.*** On this occasion, the threat of a strike arose over a dispute between the Brotherhood of Engineers and the Brotherhood of Locomotive Firemen and Enginemen on the one hand, and the ninety-eight western railroads on the other. The two Brotherhoods presented demands involving working conditions and increased wages. The carriers

---

*For the origin, ideology and practices of the National Civic Federation, see Philip S. Foner, History of the Labor Movement in the United States, New York, 1964, 3:61–111.
**According to the statement in his autobiography, Samuel Gompers would have resigned from the National Civic Federation had not this provision been dropped. (Seventy Years of Life and Labor, New York, 1925, vol. II, p. 1143.)
***There was even a threat of a strike immediately after passage of the Newlands Act. This arose when the carriers announced that they were going to submit "all questions of rates of

immediately countered with several demands of their own. After several months of fruitless conferences, the negotiations were broken off on July 14, 1914, and the workers prepared to go on strike.

At the request of the carriers, the Board of Mediation and Conciliation entered the dispute. For several days, the Board attempted, without success, to bring the parties to an agreement. At that point, the Board, as provided by the Newlands Act, suggested that the parties submit the dispute to arbitration. When the employers insisted that their demands be arbitrated, as well at those of the men, the plan was rejected by the Brotherhoods. The suggestion by the Board that only the demands of the men be arbitrated was refused by the carriers.[12] When the Brotherhoods announced on July 31 that the strike would begin on August 7 unless the carriers agreed to the arbitration plan proposed by the Board, President Wilson immediately called the parties to a conference at the White House. On August 1, the President held separate conferences with the carriers and with the Brotherhoods, but the carriers refused to concede their demands.[13]

The following day, after the outbreak of war in Europe, the President wrote to A.W. Trenholm, chairman of the Conference Committee of Railway Managers, warning that because of the world crisis, a strike would be of "incalculable magnitude." He appealed "with confidence to your patriotism and to your regard for the public welfare to make whatever sacrifice is necessary to avert a national disaster."[14] Under this pressure, the carriers gave in, and on August 3, 1914, Trenholm informed the President that the carriers had agreed to accept the plan of arbitration proposed by the Board because "of the situation as you have presented it, and of your appeal to our patriotism. . . ."[15] At two o'clock in the morning of August 4, 1914, after several hours of negotiation, an arbitration contract was signed.[16]

The strike was averted, but the developments that followed in the dispute were to have momentous consequences for the future. When the abitrators appointed by the Brotherhoods and the carriers failed to agree upon the selection of the two "neutral" members, as provided by law, the Board appointed Judge J. C. Pritchard of the U.S. Circuit Court, and Charles Nagel, a St. Louis attorney. Shortly before the decision was to be announced, the Brotherhoods learned that Nagel was co-executor for an estate which owned stocks and bonds in twenty-one railroads. The Brotherhoods immediately filed protest with the Board and with President Wilson. On April 30, 1915, the day the decision was to be

pay and working conditions" to arbitration, as well as the specific dispute then at issue. The Brotherhoods immediately theatened a strike unless all new issues were withdrawn. Finally, after several days, Seth Low of the National Civic Federation persuaded the carriers to arbitrate only the "pending" issues, and the strike was averted. (*New York Times*, July 17-20, 1913.)

announced, the President held a conference with Judge Knapp of the Board of Mediation and Conciliation, after which he declared that the decision of the arbitrators should stand, since the Brotherhoods had known of Nagel's connection when he was appointed and had not protested at that time. The Brotherhoods promptly denied this and retorted that they had been "grossly deceived" in the selection of the arbitrators. After protesting bitterly against the award, which fell far short of their demands, the Brotherhoods accepted it and dropped their protest.[17] However, the incident further strengthened their determination that disputes should not be arbitrated. It also gave impetus to the movement to bring about joint negotiations by all four Brotherhoods on a national basis.[18]

This movement for concerted negotiations had been slowly developing since the defeat and disappearance of the American Railway Union, the first and only industrial union of railroad workers, whose promising career was cut short during the smashing of the Pullman strike in 1894, the dismissal and blacklisting of its members, and the arrest and imprisonment of its President, Eugene V. Debs, for having violated a federal court injunction issued under the Sherman Anti-Trust Act.* Before the turn of the century, negotiations with the carriers had in the main been conducted by each Brotherhood individually on a local or system basis. For several years thereafter, however, there had been a gradual change from local or regional negotiations, and simultaneously, the Brotherhoods began to cooperate with each other in their bargaining demands.[19] This, of course, met with stiff opposition from the railroads. As long as the unions negotiated on a road-by-road, Brotherhood-by-Brotherhood basis, the carriers were in the driver's seat. They therefore rejected all efforts of the Brotherhoods to negotiate with all the carriers on a national basis in a "concerted movement." Nevertheless, the movement for joint negotiations by all four Brotherhoods on a national scale continued. Although the movement was not to culminate until 1916, by 1913 it had reached a point where the *Locomotive Firemen & Engineers Magazine* called the employers' resistance the most important obstacle to be overcome by the Brotherhoods. Its editorial on this vital issue merits reprinting in full:

> Our experience during recent months with the Eastern Railroad Companies as well as that of the B. of L. E. is fraught with some weighty lessons for all railroad labor organizations.
> It would seem that as though the General Managers Conference committee realizing that protracted negotiations meant enormous expense to our Brotherhood prolonged them to as great—to as tortuous—a length as was

*See Foner, *op. cit.*, 2: 262-78.

possible for them to do. This has been a conspicuous feature of our negotiations with railroad companies for some years past. Evidently its purpose is twofold—to pile up expense on our Brotherhood and to make the negotiations as wearisome to our representatives as possible; also to defer a settlement to the last minute with a view to saving the company the wage increase from the period covered by the enforced delay. The experience of other railroad labor organizations in this particular has been similar to our own.

For this state of affairs—for the prompt consideration of our demands for wage betterment and improved working conditions, as well as for the success of our efforts in securing these concessions the only or at least by far the most effective remedy is *Federation*— a federation in fact as well as in name—a federation that would make one general contract for all train service employees secured by a Joint Federated Board representing all of the organizations— a federation that would mean that if it became necessary to strike to enforce our demands, one organization of train service employees would not be striking while the other organizations would be working with strikebreakers, but that, should a strike be declared all train service employees would leave their posts together—true to each other as men and brothers, acting unitedly in defense of their common industrial and economic interests.

Thus would it be absolutely impossible for the railroad companies to even attempt to operate their roads until they had agreed to give their employees a just—a fair proportion of the wealth that these employees made it possible for the railroads to earn. . . .

Let us make it as firm, as indissoluble, as compact as the federation that binds together in an impregnable offensive and defensive alliance the interests that own the Steel Trust, the Railroads, the Standard Oil Trust, the Harvester Trust, the Meat Trust and other great monopolies—the interests that control the country's finances.

Of late we have been hearing much of the money trust and the big business combination recently unearthed by the Pujo Committee of the United States Congress, which combination controls twenty-five billion dollars ($25,000,000,000) and operates through 155 interlocking directorates.*

When we consider the prodigious power by this combination and its stupendous political influence we can the better realize the folly of the railroad labor organizations continuing to operate single-handed in protecting the industrial interests of their membership.[20]

*The Pujo Committee, a U.S. Senate body, investigated the charge that there was a "money trust," and heard testimony which revealed the manner in which banking tycoons, headed by J.P. Morgan, were able to control the assets of numerous financial houses and industrial corporations by representation on their boards of directors. They were able to lend money to themselves and withhold it from others in a manner which amounted to a trust. Moreover, through interlocking directorates, they were able to dominate the chief industrial, transportation, and financial companies in the United States. For a summary of the findings of the Pujo Committee, *see* Louis D. Brandeis, *Other People's Money* (New York, 1913.)

Unfortunately, the appeal omitted any reference to the non-operating railroad workers, who were still being ignored by the Brotherhoods. Nevertheless, it did mark an important advance in the thinking of the Brotherhoods. Three years later, the editorial's vision became a reality. In 1916, the Big Four Brotherhoods united in a concerted movement to achieve the demand for an eight-hour day for all 400,000 operating railroad workers at ten hours' pay, and time-and-a-half for overtime.

The Brotherhoods had reached the conclusion that a sixteen-hour maximum was too long, particularly when many other occupational groups enjoyed the benefits of an eight-hour day. In 1907, the Hours of Service Act, with its provision for a sixteen-hour day followed by eight hours rest, was viewed as a significant step forward. But by 1915, it was viewed as a grossly insufficient in meeting the needs of the railroad workers.[21]

The railroads had consistently opposed the demands for shorter hours by their employees. After they had unsuccessfully fought the passage of the Hours of Service Act of 1907, which guaranteed trainmen eight hours of rest after sixteen hours of duty, they attempted to render it impotent in the federal courts. While they had little success in repealing the law or having it interpreted to their benefit, they were determined that no new agreement to reduce the working day would be accepted.

NEGOTIATIONS BEGIN; THE WAR OF WORDS

In December, 1915, the officials of the Four Brotherhoods— A. B. Garretson, president of the Order of Railway Conductors; W. G. Lee, president of the Brotherhood of Railroad Trainmen; W. S. Carter, president of the Brotherhood of Locomotive Firemen and Enginemen, and W. S. Stone, president of the Brotherhood of Locomotive Engineers— met in Chicago in order to coordinate their strategy to achieve their goal. The first step, it was agreed, was to resort to collective bargaining.[22] The Brotherhoods therefore requested the railroad managers to form a committee to represent all the nation's carriers so that negotiations might be coordinated on a national basis. The carriers agreed to the proposal for national negotiations, and both sides agreed to meet on June 1, 1916 to consider the unions' demands.[23]

Meanwhile, both parties began an extensive propaganda campaign to win public support for their positions. The publicity managers for eastern group of roads fired the first shot with a statement that the Brotherhoods were not sincere in asking for the eight-hour day. Instead, the railroads declared, they wanted higher wages and were using the popularity of the shorter work day as a means of securing this goal. Yet these workers were already "the highest paid men in the rank and file of the railroad service, many of them earning more than their division officers." Indeed, engineers on the best passenger runs "earn from $2,500 to $4,000 a year, some of them being paid more than bank presidents in the smaller communities through which they ran." The carriers second argument was that while the engineers, firemen, conductors, and trainmen were "an army of a third of a million,"* there were "more than a million and a half other employees of the railroads [who] would get no benefit" from the Brotherhoods' demands. On the contrary, if the carriers were compelled to add many millions to their payrolls because of these demands, they would have to find the money in one of four ways—"reduce the wages of the million and a half men outside the train service; reduce payments to their stockholders; curtail the betterment expenditures for new stations, reduction of grade-crossings and other non-productive improvements demanded by the public, or ask the Government to allow a proportionate increase in freight rates."[24]

The Brotherhoods established a joint Publicity Bureau in Cleveland to answer the carriers' arguments and present the case for unions' demands. The Bureau issued thousands of leaflets, each carrying a short story about the crying need of railroad workers for an eight-hour day. One leaflet was headed, "Long Hours Cause Death," and carried at the top a reproduction of a United Press dispatch about Ray Washburn, 36, an engineer on the Baltimore & Ohio Railroad, who shot and killed himself on May 31, when he became mentally unbalanced due to overwork. During the month of May, 1916, his regular time and overtime kept him at the throttle for forty-five working days. The leaflet continued:

> Railroad officials would call this man an "aristocrat of the labor world" and cite the fact that he received good pay, but they would neglect to mention the long hours he worked to enable him to earn a fair wage.
> Train crews are now compelled to work from twelve to twenty hours continuously and they are asking that their work day be shorter and their working conditions be bettered. They receive a less wage per hour than most other trades.[25]

Another leaflet emphasized that the long hours which the men on the trains had to work were not only injurious to their health, but were also the cause of many railroad accidents.[26] The leaflet reprinted excerpts from an article by John M. Gutterman in the June, 1910, *McClure's*

*This was an underestimation. There were 400,000 members of the Big Four Brotherhoods.

Magazine entitled, "Why Railroad Men Die?" Gutterman argued that the list of killed and injured among railroad workers was so appalling that it would take only a few years to maim or kill all the men working on the railroads, necessitating the recruitment of an equal number of new men to replace them. Moreover, while the percentage of those killed had remained practically constant at about ¼ of 1 percent for the period 1889 to 1910, in spite of the introduction of safety devices, during that time the percentage of those injured had quadrupled:

> Whereas once in two hours, month in and month out, a conductor, brakeman, switchman, or railway laborer perished by accident, one is maimed every six minutes. Last year (1909) 6.4 per cent of all the railway employees in the United States were injured: thus the chances are that no man can escape accident for nine years. . . . In spite of double-tracking and safety devices and palliative legislation, matters have come to such a pass that if the injured of one bad year could all wait in line before one hospital door, the queue would reach the length of Manhattan Island, from the Battery to Spuyten Duyvil Creek, back again to the Battery, and up once more as far as Madison Square, while the dead, if laid side by side, would make a row nearly two miles long.

The carriers' publicity department immediately replied that it was the Brotherhoods who were largely responsible for accidents by failing to condemn carelessness and negligence upon the part of those members who disobeyed safety rules, and that the railroads had launched and supported safety movements to educate the workers on the avoidance of accidents. The Brotherhoods could solve the safety problem by cooperating in this campaign, and not by seeking to bankrupt the railroads through the demand for the eight-hour day and time-and-a-half for overtime.[27]

However, this argument did not prove very convincing. Even the *Railroad Age Gazette,* the organ of the carriers, conceded that "the ultimate responsiblity for maintaining discipline rested with management."[28] As for the carriers' concern for safety, the Brotherhoods responded, this had only surfaced when their usual indifference to this problem began to cut into their profits.* Finally, accidents were still a major problem for railroad workers, and only a shorter working day, specifically the eight-hour day, could make a serious dent in it. In short,

---

*As Kurt Wetzel points out, "Management's overdue attempt to improve safety showed that as an end it itself, safety was a low priority. Only when accidents came to have serious negative financial consequences was the industry willing to make the effort necessary to deny and evade responsibility for accidents; the safety movement was the first good faith effort by management to act on its assertions that accidents were primarily a human problem not an equipment problem." ("Railroad Management's Response to Operating Employees Accidents, 1890-1913," *Labor History* 21 [January, 1970]: 368.)

the real threat to safety came from extended work time without sufficient time for rest.[29]

In their publicity campaign, the Brotherhoods emphasized that the eight-hour demand had not been sprung suddenly on the railroads. "The idea of having an eight-hour day for men . . . in engine, train and yard service, is not a new thought," the *Railway Conductor* editorialized. "It has been discussed for several years in Lodge and Division and among groups of members of the four great railroad labor organizations employed in engine, train, and yard service throughout the United States and Canada. . . . The Conductors and Trainmen were ready two years ago to take part in a movement similar to the present one, but the Engineers and Firemen were not then at liberty to cooperate with us, and thus the movement was held back until now."[30]

Further proof that the eight-hour day was not a new idea lay in the fact that it had already been put into effect on several Southern railroads, and, the Brotherhoods emphasized, without the paralyzing economic effects predicted in the carriers' propaganda.[31] Finally, to the main argument of the carriers, namely, that the real aim of the Brotherhoods was higher wages and not an eight-hour day, the presidents of the four big unions each delivered a stinging reply which was circulated in a widely-distributed leaflet that was reprinted in the labor and Socialist press. It was headed, "Chiefs of Great Brotherhoods Tell Why Men Fight for Eight-Hour Day Rather Than Wage Increase!" and included the following statements:

A. B. Garretson, President of the Order of Railway Conductors: What the eight-hour day means to the trainmen and engineers of the country is the opportunity to live in human companionship with their families, to have some of the privileges of leisure that men engaged in other pursuits enjoy, to be relieved of inhuman hours, to gain the benefits, social, hygienic and industrial, that come with a reasonable time for employment, for rest, and for recreation.

The punitive overtime is nothing but the effort to make the employment of men for long hours uneconomic, and therefore, from the employers' standpoint, undesirable.

An increase in the rate of wages would mean more money to spend. This would not compensate the men for the onerous conditions under which they serve, and they are thus placing betterment of conditions above a higher rate of pay in the scale of desirability.

The other three Brotherhood chiefs made more or less the same points in their statements. However, W. S. Carter, president of the Brotherhood of Locomotive, Firemen and Enginemen, insisted that for the men in terminal and freight service, an eight-hour day would mean, "in many instances an actual reduction in their earnings. In terminal work, where men are now earning one and one-half day's pay in fifteen hours, they will earn but one day's pay for eight hours' work, because when railroads are required to pay time and one-half for overtime, after eight hours, no man will be required to work overtime." And should they be required to do so, wrote W. S. Stone, Grand Chief of the Brotherhood of Locomotive Engineers, the railroads should be penalized:

> Overtime in road service is due almost wholly to railroads overloading trains so they cannot make their mileage within time limits. The railroads are doing this for profit; they do not deny it, and if they propose to demand extra service at the sacrifice of the health and future earning ability of the men they should pay extra for it.[32]

THE PRESS JOINS THE WAR OF WORDS

At the same time that the battle of publicity releases and leaflets was raging, the newspapers began to line up behind the carriers or the Brotherhoods, with the vast majority rallying to the side of the railroads. (As the *Railroad Trainman* noted, "it only needs the action of a body of businessmen for or against anything to bring the press generally to their support."[33]) The New York *Journal of Commerce* could not see how the railroads could possibly meet a demand for $100,000,000 a year in increased wages if they granted the Brotherhoods' demands. "The railroads may be forced by circumstances to reduce their expenses and curtail their operation, and the weaker ones may be driven into bankruptcy; but what good will that do?"[34] On the other hand, the New York *American*, a Hearst paper, thought the Brotherhoods had made "a reasonable request which should be cheerfully and immediately conceded." There need be no further dispute and certainly no strike as a last resort, the *American* continued, "if the railway managers will do the right thing." In the *American's* opinion:

> The eight-hour day is a LEGITIMATE DEMAND and should be conceded by the railroads.
> The railroads have received all sorts of concessions and aid from the Government.
> They have, within these few months, been permitted to increase freight-rates.
> They are given the mails to carry at rates which virtually amount to subsidies.
> They are now in prosperous times and making a great deal of money.
> They make this money out of the people of the country and through Government concessions which come from the people.
> It is only RIGHT that they should divide a part of these benefits with the people—with their employees, who are large a part of the nation's workers.[35]

Interestingly enough, the *American's* assertion of abundant railroad prosperity was confirmed by the *Commercial and Financial Chronicle,* the leading pro-business journal published in New York City. It noted the increase of 27 percent net and 73 percent gross railroad earnings for November, 1915 over November, 1914. To cite a few examples, the Atchison's net earnings for November, 1915, exceeded those of November, 1914, by $1,000,000; the Erie showed a gain of nearly $2,000,000; the New York Central, nearly $4,000,000; the Pennsylvania, $2,500,000; and the Southern Pacific, $1,500,000. Virtually all the roads showed handsome gains. The *Chronicle* pointed out further:

> The transformation has come all of a sudden. Even three months ago no one would have conceived that such a wonderful metamorphosis was possible. . . . But, about the middle of September, traffic and revenues began all at once to increase, and in a very rapid way, too, tho at first it was particular systems rather than the railroads as a whole that gave evidence of the fact. Having once begun, however, the movement quickly gained increasing headway.[36]

The reason for the "sudden" transformation was the great increase in the volume of rail traffic because of the demands for goods from war torn Europe, particularly the Allied Powers. While the *Chronicle* did not spell it out, it was clear that the high rail revenues enabled the carriers easily to meet any increased costs that might arise from the institution of an eight-hour day.

THE NEGOTIATIONS

On June 1, 1916, a negotiating conference opened in New York City. A. B. Garretson, head of the conductors, spoke for the Big Four. He was backed by the presence of 640 division chairmen of the Brotherhoods' locals, representing every division in the country. Heading the National Conference Committee of Railroad Managers—the group formed at the suggestion of the Brotherhoods—was Elisha Lee, general manager of the Pennsylvania system and a long-time foe of unionism. The paramount issue involved both shorter hours and higher pay. The unions demanded the eight-hour day with no reduction in pay from the existing ten-hour standard basis. They insisted that these issues could neither be arbitrated nor compromised. The railroads responded by insisting that the union's demands be arbitrated either under the Newlands Act or by the Interstate Commerce Commission. Along with these demands should go the employers' "contingent proposition", which involved changes in the working rules. The carriers' "contingent proposition" was supposedly not a counter-proposal but to be applied only where there was a change in the basis of pay brought about by the Brotherhoods' demands. But when the Brotherhoods asked the carriers to spell out the work rules changes they would be requesting, it became clear that the "contingent proposition" could be used to sweep away all of the existing rules, as well as to nullify any pay increases under the eight-hour day.

After two weeks of fruitless bargaining, during which the Big Four made clear their opposition to arbitration, on June 14 the unions requested a definite answer as to whether the managers would accept their demands. The following day, the managers announced their refusal and again proposed arbitration. The Brotherhoods replied that the eight-hour day and working rules were not arbitrable issues. Furthermore, even if they were, arbitration could not be invoked under the Newlands Act until "a strike was threatened," and as yet no strike vote had been taken. Fundamentally, the Brotherhood chiefs argued that arbitration was undesirable because it was difficult to find public representatives conversant with the technicalities of the issues.[37]

As neither bargaining team was willing to allow any major concessions, negotiations were broken off on June 16. The representatives of the Brotherhoods and the carriers did not meet again until August 8. In the meantime, to bolster their bargaining positions and in keeping with their constitutional provisions, the four Brotherhoods took a strike vote among their members. The railroad officials cherished no illusions that the result would be favorable to them. They proved to be correct. The figures announced on August 8—the same day negotiations resumed—revealed that ninety-four percent in the four unions favored a strike to begin on Labor Day, September 4, 1916, for the eight-hour day. The vote broke down as follows:

UNION	PERCENTAGE FOR STRIKE
Brotherhood of Locomotive Engineers	94.57
Order of Railway Conductors	85
Brotherhood of Railway Trainmen	97
Brotherhood of Railway Firemen and Enginemen	98.03
Average for the four unions	94.38

The headline in the *Literary Digest* announcing the strike vote read: "Facing Our Greatest Labor War," and the magazine quoted the New York *Call,* the Socialist daily, as stating that with 400,000 workers on 255 railroads prepared to strike if necessary, the nation faced "the greatest attack on capital that has ever been maneuvered in all history."[39] But evidently this prediction did not frighten the *Railway Age Gazette:* it announced that regardless of the strike vote, "Any railway officer who would suggest making any concession whatever, except after arbitration, ought to be branded as a coward, and as a traitor to the interests of the railways and the country. If the choice is between further concessions and a strike, then the strike should be allowed to come."[40]

This was the atmosphere when the negotiations resumed in New York City. The Brotherhoods' representatives were described by the New York *World* as being in a strong position, "stiffened by the most overwhelming vote favoring a strike ever taken in the four big brotherhoods."[41] Backed by the vote, the Brotherhood representatives renewed their demand for an eight-hour day. The managers, however, remained unyielding and simply reemphasized their demand for arbitration, even asking the unions to join them in an appeal for arbitration to the United States Board of Mediation and Conciliation, now that a strike was imminent. The Brotherhood chiefs refused to join in such an appeal, but they did consent to mediation by the board.[42]

FAILURE OF MEDIATION

The Board of Mediation and Conciliation had been standing by since it had become aware of the dispute early in 1916. On July 26, Judge William Chambers, the Board chairman, noted:

> "In the present nation-wide controversy the information reaches the Board that the parties contemplate further negotiations. If the vote now being taken results in favor of a strike and the parties should not invoke the service of the Board, you may be assured that the Board will promptly proffer its services, with confidence that such services will be accepted by the parties."[43]

Actually, the Board had little "confidence" that a settlement could be reached. It held one conference with the Brotherhoods at Webster Hall in New York City on the morning of August 10 and a second conference with management that afternoon at the Biltmore Hotel. At the conclusion of the two conferences, none of the Board members had any progress to report. Supplementary conferences were no more fruitful. The Brotherhoods took the position that since the managers had requested mediation, it was up to them to make some concession that would lead to further discussions. They also maintained that the eight-hour day and working conditions were not arbitrable questions. At no time, however, did the Brotherhoods refuse to arbitrate questions of pay if the eight-hour day were granted. The managers, for their part, refused to make any concessions. They continued to demand arbitration of the eight-hour issue as well as of their own "contingent proposition." The Brotherhoods, however, claimed that the carriers by insisting upon the "contingent proposition" were not really sincere in offering to arbitrate because they realized that the unions would have to refuse to arbitrate a demand so broad and sweeping in its implications.[44]

Judge Chambers had informed President Wilson almost immediately after arriving in New York that negotiations were likely to fail and that it was very doubtful the Board could secure an agreement. On August 9, the President wired Chambers that should his fears be realized, he should inform the parties that the President desired a conference with them before the final break. On August 13, the Board announced its inability to produce a settlement. That same day, Chambers notified the President that the break was near and that he should send his request immediately.[45] Also on that same day, Joseph Tumulty, Wilson's private secretary, was dispatched to New York City to request formally that both parties confer with the President in Washington. Tumulty arrived in New York with a communication to the Board of Mediation and Conciliation, and later that afternoon, the information was released that he had brought with him messages inviting both parties in the dispute to confer with the President at the White House. In the message to the Brotherhoods, Wilson declared that he had "learned with surprise and keen disappointment that no agreement had been reached," and since "a general strike might be disastrous, I feel that I have the right to request, and I do hereby request, as the head of the Government, that before any final decision is arrived at, I may have a personal conference with you here."[46]

Austin B. Garretson of the Railway Conductors gave the Brotherhoods' reply in the name of "the 400,000 railroad men of the United States." He pointed out first that at no time during the dispute had the carriers "made any counter-proposal whatever looking for a settlement," even though they knew very well "we would not consent to arbitrate those proposals." Under these circumstances, the Brotherhoods' representatives were preparing "to proceed in accord with the methods . . . to effect a settlement of the points of contention between us. That is to say, if need be we would withdraw our men from service." At that point, he went on, they were presented with the President's request for a conference of both parties at the White House. He then announced that the four executives, accompanied by a representative committee of the men, thirty in number, would be in Washington the next day, "at the disposal of the President of the United States for the purpose indicated."[47]

Actually, the Brotherhoods were quite pleased that their dispute with the carriers had been transferred to the White House. Remembering the way President Wilson had intervened in their favor twice before, they were hopeful that a positive settlement would emerge from this session as well. The carriers' representatives, however, were split. Several were resentful at the President for intervening, fearing that, as in the past, the Brotherhoods would emerge with the better part of any settlement forced upon them. Others had no objection to the President's action, since they were determined not to yield under any circumstances, not even in the event of a strike. All the rail executives were in agreement that no wage increase should be granted without a corresponding rate increase. They were hopeful, too, that in any general settlement, they might be able to get rid of a group of work rules that they thought "unduly restrictive and expensive."[48]

THE WAR OF WORDS CONTINUES

In order to put pressure on the President to see things their way, the carriers intensified their propaganda campaign. The refusal of the Brotherhoods to agree to arbitration provided them with a new argument. Although they continued to maintain that the Brotherhoods were not sincere in their demand for an eight-hour day and that the shorter work day was not physically possible on the railroads, the carriers now began to concentrate their attack upon the refusal of the Brotherhoods to agree to arbitration. They flooded the country with literature emphasizing that this meant that the Brotherhoods were prepared to thrust the nation into chaos and industrial warfare.* The only solution to the difficulty, the leaflets emphasized, was for the President to either insist upon arbitration or to support the proposal for an investigation by the Interstate Commerce Commission during which there could be no strike.[49] To bolster their argument, the carriers distributed the statement of James Cardinal Gibbons, in which, while refusing to discuss the specifics of the railroad dispute, he expressed the opinion that it should be settled by arbitration, adding: "The laborer is worthy of his hire, but if we are too severe toward capital we will beggar the nation."[50]

Finally, on the eve of the White House conference, the carriers' publicity department distributed two leaflets nationwide. One was directed to the railroad workers, operating and non-operating alike, and read:

> Do you realize that if a joint strike is called the government will take charge of the railroads and operate them, if necessary, to insure uninterrupted transportation and save the public loss and inconvenience?

---

*According to the *New York Times*, the carriers sent thousands upon thousands of copies of their appeals to all parts of the country (Aug. 3, 1916.) Edwin C. Robbins, in a contemporary study, estimated that the carriers spent a half million dollars on this propaganda. ("The Trainmen's Eight Hour Law—II," *Political Science Quarterly* 32 [September, 1917]: 426.)

> Do you prefer working for the government under its discipline rather than to continue as at present a free American citizen?[51]

The other leaflet was directed to the businessmen of America and featured the following statement of a railroad manager:

> This fight is to industry in America what the war is to Europe. The future of the railroads depends on the outcome and if the strike is called the railroads will not give in easily. Write or telegraph the President to insist either upon arbitration or an investigation of the issues in the dispute—during which there should be no strike.[52]

The business community responded quickly to the appeal. Chambers of Commerce throughout the nation, the National Association of Manufacturers, and leading businessmen joined the carriers in the demand that either the issues be arbitrated or that the Interstate Commerce Commission investigate the controversy. Henry Ford warned that his factories would have to shut down if rail traffic ceased. Charles F. Wood, President of the Boston Chamber of Commerce, urged that the Interstate Commerce Commission be allowed to pass judgment in this dispute. California fruit and sugar beet growers expressed fear that they would not be able to get their crops to market. Several businessmen urged compulsory mediation; others called for government intervention as President Cleveland had intervened during the Pullman Strike, and most protested against any settlement that would bring higher freight rates. Only a handful of businessmen believed that labor's demands were justified.[53]

As they had done during earlier negotiations, many newspapers joined the business community in rallying behind the railroads. "Eight-Hours, or More Pay?" the Providence *Journal* asked, and the *New York Times* answered: "The only question is increases in pay, which as everyone knows is really what the brotherhoods have demanded." The *Times* carried a lengthy article which favored compulsory arbitration as the only way to settle the dispute.[54]

A few papers still supported the Brotherhoods. The St Paul *Dispatch* commented ironically in its editorial, "Long Live Arbitration": "Did you ever notice that the fellow underneath is always clamorous for the principle of arbitration."[55] The *Springfield (Mass.) Republican* saw in the carriers' insistence on arbitration a plan to disrupt the railroad unions. Seeking to explain the Brotherhoods' position on arbitration, the New York *Evening Post* reported that "spokesmen for the employees have been careful to point out that they have not rejected the principle of arbitration, that they had only objected to the kind of arbitration proposed."[56]

The Socialist New York *Call* was by far the most consistent and persistent supporter of the Brotherhoods. This was not surprising, since Socialist Party platforms consistently pressed for the eight-hour day and the *International Socialist Review, Masses,* the New York *Call* and other socialist periodicals raised the issue repeatedly. The *Call,* in fact, was so enthusiastic in its support of the Brotherhoods that it did not even once mention that they had made no attempt to either include the non-operating railroad workers in their demands or to cooperate with them in any way. It pointed out that the railroads had set up "one of the most costly publicity bureaus ever organized by Big Business to warp the minds of the people of the nation," including the use of "big advertisements in all the large capitalist newspapers of the country . . . filled with false statements." In this way, "the railroad magnates hope to arouse the customers of the railroads against the four brotherhoods." To offset this propaganda, the *Call* announced it would devote a major part of each issue during the dispute to the publication of material explaining and defending the Brotherhoods' demand for the eight-hour day.[57]

The *Call* used a variety of devices to carry out this pledge, publishing cartoons, reprinting leaflets issued by the Brotherhoods, debunking leaflets of the carriers, and relating the long struggle for the eight-hour day, even arguing that *"the eight-hour day was the standard in the fifth century!"* One of the cartoons was headed, "In Four Hundred Thousand Homes!" and depicted a woman holding a child while a sign clings to her fingers reading, "Railroaders Demand 8-Hour Day." The child asks, "Won't Daddy Ever Come?" In one issue, the headline asked: "Where Do Railroad Men Now Work Eight Hours A Day?" The answer: "In Mexico." Then followed: "Gentlemen who own railroads and Mexican ranches and who want the United States to 'clean up Mexico' probably would be slow to admit that Mexico can show us anything in industrial or governmental operation. To these persons who are loudly protesting that the American railroads would be bankrupted if they worked their men only eight hours a day, we offer this information: Mexican railroads have just granted their employes an eight-hour day."[58]

THE AFL AND THE BROTHERHOODS' DISPUTE

In the main, the labor movement rallied to the support of the Brotherhoods. There had been some question as to what stand the AFL would take. At its 1914 convention in Philadelphia, a resolution had been favorably reported to the delegates from the Organization Committee which declared that there were still national and local unions not affiliated with the Federation, that they were a menace to some of its unions, and that efforts to have them affiliate had failed. The resolution went on to instruct the officers of the Federation to "proceed to organize such local or national unions, if such is possible." Speaking in favor of the resolution, J. R. Connors of the Switchmen's Union of North America, made up of non-operating railroad workers, cited the fact that the four Brotherhoods had in "some instances assisted railroads to defeat the switchmen in strikes."

Gompers, however, claimed that the favorable report had been a mistake and vigorously opposed the resolution. He charged that it permitted the setting up of rival unions which "amounted to nothing less than a declaration of war." He favored the association of the Brotherhoods with the AFL as a major step in achieving "the solidarity of the labor movement in the United States," but he would not for a moment "think of invading the sovereignty of national labor unions." Actually, he noted, there had emerged during the last ten years a better feeling between the Brotherhoods and the Federation, with the result that the railroad organizations had been of great assistance in getting certain labor legislation through Congress. The adoption of the resolution, he argued, would destroy the developing unity between the two organizations.

In vain the delegates from the Switchmen's Union pleaded for adoption, again arguing that "certain brotherhoods" (not all) had opposed their union in strikes. At Gompers' insistence, however, the resolution was returned to the Committee on Organization, where it died.[59]

Gompers now had a free hand to support the Brotherhoods in their battle for the eight-hour day, and in the summer and fall of 1916 the aid the railroad unions received from the AFL, not only brought the organizations more closely together than ever before, but even produced serious talk of Brotherhood affiliation with the Federation.[60]* On August 2, 1916, Gompers wrote to the chiefs of the four Brotherhoods that the AFL fully supported them in their demand for an eight-hour day and that the Federation would combat vigorously any attempt to compel the railroad unions to submit their demands to "compulsory arbitration." Ten days later, Gompers announced publicly that the Federation would support the Brotherhoods in the event of a strike. Speaking in the name of the AFL Executive Council, he declared:

> It is our most earnest hope that the railway companies may be induced to take a broad-minded and humanitarian view of your demand. When the railway companies understand the full meaning of the eight-hour day and

*No such organic unity ever occurred.

realize the material, moral and social advantages that will inevitably result from its establishment, they can not refuse to concede to the workers the boon of the eight-hour day and concede without imposing upon the workers the necessity of cessation of work in order to establish your demand.

But, regardless of whether your purpose is secured by the voluntary agreement of railway companies or whether it is necessary for the railway men to strike to obtain this just and necessary protection, the American Federation of Labor pledges to the brotherhoods its support and sympathy in the effort to accomplish that which is fundamental for the protection and betterment of the railway men. . . .[61]

Still there were dissenting voices. Non-operating railway workers, whether organized or unorganized, not only did not give strong support to the Brotherhoods, but even criticized the AFL for rendering such support uncritically. These workers pointed out that they would gain nothing directly from any reduction in hours or increase in pay for the operating crafts. On the contrary, they stood to lose wages if the railroads were struck.[62]

In responding to such criticism, Gompers wrote:

Every new success in shortening the working hours for any group of workers is felt by all workers. There is a big principle involved in the fight the road Brotherhoods have been making, a principle which is of paramount importance to all wage earners. When a fundamental principle is involved differences which do not concern essentials must be subordinated to the principle which affects the interest and welfare of all. . . . The benefits that will result from the establishment of an eight-hour day for all railroad workers will be extended far beyond the members of the Railroad Brotherhoods. No one effort could accomplish more for the establishment of a general eight-hour work day than the success of the Railroad Brotherhoods in establishing the eight-hour day through the power of their economic movement.[63]

As we shall now see, while the "economic power" of the Brotherhoods was crucial in their final victory, the eight-hour day itself was established through Congressional legislation.

CHAPTER 10

An Eight-Hour Day for the Railroad Brotherhoods, II: The Adamson Act

On February 22, 1916, President Woodrow Wilson wrote to Senator William J. Stone: "I have been not a little concerned about the matter [of the dispute between the Brotherhoods and the railroads]. . . . A general strike on the railroads just now would be nothing less than a calamity and I am already seeking not only information, but some way to use my good offices."[1] Three months later, on April 7, he wrote to Senator W. C. Adamson: "I am only too keenly aware of the trouble that is now impending in the railroad world and I have been casting about to see if there is anything I could do."[2]

BACKGROUND TO THE WHITE HOUSE CONFERENCE

The President did not lack for advice on how he should deal with the coming crisis. Democratic Senator James Reed of Missouri urged Wilson to confer directly with the labor leaders. Secretary of the Treasury William G. McAdoo thought that Congress should take "certain anticipatory steps," but did not specific exactly what. Other than that, he believed that Assistant Secretary of Labor Louis F. Post might be able to devise a solution. Richard B. Olney, who had been instrumental in breaking the Pullman Strike of 1894, felt that in case of a strike, the federal government should appoint receivers for the struck lines and operate them openly and nationally as a strikebreaker. Democratic Senator Ben Tillman of South Carolina urged the government "to step in between capital . . . and labor . . . and take both by the throat and shake them into decency."[3]

Meanwhile, on advice from Secretary of Labor William B. Wilson that the dispute would be submitted to mediation and that there was a good chance a settlement would then be reached, the President decided to do nothing concrete but to pursue a course of watchful waiting.[4] But by the end of July, he was being subjected to intense pressure from business groups and from several members of his own cabinet to either intervene personally in the dispute or to support the Newlands resolution which called for a public investigation of the issues while both parties refrained from any action until it was completed.[5] Late in July, Harry A. Wheeler, Chairman of the National Chamber of Commerce Committee on the Railroad Situation, wrote in alarm to the President that after conferring with the railway executives, he was positive that a strike would occur unless Wilson intervened. Wheeler assured the President that all business groups in the country supported the Newlands resolution.[6]

Under this pressure, Wilson turned once more to his Secretary of Labor for advice. The latter, meanwhile, had received information from Assistant Secretary Post which only appeared to confuse matters. Post had talked about the situation with P. J. McNamara, vice-president and legislative representative of the Brotherhood of Locomotive Firemen and Enginemen. According to Post, McNamara had told him that the Brotherhoods were not really sincere in their demand for an eight-hour day; that their members were not so much interested in the shorter work day, but were really after pay for more than eight hours, thus implying that a wage increase by itself could settle the issue. In fact, Post reported that McNamara told him that if Congress did not interfere by passing the Newlands resolution and left the parties alone, he was certain there would be no strike.[7]

Although everything said and done by the Brotherhoods since the beginning of the dispute had contradicted McNamara's evaluation, Wilson enthusiastically accepted Post's report as accurate. He immediately advised the President that it would be a mistake to support passage of the Newlands resolution or to have the Interstate Commerce Commission interfere in any way. Much of the hysteria, he continued, was caused by the impending strike vote, which had to be taken only because it was necessary before the carriers or the Board of Mediation and Conciliation could recognize that a dispute existed. Of course, it was to be expected that the vote would reveal an almost unanimous determination to strike if negotiations failed, but Wilson assured the President that a strike vote did not mean that there would be a strike, since there was usually a big difference between a union's demands and what it was willing to settle for.

Having given the President a lesson in how unions, including his own

United Mine Workers, often operated, but at the same time, having completely underestimated the Brotherhood's determination to achieve the eight-hour day, the Secretary then pointed out to Wilson that the Board of Mediation and Conciliation had compiled a very successful record, and that it had a very good chance of settling the dispute. A public investigation, on the other hand, would destroy all chances of successful mediation. Meanwhile, the Department of Labor, while not interfering, would place a representative on the spot to keep in touch with the proceedings.[8]

The President was evidently impressed by this assurance, for he replied that the Secretary of Labor was "entirely right in your judgment about a special investigation," and that such an inquiry would "be a very great mistake at this time." He also expressed satisfaction that the Department was keeping in touch with developments and asked the Secretary to inform him "the moment it seems wise for me to do anything in this matter."[9]

Events soon demonstrated that the years that William B. Wilson had spent removed from actual involvement in the labor movement had caused him to seriously miscalculate the situation. He simply did not recognize either the intense determination of the carriers not to yield to the Brotherhoods' demands, or the sincerity of the railroad workers' desire for the eight-hour day and their equally intense determination to obtain it by a general strike if necessary. Nor did he properly understand the Brotherhoods' lack of confidence in the Board of Mediation.

On the same day on which he had written to his Secretary of Labor agreeing with him about the inadvisability of a Congressional investigation, President Wilson also replied to leaders of the Chamber of Commerce who insisted again that he support the Newlands resolution and compel the parties to wait until the investigation was completed before taking any action. To this reiterated demand, Wilson replied that he neither had the power to compel the parties to await the results of an investigation, nor did he think it wise that such an investigation be undertaken.[10]

However, the options remaining to the President were quickly running out, and by the time the Mediation Board left for New York City, Judge Chambers had conferred with him, and was told to expect the call inviting the parties to the White House if, as was by now anticipated, the mediation efforts failed.[11] Certainly by this time, with the presidential campaign of 1916 getting under way, and a contest shaping up between Wilson and Charles Evans Hughes, the Republican nominee, it is clear that political considerations were not absent from the chief executive's decision. However, they were not the prime motive for

Wilson's action—the serious damage a railroad strike would inflict on the nation's economy and the Wilson preparedness program was a significant factor influencing his thinking—but the political considerations were also important. Also not to be ignored was the fact that Wilson was disposed to favor shorter hours of work long before the railroad dispute developed, and he appeared to be convinced that public sentiment supported him in this stand. Shorter hours for workers had been one of the reforms of the "New Freedom," and he had mentioned it several times in the 1912 campaign.[12] Furthermore, as a one scholar has argued, "Wilson's history of dealing with the railroads could well have predisposed him to favor the brotherhoods' demand. In some of his early strong ideas against trusts, part which derived from Louis Brandeis, railroads figured prominently. . . . One of the first anti-trust cases the government acted upon in the Wilson Administration was that involving the New York, New Haven and Hartford Railroad."[13] Significant, too, is the response Wilson gave to a correspondent who criticized the operators' intransigence in the dispute over the eight-hour day. "I think you are right about the railroad men," Wilson wrote. "They do not seem to know how to lift their eyes from the immediate task, and I must say it is rather discouraging dealing with them."[14]

Finally, as we have seen, Wilson, when called upon, had already intervened twice in issues affecting the Brotherhoods and carriers and had thereby opened the door for similar intervention to try to resolve the latest dispute.[15]

THE WHITE HOUSE CONFERENCE

The White House conference began on August 14. The explosive tensions between the two parties was illustrated when the President met in the Green Room with labor representatives in the morning, and with management representatives in the afternoon. Garretson, spokesperson for the Brotherhoods, refused to budge even after Wilson reemphasized the harmful effects of the threatened strike action on the public. In the afternoon, the carrier representatives stressed the tremendous costs to the lines and their stockholders should labor be allowed to have its way. Wilson did not deal with the cost to the railroads in dollars, but he did urge the managers to consider the cost of ignoring the public's interest. Both conferences broke up with the President still hopeful of compromise, but with the Brotherhoods just as determined as ever.[16]

On August 15, Wilson put forth his own proposal for a settlement. The eight-hour day, he declared, was a just demand and the railroads should grant it. However, all questions of punitive overtime pay would have to await the results of a study of costs by a commision specially authorized to investigate the matter.[17] The President explained his statement on the eight-hour issue a few days later. "I made this recommendation," he informed Senator Newlands, "because I believe the concession right. The eight-hour day now undoubtedly has the sanction of the judgment of society in its favor and should be adopted."[18]

Railroad labor's chief goal had certainly gained a powerful supporter. Nevertheless, as Allen La Verne Shepherd points out, "his [Wilson's] endorsement of that goal was tempered by political necessity. His action was a middle-of-the road maneuver, designed to placate both parties yet not wholly satisfactory to either one."[19] Dallas L. Jones views the recommendation somewhat differently:

> The proposal, essentially a middle-of-the road compromise, brought the issues into focus. The Brotherhoods were taken at their word that the eight-hour day rather than higher pay was the essential question, and it met the carriers' argument that the Brotherhoods did not want the eight-hour day and that there should be arbitration. It made both sides take a definite position.[20]

The Brotherhoods' position was that they did not have the power to settle for less than what they had demanded. Wilson promptly requested that the 600 chairmen still at their home posts be brought to Washington to vote on his proposal. On August 17, these men arrived in Washington and immediately met with the President. Wilson told them that he had not asked the railroads to grant the eight-hour day merely to avoid a strike, but because he believed the demand was just. He then added that he also believed it right that the question of pay should be arbitrated.[21]

After the conference with the President, the chairmen held a closed meeting to consider his proposals. In spite of the Brotherhoods' chiefs' desire to secure approval of the proposals before the next meeting with the President,* the chairmen failed to take action. Many of them believed that they should continue to insist upon their full demands.

When the President first submitted his proposals to the railway managers, they replied that they could not grant the eight-hour day without a guarantee of increased rates. Wilson answered that he had no assurances that there would be a rate increase, but that he was positive that the findings of the commission he would appoint to consider the question of cost would carry great weight with the Interstate Commerce

*On the previous day, Gompers, Garretson and Stone conferred on the situation. It was after this conference that the two chiefs appeared to be more favorably inclined to the President's proposal. According to the *New York Times*, this was the result of Gompers' urgings. The AFL president was eager to help Wilson settle the dispute, and for the Brotherhoods to do all they could to aid the President. (*New York Times*, Aug. 17, 1916.)

Commission if it were found that rate increases were necessary. The managers refused to give Wilson a definite answer to his proposal. But later, in public statements, they accused the President of playing politics by attempting to avoid doing the right thing until after the election. (By the right thing, of course, they meant calling for the entire dispute to be arbitrated.) They also declared that the President was not concerned about the welfare of the railroads because he thought that the people who controlled the lines were unfriendly to him.[22]

While the Brotherhoods were still debating the President's proposal, the managers told Wilson on August 17 that they would not accept his proposal because it was necessary to maintain the principle of arbitration. "If arbitration is rejected what hope can there be for industrial peace?" they asked in justification of their refusal. Upon receiving the managers' rejection of his proposal, Wilson immediately summoned the presidents of some of the larger roads to Washington in order to appeal to a higher source of authority. At the same time, he issued a public statement explaining the proposal he had advanced:

> I have recommended the concession of the eight-hour day—that is, the substitution of an eight-hour day for the present ten-hour day in all of the existing practices and agreements. I made this recommendation because I believe the concession right. The eight-hour day now undoubtedly has the sanction of the judgment of society in its favor and should be adopted as a basis for wages even where the actual work to be done can not be completed within eight hours.

Turning next to the questions of costs "to the railroads and their stockholders" of such an innovation, he noted that "the railroads which have already adopted the eight-hour day do not seem to be at any serious disadvantage in respect of their cost of operation as compared with the railroads that have retained the ten-hour day." But only experience and practice could really solve that question, and therefore he had proposed that a commission look into the problem, and that all other issues in the dispute, such as "the demand for extra pay for overtime made by the men and the contingent proposals of the railroad authorities be postponed until facts shall have taken the place of calculations and forecast with regard to the effects of a change to the eight-hour day."[23]

On the same day, President Hale Holden, of the Burlington, acting as spokesperson for the railroad executives, issued a statement explaining why the roads could not accept the President's proposal. He began by asserting that the common acceptance of the principle of arbitration had put the right to claim arbitration as a method of settling labor controversies "beyond dispute." The eight-hour day, he continued, was "when considered in connection with railroad train service, a question upon which minds may differ and [is] therefore a subject for arbitration." He repeated the willingness of the railroads to submit the question either to the Interstate Commerce Commission or a special tribunal. And he concluded:

> To say such a demand as that now presented for a revolutionary change in the arrangemnts that have grown up in the development of the railroad business and involving so many complicated facts and relations, and such vast additions to the cost of the country's transportation, is not arbitrable, is to destroy the principle of arbitration, and if successful would in our judgment tend immediately to discard all of the legislation, States and National, which has been enacted in recent years, and set the country back to the old days of strikes, lockouts, public disorder, and business anarchy for the settlement of questions inherent in the relation of employer and employee.[24]

Ignoring the apocalyptic prophecy of the railroad executives, the Brotherhoods, on the following day, accepted the President's proposal. But the railroad president merely requested more time to study the plan. The following day, the presidents rejected the proposal. Immediately President Wilson sent out a call for the presidents of additional roads to come to the conference in Washington. However, this produced no change of attitude. The railway executives again rejected the President's proposal, and told him, "We stand for the principle of arbitration for the settlement of industrial disputes. Arbitration is the ideal toward which public sentiment and legislation of this country have been steadily tending for the settlement of disputes between employers and employees."[25]

Wilson replied that he regretted that the executives appeared to believe he was opposed to arbitration. He was not. In fact, he was so much in favor of it that he believed in compulsory arbitration. Yet under the law, he reminded the executives, there was no way to compel arbitration if either side refused to arbitrate. Moreover, the railroads were asking for something impracticable in requesting Congress to pass a compulsory arbitration law at a moment's notice. "As President Wilson spoke to the officials," one newspaper reported, "he walked up and down before them in the blue room. Several times he emphasized points with a clenched fist. He spoke solemnly."[26]

Implacable as ever, the railroad presidents refused to budge. The President pointed a finger at the executives and declared, "If a strike comes, the public will know where the responsibility rests. It will not be upon me."[2][7]Then apparently losing his temper, muttering, "I pray God to forgive you; I never can,"* he terminated the meeting.[28]**

Letters and telegrams continued to pour in to the President. Those from businessmen and business groups invariably asked Wilson to compel the men to arbitrate; those from labor organizations sided with the Brotherhood. The major exception in this last category were the messages from the non-operating workers, both organized and unorganized, on the railroads who wrote that the Brotherhoods were the best paid men; that they did not deserve more, and that they [the non-operating railroad workers] would gain nothing and lose much in the event of a strike.[29]

Among the many telegrams which were sent to the President on behalf of the carriers, one was from President George C. Pope of the National Association of Manufacturers. Pope wired Wilson that though his organization was appreciative of the President's efforts to settle the dispute peacefully, the NAM wished to urge that "you will with all the power of your great office and personally assert and maintain the principle of arbitration for industrial disputes affecting national intercourse. . . ."[30]

In reply Wilson declared:

I hold to the principle of arbitration with as clear a conviction and firm a purpose as any one, but, unfortunately, there is no means now in existence by which arbitration can be secured. The existing means have been tried and have failed.

This situation must never be allowed to arise again, but it has arisen. Some means must be found to prevent its recurrence, but no means can be found offhand or in a hurry or in season to meet this present national emergency.

What I am proposing does not weaken or discredit the principle of arbitration. It strengthens it, rather. It proposes that nothing be conceded except the eight-hour day, to which the whole economic movement of the time seems to point, and the immediate creation of an agency for determining all the arbitrable elements in this case, in the light, not of predictions or forecasts, but of established and ascertained facts. This is the first stage of the

*Charles W. Eliot, president of Harvard University, wrote to the President to inquire whether he said to the railroad officials: "I pray God to forgive you; I never can." Wilson replied: "I did say to the representatives of the railway presidents in parting with them, 'God forgive you.'" (Eliot to Woodrow Wilson, September 11, 1916; Woodrow Wilson to Tumulty, attached to letter of Eliot, Woodrow Wilson Papers, Library of Congress.) However, the version quoted above is from the account widely reported in the press.
**After the conference the frustrated Wilson remarked to Tumulty: "I was not able to make the slightest impression upon these men. . . . I am at the end of my tether, and I do not know what further to do." (Wilson to Tumulty, September 21, 1916, Woodrow Wilson Papers, Library of Congress; Joseph P. Tumulty, *Woodrow Wilson As I Know Him*, Garden City, N.Y., 1921, p. 198.)

direct route to the discovery of the best permanent basis for arbitration when other means than those now available are supplied.[31]

Pope refused to be persuaded. He replied that "the maintenance of the arbitrable spirit in industrial disputes is of far greater importance than the merits themselves." Elisha Lee, chairman of the Railways Conference Committee, supported Pope to the hilt, declaring: "That the railroads should grant, under threat of a national strike, a $50,000,000 wage preferment to a small minority of their employees, without a hearing before a public tribunal, is inconceivable in a democracy like ours."[32]

FAILURE OF THE WHITE HOUSE CONFERENCE

The day after the rejection of the President's proposal, the railroads offered a counter-proposal. It called for compulsory investigation of the dispute, similar to the Canadian Disputes Act. (This Act provided that if mediation failed to settle a dispute, a governmental investigation of the facts underlying the dispute would be undertaken. During the investigation, there could be no strike or lockout. At the end of the investigation, the facts were made public and the parties were free to take action.) A second counter-proposal submitted on August 27, was intended to secure rate increases if the eight-hour day were adopted. A commission would be established to investigate both the financial and administrative impact of the shorter workday on the operation of the lines. Pending its report, two sets of books, one for the eight-hour day and one for the ten-hour day, were to be kept by each carrier.[33]

Declaring that he would not act as mediator beyond what he had already done, Wilson turned both counter-proposals over to the Brotherhoods without comment. The unions promptly rejected them and told the President that they seemed to have been "prepared with a deliberate purpose of refusing to accept all the essential features of the plan proposed by your Excellency . . . while at the same time, endeavoring to veil that refusal under a concurrence with some non-essential features of your plan. . . ." At the same time, the Brotherhoods indicated willingness to accept the President's proposals.[34]

The controversy, meanwhile, was rapidly approaching a climax. The chairmen, summoned to Washington at the insistence of the President, were growing restless as the days passed, and on August 25, Wilson was told that they could not be kept in the capital much longer. Upon receipt of this information, the President asked the railway executives to give him a definite answer as to whether they were willing to accept his proposal. On the 27th, the Brotherhoods requested permission from Wilson to allow the 640 chairmen to return to their homes and to leave in their stead, a committee with full power to act. This, they explained, would simplify matters for them. When Wilson gave his approval, the chairmen left Washington late in the afternoon of August 27, leaving a committee in charge.[35]

The Brotherhoods were now convinced that the continuation of the negotiations day after day without progess was working to their disadvantage. For one thing, they had evidence that the railroads were using the delay to perfect their strikebreaking plans, hiring strikebreakers and purchasing arms and ammunition. For another, they were convinced that the carriers were attempting to "inflame the minds of the American people against the employees."[36] In this they were receiving the full support of the majority of newspapers and magazines. Nor was this surprising, for as Gompers pointed out in this connection: "The newspapers are owned, controlled, or influenced by the forces of great wealth of America. In addition they are generally owned by men of wealth. Furthermore, the owners of the newspapers are employers of labor. As employers of labor they are not going to permit the labor side of labor's cause to have a hearing."[37]

The Brotherhoods also realized that the carriers were using the delay to bring pressure upon the President. And in this, too, they were succeeding. As the *Railway Age Gazette,* the organ of the railroad officials pointed out with satisfaction: "the business interests of the country are backing the railways in their insistence on arbitration with an outspokenness, an energy, and a unanimity which has been surprising. Moreover, a very large part of the press is savagely denouncing Mr. Wilson, and declaring that by his abandonment of the principle of arbitration he has dealt a heavy blow to the cause of industrial peace, which will tend to cause strikes, lockouts, and anarchy in every branch of business. In fact, both the business community and the press are now convinced that not only the future of the railways, but to a great extent the industrial future of the United States, has been put at stake by the form this controversy has been given by President Wilson—and they are not hesitating to let the President know it."[38]

But the Brotherhoods' supporters were also letting the President "know it." In an authorized statement published by the New York *Call,* Senator Robert L. Owen of Oklahoma, chairman of the Senate Committee on Banking and Currency, and a sponsor of the Federal Child Labor Bill in the Senate, urged Wilson to stand firm in favor of the eight-hour day for the Brotherhoods. Asserting that he was with the railroad workers to the finish in their fight for a reduction of the normal working day to eight hours, he urged that "the greed for more of those already too powerful commercially and financially, should not be allowed the fix the national policy of the eight-hour day." He summed up his position:

> The eight-hour day, demanded by the railroad brotherhoods, marks an epoch in the ever-increasing recognition of the concrete rights of man to life, liberty, and happiness.
> It has been a long, hard struggle.
> I am rejoiced the eight-hour day is so far established.
> I should like to see it the universal rule and to see society adjust to it.
> An eight-hour day of labor will produce a maximum industrial and commercial efficiency, will be a better basis of national preparedness and happiness than longer hours, which exhaust the human body and brain and bring physical decadence. . . .
> An eight-hour day will better distribute the labor to be performed and will better distribute the proceeds of that labor and thus distribute happiness and property more equitably. . . .
> The eight-hour day is coming.
> Let it come at once in every line.[39]

For their part, the Brotherhood chiefs were trying to bring pressure on the rail executives by sending the chairmen home. As long as the chairmen remained in Washington, the railroad managers were convinced that there could be no strike. It was known, moreover, that the chairmen carried with them secret strike orders. Supposedly the date and hour of the strike was not set. But the secret strike order did not remain a secret very long. The carriers learned that a strike date had been set, and they called the White House for verification of this fact. If it were true, the rail executives informed the President, they would have to leave for their home offices at once. The White House immediately called Garretson of the Brotherhoods, who confirmed the report that the strike date had been set. But he also pointed out that the date was set far enough in advance to provide additional time for negotiations. Thereupon the President appealed once again to the railway executives, but they remained adamant and insisted upon their last counterproposal.[40]

The President lamented the fact that there was now no means in existence by which to secure arbitration, and that the nation was faced with an inevitable strike unless immediate action was taken. Agreeing that this was precisely what would happen, the heads of the four Brotherhoods declared: "The real and ultimate reason that the present railroad strike will be declared was the refusal of the railroads to accept the plan of settlement proposed by the President of the United States." Gompers made the same point in a public statement, and went on to praise "the splendid fight of the 400,000 railroad men for the eight-hour work day." He assured the President and the nation that when they struck, they would have "the sympathy, good will and support of all the wage earners" who were convinced that "the effect of the eight-hour fight made by the railroad men will redound to the benefit of all wage earners in their efforts to secure the shorter work day. . . ."[41]

The President's only alternative now was to call for Congressional action. Wilson decided to go before Congress. He was not convinced that the legislators would respond to the emergency with the necessary legislation. Or as he put it, he did not know "whether it will be possible to get from Congress any action which will control, or even moderate the situation." Fearing the worst, Wilson ordered some 15,000 troops from the Mexican border in the event that Congress should fail to enact legislation and the railroads should be struck.[42*]

Edward Berman argues that there were other methods, such as an injunction which President Wilson might have used in the crisis rather than appealing to Congress; but as Dallas Jones notes: "Not only was there no assurance that these methods would succeed, but there were political factors mitigating against their use."[43] In this connection, the editorial response of the pro-railway New York *Sun* to an irate "Stockholder" is interesting. The correspondent urged that the Brotherhood leaders "be arrested and punished under the Interstate Commerce law for conspiracy in case the strike against the railroads should be called without preliminary arbitration on the grievances, and refusal to comply with the award." The *Sun* reminded its correspondent that under the Clayton Anti-Trust Act (approved by Wilson on February 12, 1913), "the labor of a human being is not a commodity or article of commerce," and the correspondent's proposal made it "if not impossible, at least extremely difficult and doubtful as an outcome." It also reminded him that "work cannot be made compulsory on individuals, except as a punishment for crime," and that "the right to strike has been upheld as an elementary principle" so that organizations and their leaders who carry out a strike "cannot be penalized if the act be lawful." Then it asked:

> But what would be the use of arresting labor leaders? They would be released forthwith on bail and their trial would not come until months after the strike had been settled one way or the other. Then what could be the chance of convicting them in cold blood? The only effect of the arrests would be the excitement and exasperation of their followers to more obstinate resistance and perhaps to vengeful excesses.

What, then, was the real answer? The *Sun* replied: "The only feasible way of dealing with a strike seems to be to let it run its course."[44]

*Wilson's Mexican policy, will be discussed in the next volume.

Reprinting the stockholder's letter and the *Sun's* response, the New York *Call* labeled them "Throwing Up the Sponge," and added: "Evidently what was possible in 1894 is not possible in 1916. What was easy for Grover Cleveland is not feasible for Woodrow Wilson. And 'there's a reason,' but it has nothing to do with the Clayton bill. The workingmen have become more united, more intelligent, more determined to get what they want and better posted on how to get it."[45]

WILSON'S PROPOSAL TO CONGRESS

On August 29, 1916 President Wilson addressed a Joint Session of Congress. After recounting the history of the dispute over the Brotherhoods' demand "that they be granted an eight-hour working day, safeguarded by payment for an hour and a half of service for every hour beyond the eight," he brought the story up to the "complete deadlock between the parties," the setting of a strike date for September 4th, and the fact that a strike would occur unless speedy action were taken to avert it. Then full of foreboding, he pictured what would follow in the event of a strike:

> It affects the men who man the freight trains on practically every railway in the country. The freight service throughout the United States must stand still until their places are filled, if, indeed, it should prove possible to fill them at all. Cities will be cut off from their food supplies, the whole commerce of the nation will be paralyzed, men of every sort and occupation will be thrown out of employment, countless thousands will in all likelihood be brought, it may be, to the very point of starvation, and a tragical national calamity brought on, to be added to the other distresses of the time, because no basis of accommodation or settlement has been found.

After assailing the rail executives for their unyielding position, and upholding the principle of the eight-hour day because "the whole spirit of the times and the preponderant evidence of recent economic experience demanded it," Wilson pointed out that the only arbitrable issues were those which would result from the eight-hour day, not the eight-hour day itself. He had assured the carriers that no obstacle would be placed in the way of increased rates if the facts warranted such an increase. Wilson then called upon Congress to enact a six-point program: (1) the enlargement and administrative reorganization of the Interstate Commerce Commission to enable it to deal more promptly and effectively with the industry's possible financial problems resulting from either a strike or wage increase, (2) establishment of an eight-hour day for all operating employees; (3) appointment of a commission to study the impact of a shorter work day; (4) consideration by Congress of an increase in freight rates if the ICC deemed it necessary; (5) amendment of the Newlands Act to include provisions for prohibiting both strikes and lockouts until the investigation of a dispute could be made; (6) authority for the President to take over and operate the railroads and draft personnel "in case of military necessity." Another recommendation, listed separately, urged that arbitration awards be interpreted by courts of law and not by the parties themselves.[46]

The first reaction of the Brotherhoods and of the labor movement as a whole to the President's message was anything but enthusiastic. Headlines in the labor press read: "Wilson Urges No-Strike Law"; "Special Message Calls for 'Slave Act.'" The objection was specifically to Wilson's recommendation of a law declaring strikes unlawful pending investigation by a federal commission of disputes between the carriers and railroad workers. The fact that the proposal seemed to be based on the Canadian Industrial Act did not make it any more appealing to labor. "Since the abolition of slavery," declared the heads of the four Brotherhoods, "no more effectual means has been devised for insuring the bondage of the working men than the passage of compulsory investigation acts of the character of the Canadian disputes act."[47]

It has been argued that this was only a minor aspect of the unions' opposition, and that "the Brotherhoods were completely opposed to the President's action in appealing to Congress for legislation to put the eight-hour day into effect." They took this stand, goes the argument, because they did not want working conditions and hours to be established through "legal enactment," insisting that such advances must come through "economic power." Underlying this reluctance, the argument continues, was their fear of the future impotence of their organizations if shorter hours and improved working conditions were established and protected by law instead of by collective bargaining— trade unionism and strikes.[48]

Certainly this was the position taken by Samuel Gompers in supporting the Brotherhoods. Ignoring, as was his and the AFL's wont, any history of eight-hour activity before the formation of the Federation, he declared publicly:

> Beginning with the declaration of the American Federation of Labor convention in 1884, establishing the eight-hour day as the primary purpose to be secured by the economic organization of the workers, a revolutionary force was injected into industrial and commercial organization and relations.*

*For the resolution adopted at this convention and the events and results that followed, *see* Philip S. Foner, *History of the Labor Movement in the United States,* New York, 1955, vol. II, pp. 98-105.

The first great concerted campaign for eight hours was that of 1886,* when the efforts of all labor organizations were concentrated on securing the shorter work day in their own trades.

The splendid achievements of the first great effort, gained through the economic power of the trade union movement, disclosed the way to secure eight hours for all. Whatever progress has been made in reducing hours of work has been due to organized economic power.[49]

Gompers' statement was written especially for the Socialist New York *Call*, which seems to have been so overwhelmed by this fact that it did not bother to correct his statement about the first united action having occurred in 1886.

It is strange, too, that the *Call* did not take issue with Gompers' whole approach to the eight-hour day since the Socialists generally proposed a political solution, in the form of legislation, for long hours.** At the 1915 AFL convention, a Socialist-led coalition challenged the position of the Gompers leadership, endorsed by the AFL convention during previous years, that only economic methods (i.e., collective bargaining) would be used to usher in the shorter working day. Arguing that labor opposition to legislation had actually caused the defeat of hours laws in some states, socialists and their allies on this issue held that tactics should be flexible and varied. William Green, an AFL vice-president (and later president) broke with Gompers on this score. "Is there anyone here," he asked, "who believes the man who enjoys the benefit of the eight-hour day through . . . economic organization . . . enjoys it more than the man who secured it through legislation." John Fitzpatrick, head of Chicago Federation of Labor and one of the most astute trade union strategists of the period, spoke for the eight-hour day by legislation, both industrially and politically, a position endorsed by the Illinois Federation of Labor. Gompers' supporters won a close vote (8,500 to 6,396 with 4,061 abstentions) on the issue, but labor bodies continued to battle for the eight-hour day on both the economic and legislative front. (*Proceedings, AFL convention, 1915*, pp. 132–48, 224–56.)

It is true that in private correspondence and public testimony during the hearings on "The Threatened Strike of Railway Employes," conducted by the Senate Committee on Interstate Commerce on August 31, 1916, the chiefs of the Brotherhoods and Gompers, whom they invited to appear with them, maintained a certain amount of opposition to

*For the eight-hour movement before 1886, *see* Philip S. Foner, *History of the American Labor Movement in the United States*, New York, 1947, vol. I, pp. 371–82.
**Moreover, the Socialist Party's National Executive Committee issued a pamphlet entitled *Are the Workers of America Opposed to an Eight-Hour Law? (American Socialist*, Aug. 21, 1915.) Gompers thought the pamphlet influential enough to devote 28 pages of the August, 1915 issue of the *American Federationist* to answering it.

legislative enactment of an eight-hour law. But the Brotherhoods' leader made it clear at the same time that, once Congress did pass such a law, they could take the necessary steps to call off the strike set for September 4th. In fact, W. G. Lee, president of the Brotherhood of Railway Trainmen, urged speedy action so that at least one point of the President's six-point program—the one calling for the eight-hour day—could be adopted swiftly. "I hope," he declared, "it can be enacted before the close of Saturday's work day (September 2)." He continued:

> If so then we can stop this calamity by wiring all of our general chairmen the message, "Satisfactory settlement effected," and explain that it is just about what he suggested, the eight-hour day, an investigation of the other things, and put them in if they are found to be fair or dispose of them in a fair and equitable way as Congress may say, or some one else. We are ready to do that, gentlemen, and all criticism to the contrary should be forgotten.
>
> But I want to impress upon you how absolutely impossible it is to send word to those chairmen that a satisfactory settlement has been made until first the eight-hour day is established.

When Senator Pomerene interrupted Lee with the suggestion that the Brotherhoods should withdraw the strike order and then give Congress time to investigate the merits of the controversy, the Brotherhood chief replied that Congress had had "ample time" to initiate its investigation during the eleven days that the unions were the "guests" of President Wilson. He firmly repeated it was possible to withdraw the strike order now in only one way, namely, by a wire to the chairmen announcing that the eight-hour day had been secured by Congressional action.[50]*

It would appear that it was not so much Congressional legislation for an eight-hour day that the Brotherhoods opposed publicly but the absence of such a law.

THE ADAMSON ACT

While the Hearings on "The Threatened Strike of Railway Employes" were taking place, President Wilson was meeting with Speaker Champ Clark, Majority Leader Claude Kitchen, Minority Leader James R. Mann, chairman W. C. Adamson, and other Commerce Committee

---

*In his testimony Lee charged that the railroad managers had used the eleven-day truce during the conferences with the President to prepare themselves for war with the Brotherhoods. During this period, the Brotherhood chiefs received "wires, affidavits, and letters from our members by the hundreds directing our attention to the hostile activities of the railroad companies," including information that the carriers planned to use non-operating railroad workers "as scabs-strikebreakers." U.S. Congress, *Committee on Interstate Commerce, Hearings on the Threatened Strike of Railway Employees*, 64th Congress, 1st Session, pp. 143-44. (New York *Call*, Sept. 27, 1916.)

members. The President insisted on adoption of his entire six-point program, and urged inclusion of the compulsory investigation during which there could be no strike. But Adamson informed Wilson that passage of a rate increase and the strike ban during compulsory investigation were impossible at that time. He made it clear that the combined opposition of the Brotherhoods and the AFL doomed any chance of winning Congressional approval of the compulsory investigation provision. The evidence supporting this conclusion was clear. The Brotherhood chiefs and Gompers had vigorously opposed the provision during the hearings on the impending strike. Then at a meeting called at the AFL building, attended not only by labor leaders of the Brotherhoods and the Federation, but also by the "labor congressmen" and Secretary of Labor Wilson, plans were discussed for blocking the proposal.

Gompers wired all of the Central Labor Unions and State Federations of Labor affiliated with the AFL urging them to

> . . . telegraph both your United States Senators and your Congressmen in Washington, insisting upon the eight-hour work day at present compensation, and in your telegram emphatically protest against enactment of any law imposing upon American workers involuntary servitude, even for a day. Please have the labor and other press in your community send similar telegrams.[51]*

This unified opposition of the Brotherhoods, AFL, and the "labor Congressmen" meant that no compulsory investigation provision could be included in Adamson's bill which meant, the Senator made clear to Wilson, that the best that could be hoped for was passage of an eight-hour law with a commission to study its effects.

The President still refused to give support to Adamson's measure. But when he was informed by the Senate leaders that there was no hope of securing more before Congress convened on August 1, Wilson sent word to Adamson to go ahead with the bill he had drafted.[52]

Whether or not the Brotherhoods really opposed the President's action in appealing to Congress for legislation for an eight-hour day, their testimony indicating that such a law was the only way to call off the impending strike did have the effect of speeding action on the Adamson bill. The House Committee on Interstate Commerce and Foreign Commerce reported the measure favorably; the House passed the bill the same day by a 239 to 56 vote. On September 2, 1916, after a day of bitter debate and with all of the Republican Senators, except Robert M. LaFollette, voting against the measure, the Senate voted 43 to 28 to enact the measure. President Wilson signed the Adamson Act in his private

---

*There is not even a hint in these telegrams that Gompers frowned upon an eight-hour day obtained through Congressional action.

railroad car at Union Station before leaving Washington to deliver an address in Kentucky. The four pens used were given to each of the Brotherhood chiefs.[53]

Entitled a law to "Establish an Eight-Hour Day for Employes of Carriers Engaged in Interstate and Foreign Commerce and for Other Purposes," the Adamson Act declared that beginning January 1, 1917, "eight hours shall be deemed a day's work and the measure of standard for the purpose of reckoning the compensation actually engaged in the operation of trains and for the transportation of persons or property" in interstate commerce. The law instructed the President to appoint a commission of three to "observe the administrative and financial effects of the institution of the eight-hour standard work day." The commission was instructed to carry on this study during a period of not less than six months and not more than eight, and was required to make its report not later than thirty days thereafter. During the seven or nine months required to make the investigation and file the report, the railroad managers were forbidden to reduce the wages of the trainmen working the eight-hour day below the existing day's standard wages for ten hours. Overtime after eight hours was to be paid on a pro rata basis for such standard work day. Originally the bill had called for time-and-one-half for overtime, but it was changed to straight time.

Anticipating the President's approval, the Brotherhoods canceled the strike immediately after the Senate had acted to adopt the Adamson bill.[54]

On the same day the railroad unions took this action, Gompers' secretary, writing for the AFL president, emphasized: " . . . the railroad brotherhoods still maintain their opposition to the legislative methods. Undoubtedly, the precedent established will give a bad twist to the labor movement. Of course, the quasi-public nature of the railroad business is a mitigating element, but undoubtedly trouble will result in the end. . . ."[55] How much of this reflected Gompers' view or that of the Brotherhoods is impossible to tell. As for Gompers, however, it is worth noting that in spite of his disapproval of the legislative method of securing the eight-hour day, once the Adamson Act was adopted, he urged the railroad unions affiliated with the AFL to act swiftly to secure inclusion within its provisions.[56]

Whatever the Brotherhood officials may have felt personally about securing the eight-hour day through Congressional legislation,* they

*Warren S. Stone of the Engineers and W. G. Lee of the Trainmen later declared that they did not like the Adamson Act and expressed the wish "that the brotherhoods had gone ahead with the strike." (W. S. Garretson, "Truth About the Passage of the Adamson Bill, *Railroad Democrat*, Aug. 21, 1919; Allen La Verne Shepherd, "Federal Railway Labor Policy, 1913-1926," unpublished Ph.D. Thesis, University of Nebraska, 1971, p. 90.)

had no choice but to call off the strike once the Adamson Act was passed. For one thing, they had already stated publicly before a Congressional Committee that once such a law became a reality, they would act immediately to have the strike called off. For another, they did not want to embarrass the President politically in the midst of a campaign for re-election.* While three of the chiefs were Republicans,** they knew that the Wilson administration had been friendly to railroad labor, and that the workers had gained more under the Democrats than they had under previous Republican administrations. To have gone ahead with a strike after enactment of the law would have made Wilson look foolish and turned public opinion against the Brotherhoods. Certainly there would have been little sympathy for the explanation that their future as trade unions would be jeopardized if the workers achieved so important a victory as the eight-hour day through legislation.[57]

In his study, "Federal Railway Labor Policy, 1913-1926," Allen La Verne Shepherd argues that Wilson could not get all he wished included in the Adamson Act because the Democratic party in 1916 was "rent by factionalism that extended deep into Congress." While reports of a revolt by Champ Clark and the anti-war elements, as well as of Bryan's growing hostility to the Preparedness program, had declined by August, "the breach over foreign affairs was not healed." This weakened the possibility of winning the support of the dissidents for the complete package, while the Democratic party's eagerness to gain the support of organized labor and "attract many ex-Bull Moosers into its fold for the fall elections," made it politically unwise to propose a ban on strikes during compulsory investigations; also, the idea of raising railroad rates would hardly appeal to farmers and small businessmen. Adamson, Shepherd concludes, could promise passage of the two provisions in his bill "because the Democrats, despite Republican gains in 1914, still controlled both houses of Congress and because the Republicans were just as much divided by dissension in foreign affairs as the Democrats. They could also be expected to oppose any concessions to labor unions on the domestic front, thereby presumably antagonizing the uncommitted progressives."[58]

*In his testimony before the Senate Committee on Interstate Commerce, Lee denied that partisanship toward Wilson as a Democrat, as was charged in some papers, had any influence in the Brotherhood's support of the President's proposals. "With three of these chief railroad executives lifetime Republicans, the press or any one else referring to it as a political trick is unfair, unjust, and should not be mentioned." (New York *Call*, Sept. 27, 1916.)

**The impact of the Adamson Act on the presidential election is discussed below, *See* chapter on the Election of 1916.

It is helpful of Shepherd to include "presumably antagonizing the uncommitted progressives." While most Republicans opposed Adamson's bill because of their bias in favor of the railroads or purely on partisan grounds, Senator Albert B. Cummins, progressive from Iowa, opposed it on the principle that the rail unions were browbeating Congress and the country into accepting their demands. Cummins' progressivism was typical of those in the movement who either viewed organized labor as a menace equal to that of big business, or in too many cases, as an even greater evil.[59]*

IMPLICATIONS OF THE ADAMSON ACT

Regardless of what factors were responsible, in September, 1916, 400,000 workers on the railroads gained the eight-hour day, and a nationwide rail shutdown was averted. Moreover, the influence of the Adamson Act in extending the eight-hour day was considerable. The railway switchmen soon demanded the eight-hour day and it was awarded to them through arbitration, which set off a day of celebration. Other railroad workers showed less enthusiasm since they were still not included in the Act; but they too hoped that the gains achieved by the operating men would gradually filter down to them.[60]

Of this, Frank P. Walsh, chairman of the Industrial Relations Commission, had not the slightest doubt. In fact, he saw in the passage of the Adamson Act the opening up of a new era for labor throughout the world. "The eight-hour day is inevitable in the United States," he wrote, in a special message to the New York *Call*, "and when the workers of Europe leave the trenches I predict a world-wide refusal to work at any employment for more than eight hours a day." Pointing out that "every governmental body, hygienic association and society of scientific and economic research" that had investigated industrial conditions for the past decade had "found that the physical well being, necessary opportunity for mental development, and the recreational needs of human beings" demanded that "no man or woman should be permitted to work for more than eight-hours a day," Walsh insisted:

Eight hours should be recognized by society as a sufficiently long work day.
 THE EIGHT-HOUR DAY AND THE LIVING WAGE SHOULD NO LONGER BE SUBJECT TO ARBITRATION!

*For a discussion of this aspect of the Progressive Movement, *see* Philip S. Foner, *History of the Labor Movement in the United States*, New York, 1980, vol. V, pp. 61-62, 87.

Who gave the eight heads of railroads the power to decide how long the trainmen should spend with their wives and children?*. . . .

This stand of the trainmen is not a revolution, but there are 400,000 men who are intelligent enough to say they will work no more unless as free men.

The year 1916 marks the beginning of the end of an industrial despotism which allows a few men to exercise autocratic control over the lives, mental aspirations and craving for happiness of countless producers.

Wilson's Eight-Hour Day Plea Will Become the Demand of the Whole World's Workers.[61]**

RAILROADS FIGHT THE ADAMSON ACT

Such euphoric phrases left the railroad managers cold. Indeed, it soon became clear that passage of the law marked only a temporary cease-fire in the war between the Brotherhoods and the railroads. Shortly after the Adamson Act was passed, the Brotherhoods requested a conference with the carriers to put the eight-hour day into effect. At the conference, the railroad managers refused to discuss the matter and told the Brotherhoods that they intended to test the Act's constitutionality.[62]

All of the railroad presidents applauded this intransigent stand. Typical was the circular sent to their stockholders by the Atchison, Topeka, and Santa Fe Railroad in which President E. P. Ripley declared the Adamson Act unconstitutional, and recommended to all the railroads that "steps should be taken to resist it in every lawful manner." He also urged stockholders of every road "to use their influence in favor of appropriate remedial legislation."[63]

At the end of November, 1916, all the railroads announced jointly that they were in agreement "to fight to the end." To this open defiance of the law, W. G. Lee, head of the Trainmen, responded for all the Brotherhoods by reminding the carriers that "a strike vote is still in effect," and "if the railroads do not live up to the very spirit of the law, there is no reason why the brotherhoods should not take advantage of their strongest card."[64]

Gompers backed the Brotherhoods again, declaring angrily that "whatever steps the railroads may take to kill the Adamson Law, that

---

*In a letter to the New York *Call*, Julia Lathrop, chief of the Children's Bureau of the Department of Labor, noted: "Children need the companionship of fathers as well as mothers, and they can have neither in any real sense if long hours of work exhaust energy and leave no time away from work save that required for the business of eating and sleeping." (New York *Call*, Sept. 13, 1916.)

**Walsh added: "The wisdom and bravery of the President in making this pronouncement is unparalleled in the annals of statesmanship." (New York *Call*, Sept. 3, 1916.) Clearly the IRC chairman was not inclined to understatement.

law is going into effect on January 1, and will be enforced." He issued a
warning, using a Shakesperean quotation to make his point: "Men of
wealth, I say to you, be careful how far you go. There is a limit even to
human endurance. You throw down the gauntlet and we accept the
challenge. When the time comes, it will be another case of 'Lay on
Macduff, and damned be him who first cries 'Hold, enough'!'"* Gompers
cited the fact that the Louisville *Post*, which in response to the declaration
that the railroads were in agreement "to fight to the end," remarked:
"The railroad oligarchy is as blind as ever was the slave oligarchy, which
resisted every suggestion of gradual or compensated emancipation."[65]**

Both Gompers and the Brotherhood chiefs soon had another reason to
feel bitter. Although Wilson had reluctantly accepted the Adamson Act
without his pet scheme for compulsory investigation during which there
would be no strikes, in December, 1916, when he addressed the opening
session of the Sixty-fifth Congress, he renewed his request for such
legislation. Since the opposition of Gompers, the AFL, and the Brotherhoods had not deterred the President from pushing his compulsory
arbitration proposal,*** organized labor enlisted the support of Republican legislators and even businessmen. Through Frank Feeney of
the elevator constructors, Gompers arranged for a conference with
Republican Senator Boise Penrose, who also opposed the President's
legislative proposal. Gompers urged Penrose to advise Republican

---

*The quotation is from *Macbeth*.
**"The *Post* cited the following facts of the history of the railroads to make its point event
stronger:
"The railroads fought to the end the adoption of the Interstate Commerce Act.
"The railroads fought to the end every attempt to give the Interstate Commerce Commis-
sion anything more than advisory power over the regulation of rates or the eradication of
abuses.
"The railroads fought to the end all attempts of State legislatures and of Congress to
abolish rebates or put an end to the pass evil, which had grown to large proportions.
"The railroads fought to the end the passage of the Hepburn Law, which they declared to
be confiscatory and unconstitutional.
"They fought to the end the National Workmen's Compensation Act.
"They fought to the end the law requiring the application of safety-appliances first to
passengers—and then to freight-trains.
"They fought to the end all legislation putting a limit to the continuous service of railroad
employees." (Reprinted in *Literary Digest*, December 2, 1916, p. 1148.)
***The Philadelphia *Public Ledger* reported on December 6, 1916: "Undaunted by the
menacing attitude of the brotherhoods and the Federation of Labor, the President renews
practically the whole of his original suggestions for dealing with the problem of compulsory arbitration, when it was in its most acute stage last August." Wilson himself wrote to
Judge Chambers: "I would not in any case have consented to a postponement of the
legislation, and I am taking steps now to press it as far as possible." (Wilson to W.L.
Chambers, December 21, 1916, Woodrow Wilson Papers.)

Senators to cooperate with those Democratic lawmakers who were unwilling to force compulsory arbitration on the workers. He suggested, too, that it would not hurt the Republican Party to support labor in this matter.

As a result of the united labor opposition, aided by Democratic and Republican law makers, nothing came of Wilson's new request for compulsory arbitration. But the fact that the President had continued to urge it upon Congress made the Brotherhoods more determined to have the eight-hour day immediately.[66]*

Meanwhile, an "Eight-Hour Commission" was appointed to report on the feasibility of the shorter workday. It was composed of General George Goethals of Panama Canal fame, Edgar E. Clark of the Interstate Commerce, and George Rublee, friend of Supreme Court Justice Louis D. Brandeis and co-framer of the Federal Trade Commission Act.[67] The "Eight-Hour Commission" made its report on December 29, 1917. It found that an eight-hour day was feasible in the railroad industry, and recommended that the Adamson Act be implemented on January 1, 1917, as provided for in the law.[68]

But the railroads continued to ignore the law, and by March, 1917, the dissatisfaction of the men forced the Brotherhood officials to take action. The chiefs notified the carriers that if the eight-hour provision of the Act were not put into effect by March 17, a strike would take place. On March 15, negotiations between the carriers and the four unions were resumed, but the managers refused to concede anything until the Supreme Court acted. The carriers again proposed arbitration if the court declared the law unconstitutional. The Brotherhoods rejected the proposal, and negotiations were on the point of being broken off when President Wilson, inaugurated for a second term only a few weeks before, again intervened.[69]

With the country on the verge of war, the situation was very different from that of the preceding September. When Wilson appealed on March 16 to both parties to settle their differences, he based the question squarely on the issue of patriotism and asked them to consider the gravity of the situation. At the same time, he informed them that he had appointed a mediation committee of the Council of National Defense to help the parties reach a settlement.[70]** The Committee consisted of Secretary of Labor William B. Wilson, railroad executives Franklin K. Lane and Daniel Willard, and Samuel Gompers. All four joined at once

---

*As we shall see in the next volume, Wilson did not hold Gompers' outspoken opposition to his compulsory arbitration proposal against the labor leader. Far overshadowing every other issue was Gompers' support for Wilson's war policies.

**The formation of the Council of National Defense is discussed in the next volume.

in asking the Brotherhoods for a forty-eight hour postponement of the strike—a request which was promptly granted.[71]

Meanwhile, Attorney General Thomas W. Gregory and a number of law officers in the Army's Judge Advocate General's office, began studying the Debs case in the Pullman Strike of 1894, planning to use it as the basis for recommending that the President take strong action against the Brotherhoods and their leaders if mediation failed. Indeed, Tumulty, Wilson's secretary, placed an article from the *New York Times* on Wilson's desk, with the attached penciled notation, "You will be interested in this." The article was entitled, "Debs' Case A Precedent."[72]

But such drastic action proved to be unnecessary. On March 18, as war approached even closer, the President notified the parties that in view of the aggravated international situation, under no conditions could a strike occur. That night the parties met in continuous session, and in the early morning, of March 19, 1917, an agreement was reached to put the basic eight-hour day into effect immediately. Thus ended what one journal called "The Railroad Labor War."[73]

Ironically, on the same afternoon, in a five-to-four decision, the Supreme Court upheld the constitutionality of the Adamson Act. The decision, which interpreted the Act as a wage law, gave the federal government power to regulate all phases of interstate commerce.[74]* Another irony was the fact that the Railroad Brotherhoods had finally won the eight-hour day by using their federated power. For it had been the great shopmen's strike on the Harriman System for recognition of the federation method of collective bargaining—the longest railroad strike in history, lasting from September 30, 1911 to June 28, 1915,**— which the Brotherhoods had helped to smash,*** that paved the way for the Brotherhoods' triumph two years later. At the final capitulation of the railroads, one of the men who had been active in the Harriman strike wrote:

The principal feature of these strikes was forcing the companies to do

*It was believed at the time that the decision would go far to reverse the *Adair* decision, but that proved to be a vain hope. One aspect of the decision in the Adamson Act case angered labor, and that was the *obiter dicta* opinion of the justices in favor of compulsory investigation of disputes during which there could be no strike. In other words, the court not only ruled on legislation already passed by Congress but voiced an opinion in favor of legislation still being discussed in Congress. (*American Federationist,* April, 1917, pp. 234-35.)

**For a discussion of the shopmen's strike on the Harriman System, 1911-1915, *see* Philip S. Foner, *History of the Labor Movement in the United States,* New York, 1980, vol. V, pp. 164-81.

***Not only did the shopmen lose the strike, but many of the strikers were blacklisted in the industry and never regained their old jobs.

188 ON THE EVE OF AMERICA'S ENTRANCE INTO WORLD WAR I

business with the Federated Trades instead of with the craft organizations singly as heretofore, this being the main issue involved, and while we lost out, that is, we did not win the point, and the strikes had to be ultimately called off, still we think this fight was the one that firmly established this policy of doing business, and on all the railroads of the country. As the Brotherhoods' victory in the struggle for the eight-hour day proves, this principle has been accepted and has been triumphant.[75]*

---

*Only a small number of organized switchmen, AFL members, among non-operating personnel won eight hours in the wake of the Adamson Act. The railroad shopmen (machinists, boilermakers, blacksmiths, carmen, sheet metal workers and railway employees), who pioneered in federated bargaining in the bitter, 45-month Harriman System strike, still did not gain the eight-hour day.

CHAPTER 11

Women Workers on the Eve of America's Entrance into World War I

"We have come to the American Federation of Labor," declared Rose Schneiderman in 1915, "and said to them, 'Come and help us to organize the American working girl' . . . but nothing was done."[1] Actually, something was started, but nothing came of it. At the AFL's 1913 convention, the time seemed propitious for at last inaugurating an aggressive movement to organize the great army of women in industrial life. For this purpose, the Executive Council was directed to levy "at whatever time it may see fit during the year 1914—an assessment of one cent . . . upon the membership of all affiliated unions, the money derived therefrom to be expended by direction of the Executive Council in whatever manner it may deem best and of the greatest advantage in the organization of the wage-earning women of our country."[2]

ECONOMIC CRISIS

The financial records of the AFL indicate that the assessment was levied, but nothing was done with the funds collected. By the time the resolution was adopted, business failures were increasing, and by the end of 1913-1914, an economic crisis was in full swing. It was to increase in intensity after August, 1914, when the war broke out in Europe, severely disrupting American industry and causing food prices in the United States to skyrocket. The economic crisis reached its worst stage in the winter months of 1914-1915, when from 400,000 to 440,000 wage earners in New York City alone—18 percent of the 2,455,000 wage earners in the city—were unemployed, to say nothing of those workers who were kept on part-time. According to surveys, unemployment in other cities was pretty much in the same proportion as in New York. Maxwell Bertch has estimated that the total number of unemployed in the winter of 1914–1915 "reached as much as 4,000,000 and possibly higher." In addition, there were several million working only part time.[3]

With the onset of this latest economic crisis and the rapid increase in unemployment, the usual cry of "Get the women out of the factories and shops!" began to be heard again in AFL circles. A group of embittered delegates to the 1914 convention of the AFL opposed any appropriation for organizing women and insisted that the employment of women and children was creating enforced idleness among men. They introduced a resolution declaring that "these conditions are destructive of the individual, the family, and our race," and resolving "that we do our utmost to restore individual, social, and racial health by restoring woman to the home." The convention did modify the resolution, but the original plan to organize women was shelved.[4]

THE UNEMPLOYED

Apart from seeking to eliminate women from industry, the AFL had no program for dealing with the problems of the unemployed. Indeed, even though the percentage of idleness among representative unions in New York had leaped from 17.5 percent in January, 1913, to 31 percent in January, 1914, and the percentage of unemployment among the organized workers in Massachusetts had increased from 11.3 to 16.6 percent during the same period, Gompers seemed blissfully unaware of the situation.[5]

It is to the credit of the IWW that it was the first organized group to recognize the existence of an unemployment problem, to call attention to the growing bread lines throughout the country and the increasing number of homeless men and women sleeping in doorways and cellars, and to point out that practically nothing was being done by federal, state, and local governments to relieve the suffering and distress of the unemployed.[6]* IWW agitation among the unemployed started on the West Coast. Conditions in San Francisco were desperate. A large building on Market Street was converted into a shelter for the unemployed, and over two thousand men slept nightly in this vermin-infested place. Throughout the city, men, women and children slept in "flops." An estimated 65,000 people were unemployed in San Francisco, and 10,000 a day were getting food on soup lines.[7]

*For a detailed discussion of the work of the IWW among the unemployed, see Philip S. Foner, History of the Labor Movement in the United States, vol. IV, The IWW., 1905–1917, New York, 1965, Chapter 19.

On the night of January 20, 1914, a crowd of unemployed workers, led by the IWW, gathered in Jefferson Hall to hear Lucy Parsons, widow of the Haymarket martyr, Albert R. Parsons. The proprietor refused to let the crowd in, claiming that the hall rent had not been paid. Parsons led the crowd across the street and began speaking from the curb. She was immediately arrested and charged with inciting a riot, but not before the unemployed had voiced demands for work at $3 for an eight-hour day and had called upon Governor Hiram Johnson to convene a special session of the legislature to pass a right-to-work bill. However, the Progressive governor denied that there was an unemployment problem and blamed the demonstration on a "few leaders who preach the tenets of the IWW, who neither wish to work themselves nor desire employment for others, and who preach an anarchistic doctrine at variance with organized Government."[8]

Under pressure from the IWW, the state government finally initiated a public works project. When the project supervisors refused to deal with the IWW's Unemployment Committee, ten thousand people marched to Union Square Plaza to protest. Unemployed women were in charge of the meeting, and Lucy Parsons, Ida Adler of the Cloak Makers, and Pearl Vogel of the waitresses were the leading speakers.[9]

Lucy Parsons was also the principal speaker at Chicago's hunger demonstration of the unemployed on January 17, 1915. Above the speaker's platform was a banner with the word HUNGER on it, while other signs carried the slogans: "We want WORK not CHARITY," "Why Starve in the Midst of Plenty?" and "Hunger Knows No Law." Parsons told the fifteen hundred men and women present that "as long as the capitalists can throw cast off rags and a few crumbs of bread at the working class in the name of 'charity,' just so long will they have an easy and cheap solution for the problem of unemployment." She then led the hunger marchers in a parade through Chicago's financial district. The police brutally attacked the marchers, and Parsons, five young women, and fifteen men were arrested.[10]

In New York, Portland, St. Louis, Sioux City, Des Moines, Detroit, Salt Lake City, Providence, and other cities, the IWW established Unemployed Leagues, which called upon the jobless to join with the IWW to "force the employers to cut down the daily working hours to 6, 5, or 4 or any number that may be necessary to make room for all our unemployed fellow workers to make a living." Most of the Unemployed Leagues were strictly IWW organizations, but in a number of communities, the Wobblies cooperated with other organizations. Moreover, as the crisis deepened, AFL unions and Socialist Party locals also become active. But it was the IWW that really succeeded in calling attention to the plight of the unemployed, that stimulated the unemployed to do something for themselves rather than resign themselves to starvation, and that forced the authorities to provide some relief for the men and women out of work. Henry Bruere, New York City municipal reformer, declared in the winter of 1914–1915 that "thanks to the activities of the IWW the unemployed are no longer regarded as hoboes as they were last year."[11]

WORLD WAR I BRINGS ECONOMIC RECOVERY

Although serious unemployment persisted until 1916, the depression began to lift by April, 1915, as European war orders caused mills and factories to rehire workers. Despite this change in the economic picture, Gompers was still insisting in 1915 that women be taken out of the factories to provide jobs for men and simultaneously end the long hours and low pay for women workers, which endangered the "perpetuity of our country."[12] But American industry, which was prospering by supplying goods to combatants abroad, was actually experiencing a shortage of labor to fill positions in the ironworks, steel mils, munitions plants, shipyards, mines, meat-packing plants, transportation companies, and many other industries that directly or indirectly played a role in supplying the war needs of the Allied Powers.

Previously, the immigrant masses had supplied American industry—largely concentrated in the North and Mideast—with a cheap, available labor supply. But the war drastically curtailed the flood of immigrants to this country* and, moreover, led to the departure of many already living here to serve the cause of their homelands. Great numbers of these individuals were workingmen.[13]

In the face of these developments, industrialists began to focus their attention on two still untapped sources of common labor. One, as we shall see, was the Southern black. The second source was women. Since 1910 the number of women employed in all general divisions of occupations, other than agriculture, forestry and animal husbandry, and domes-

---

*The effect of the European conflict upon the influx of immigrants of the United States is clearly illustrated by the following table. (U.S. Bureau of Immigration, *Annual Report of the Commissioner-General of Immigration* 1913-1919):

Year	Volume of Immigration
1913	1,197,892
1914	1,218,480
1915	326,700
1916	298,826
1917	295,403
1918	110,618

tic and personal service, had increased. But on the eve of the entrance of the United States into the First World War, women still constituted only one-fifth of the wage earners in the United States.[14] If industry was to meet the demands from abroad, it was imperative that more women be drawn into the work force. Many employers had been reluctant to hire women if male help was available, unless they were bent on using female labor to lower wage standards. However, now that Europe was at war and the United States appeared to be moving toward involvement, the demand arose that employers train women to replace men who might be drafted.[15]

Many employers did not respond to any substantial degree. A study of the trend in Ohio, a major industrial state, is revealing. Both men's and women's employment began to increase in Ohio in 1915, but the increase was much more rapid for men. It was not until the middle of 1917, several months after the United States had entered the war, that the rate of increase in women's employment almost equaled that of men.[16]

WOMEN MUNITION WORKERS

However, women workers began to enter the munitions industry in large numbers even before the United States became involved in the conflict. Up to the outbreak of the war in Europe, the American munitions industry was a small operation. With the demand from the combatants and with profits soaring, the industry expanded, and many industrial plants switched from turning out products primarily for peacetime use to producing munitions. As it became evident that women were especially suited to certain types of work in the munitions industry, they began to be employed in increasing numbers. "Many operations in the manufacture of munitions can not only be as well done by women as men, but are better done by female help," declared a speaker at a convention of the American Society of Mechanical Engineers and the National Machine Tool Builders' Association. "These operations are such as involve delicate work, requiring deftness and dexterity in the use of fingers." The *New York Times* was even more specific: "The filtering of the fine screws and the insertion of tiny springs in the assembling of parts of a shell made the sensitive touch perception and delicate handling of a woman's hand really needed.[11] Florence Kelley, secretary of the National Consumers' League, charged that munitions manufacturers, eager to get women into the plants, threatened to discharge male workers "unless they induced their wives to work." "The manufacturers, of course, deny this charge," Kelley declared, "but we have found evidence of it on all sides. . . . The women, in order to conduct their homes, work at night."[17]

By January, 1917, four thousand women were already employed at a single plant in Bridgeport, Connecticut—the Remington Arms U.M.C. Company's plant—manufacturing cartridges to be shipped to the battlefields of Europe.[18]

Compared with women's rates in other industries, the rates of pay in munition factories were high, but still far below those received by men in the same industry. The women worked long hours, often until as late as ten o'clock at night; while Connecticut's labor laws forbade work for women after 10 P.M., it fixed no starting hour in the morning. Consequently, when the rush of war orders required continuous work in the munitions plants, the companies simply forced the women on the night shift to stop work from 10 P.M. until midnight and then set them to work again.[19]

STRIKES FOR THE EIGHT-HOUR DAY: BRIDGEPORT

These conditions produced what the U.S. Bureau of Labor Studies called the "munitions strikes," and these strikes, in turn, overflowed into other Bridgeport industries.[20] During the spring and summer of 1915, headlines such as the following in the *Bridgeport Post* of August 22 appeared regularly in the Bridgeport papers:

500 EMPLOYEES OF BRYANT ELECTRIC CO. LEAVE PLANT
Strike Comes as Surprise to Factory Management—Police Prevent Disorder
GIRLS LEAVE WORK AT STAR SHIRT MFG. CO.
Several Large Concerns Grant Demands. Thousands of Employes Rejoice.

The strikes began in factories like Remington Arms and Lake Torpedo Boat, then filling orders for war-torn Europe. At first 125 women workers struck at the Remington plant, but they returned after the company quickly promised an eight-hour day with increased pay "to take effect at once." On July 23, 1915, the headline in the Bridgeport papers read: "125 Girls Win in Arms Plant." A month later, by simply threatening to strike, all the other workers at Remington Arms Company won an eight-hour day. The victory was all the more remarkable since Remington Arms and Ammunition Company was "a subsidiary of the Midvale Steel and Ordnance Company, on whose board of directors sat representatives of the Chase National Bank, the National City Bank of New York, International Nickel, Badwin Locomotive, the Guarantee Trust Company, and Midvale Steel, as well as Percy A. Rockefeller himself."[21]

The victory was also remarkable for the fact that it took place in a climate of charges by the press that the strike of the women workers and the threat of a strike by all other workers at Remington Arms and Ammunition were the work of German agents bent on disrupting Bridgeport's war production. Samuel Gompers added his voice to this chorus, and was widely quoted as stating that "officers of international unions had received money to pull off strikes in Bridgeport and elsewhere for ammunition factories." When he was criticized for aiding the giant munitions corporations, Gompers denied that these were his exact words. What he said was "that authentic information had come to me that efforts had been made to corrupt men for the purpose of having strikes inaugurated," and that the "corrupting influence has been conducted by agents of a foreign government. . ."[22] AFL Secretary-Treasurer Frank Morrison tried to heal the damage created by Gompers' words. He would not deny that "German influence might be behind the strikes in Bridgeport," but he stated that the "real trouble was a demand on the part of labor for better hours and more pay. There are 9,000 women working ten hours a day at ten cents an hour [at Remington] and they and the men are striking to better their conditions."[23]

Although thousands took part in strikes in Bridgeport during the summer of 1915, few were actually union members. Many were women production workers who had been denied membership in the craft unions (and continued to be excluded after the strikes ended in victory), but who walked off the jobs along with union male workers to fight for shorter hours and better pay.[24]

The strike at Bryant Electric Co., a division of Westinghouse, was launched by 500 women assemblers and a handful of men shortly after work began on the morning of August 20. The strikers paraded around the plant and other West End shops, and then marched downtown for a mass meeting, "presenting an imposing appearance as they passed through the center of the city." Meeting at Eagle's Hall, the Bryant workers elected a committee of two from each department (with equal representation for women) to present their demands to the company for an eight-hour day, overtime pay, and a readjustment of rates. The company's response was to shut the plant, charging "rioting" by the strikers. The company expected that the non-striking workers would now put pressure to have the strike called off. But the tactic failed; the remaining two-thirds of the work force joined the strike.[25]

The strike at Bryant-Westinghouse lasted two weeks. On September 1, the *Bridgeport Post* reported that the "1,500 employees of the Bryant Electric Co. will return to work. Practically all the demands of the strikers were met by the employers, who granted the eight hour day, time and half for overtime and double time Sunday, and agreed to readjust wages."

While some of the Bridgeport strikers were forced back to work without any change in working hours, most were successful in winning the eight-hour day. Indeed, after, a thorough investigation, the New York *World* reported that "a ten-hour center like Bridgeport was converted overnight into an eight-hour community, a result that ten years of agitation under normal conditions might not have accomplished."[26]*

Soon newspapers were predicting that Bridgeport was only the beginning, and that "war-order necessities may drive American industry to a universal eight-hour day." Indeed, from Bridgeport the eight-hour strikes spread throughout New England, as men and women munitions workers went out throughout Connecticut, Massachusetts, and Rhode Island. In the summer of 1915 the strikes swept across the whole Northeast, establishing the eight-hour day in plant after plant.[27]

STRIKES FOR THE EIGHT-HOUR DAY: PITTSBURGH

In the spring of 1916 the strike wave spread to the complex of firms controlled by Westinghouse in the East Pittsburgh area. On April 21, 1916, more than two thousand men and women working on munitions at Westinghouse Electric in East Pittsburgh walked out on strike under the leadership of the American Industrial Union, which had been established in 1914 to organize "workers in all industries in Alleghney County and the Pittsburgh District, without regard to age, creed, race, sex, or craft."[28] By the afternoon, six thousand of the eighteen thousand workers in the plant complex were out, including three hundred women. Three major plants—Westinghouse Electric, Air Brake, and Union Switch & Signal, all controlled by Westinghouse—produced shrapnel shells and airplane engines.

The following morning, men and women pickets formed a human chain around the plant gates, and only a few workers crossed the picket line. A parade of six hundred strikers, led by a "dish-pan drumcorps," marched to the town's police station to demand the release of two

---

*New York *World's* reporter interviewed several leading industrialists in Bridgeport who reported that they were satisfied with the results that followed adoption of the eight-hour day. D. H. Warner of the famous Bridgeport firm of corset-makers, told him: "we are producing in eight hours fully 95 per cent of the output we made in ten hours. Our girls report more promptly and keep more steadily at their work. The greatest difference is in the atmosphere of contentment in the factory. We would not go back to the old system if we could." (New York World reprinted in *Literary Digest,* Nov. 6, 1915, pp 997-7.)

arrested pickets. By evening, thirteen thousand workers, three thousand of them women, were on strike for higher wages and an eight-hour day.[29]

On the third day of the strike, the American Industrial Union held a mass meeting in Singer Hall, attended by two thousand workers. Anna Katherine Bell, a twenty-one-year-old Irishwoman and a three-year veteran at Westinghouse, spoke on behalf of the three thousand women strikers. A Pittsburgh paper gave some indication of the pressure she was under from both the company and her family, in conducting strike activity. "Anna Bell . . . of Braddock, leader of the 3,000 women strikers," it reported, "marched to the speakers' table, laid down a suitcase which she carried, and said she had lost her home, having been ordered out of it because she refused to return to work. She said she would not return to work until her followers won the strike."[30] She then went on to voice the strikers' demand for the eight-hour day at nine and a half hours' pay, plus a share in the company's wartime profits.*

The words of the strikers' song went:

> Come on you rounders
> We want you in the AIU
> All we want is an 8-hour day
> With 9 and one-half hours' pay
>
> Put a sign on your bonnet,
> With 8 hours on it
> And we won't care what the bosses say.
> When the strike is over
> We will roam in clover
> For we'll work 8 hours a day.
>
> What are you? What are you?
> We belong to the AIU.
> What for? 8 hours![31]

By the fourth day of the strike, over eighteen thousand workers were out at both Westinghouse Electric and Westinghouse Machine. A parade of fifteen hundred strikers marched from East Pittsburgh to Wilderming to convince eighteen hundred shellmakers not to return to work. The East Pittsburgh strikers invaded the building, broke up the company's meeting, and spoke to the shellmakers. The parade homeward was led by

---

*In this connection it is interesting to note that the *Literary Digest* reporting on the strike victories in Bridgeport, noted: "Some munition-manufacturers admit that their own profits are abnormal and that labor's demand for a larger share was only natural." (Sept. 12, 1915; p. 656.)

a mysterious "Girl in the Paper Mask," who held a newpaper over her face. Some women were apparently afraid (either of the company or their own families) to have their pictures appear in the newspapers.[32]

"While picketing the Air Brake plant," one account went, "Louisa Johnbusky, a 35-year-old, 195-pound female striker, paraded through the picket line waving a revolver and called workmen leaving the plant 'scabs.' Upon refusing to pay a $10 fine, she was jailed."[33] Almost spontaneously, new women took the lead when others were arrested. One Saturday, for example, Anna Bell was arrested after speaking at an open-air rally and charged with disorderly conduct. In another part of the town, Anna Goldenberg was arrested for holding a mass meeting without a strike permit. But others took their places until they were bailed out, after which they spoke before a rally of four thousand workers from all four Westinghouse plants.[34]

Frightened by the militancy of the strikers and the growth of the AIU, the AFL's International Association of Machinists (IAM), hitherto indifferent to the need of organizing women and immigrant production workers, the backbone of the workforce at Westinghouse, sent in sixteen organizers—including two women, Mary Schully and Mary Kules—and the two organizations cooperated in conducting the strike. They won the eight-hour day. On May 1 the IAM and AIU jointly called for a regionwide general strike.[35]

On May 1, 1916, between two thousand and five thousand strikers marched through Bradddock and Rankin, hoping to bring the steelworkers at Edgar Thomson and other mills of United States Steel out on strike. But United States Steel closed its mills and armed its private police and, in anticipation of a sympathy strike, granted its workers a 25 percent wage increase.[36]

When the strikers reached the Edgar Thomson mill—some newspapers reported that as many as twenty thousand of them surrounded the mill—they were met by a thousand of company guards. Wave after wave of men and women stormed the mill, only to be beaten back and shot at by the company guards. "Four Girls Lead Frenzied Mob of Strikers in Fatal Charge Against the Company," screamed the headlines in the Pittsburgh papers. Three strikers were killed and at least three dozen wounded. Mrs. Mary Williams, the wife of a striker, was shot in the back, and Mrs. Anna Hitchin, a striker, was also wounded. The Pittsburgh papers blamed the foreign-born workers for the riot but emphasized, "Their women folk backed them up. When the men began to fall, the women rushed to the front and dragged the men away."[37]

Governor Martin Brumbaugh sent a thousand National Guardsmen to guarantee "labor peace," and not surprisingly, the troops were quartered in the Westinghouse Electric plant. From then on, the company refused to negotiate with the strikers' mediation committee. President E. M. Herr ordered all the strikers back to work by May 9, threatening that workers would lose their jobs and pensions. Gradually, the strikers drifted back to the plants, and on May 16 the strike was officially ended.

Twenty-three strike leaders were arrested and charged with inciting to riot and accessory to murder. Four women leaders—Anna Bell, Anna Goldenberg, Bridget Kenny, and Patsy Delmar—were among those arrested. Eventually, all but one of the women were acquitted. Anna Goldenberg was found guilty of inciting to riot and spent a year in Blawnox, the Allegheny County workhouse.[38] After investigating the imprisonment of Goldenberg and several of the men strike leaders, Theresa Malkiel wrote from Pittsburgh:

> At the time of the strike a secret capitalist society was formed in Pittsburgh with a fund of $75,000,000 contributed for the purpose and with the sole aim of fighting the movement for an eight-hour day to the finish. That the men at the head of it have not only the municipal but also the judicial power of the county under their control is evident from the fact that the accused were hurriedly tried and sentenced without being given a chance to work up the case for the defense.[39]

Although the 1916 strike was defeated, it marked another high point of women workers' militancy and of solidarity between men and women workers.* The "women strikes" in the garment trades of 1909-1910 in New York, Philadelphia, Cleveland, and Chicago had demonstrated that women were fully capable of labor organization. Other strikes had demonstrated their capacity to ignite and keep aflame the impulses of revolt in a largely male work force. Immigrant women had played leading roles in the celebrated struggles of Lawrence, Little Falls, and Paterson, which, like many other strikes of the period, culminating in the 1916 walkout at Westinghouse, had revealed an impressive level of cooperation between male and female workers.

BATTLING THE HIGH COST OF LIVING

The soaring cost of living brought to the surface new examples of women's militancy. After the outbreak of the war in Europe in 1914, prices in the United States skyrocketed and continued to do so

*As the following report in the *Pittsburgh Post* of May 5, 1916 indicates, this militancy spread to other women workers in the city: "Officials of the McKinney Manufacturing Company . . . yesterday posted notices of a reward of $50 for the arrest and conviction of girl strikers who are alleged to have attacked girls leaving the plant Tuesday evening, and to have ducked one in a watering trough in Chartiers avenue. A strike was declared at the McKinney plant Tuesday morning and the girls employed in the plant walked out. Those who were attacked stayed at work."

throughout the conflict. Within just two months—January and February, 1917—the price of potatoes rose 100 percent; onions, 366 percent; cabbages, 212 percent; and beans, 100 percent. "A dollar is now worth only 12 or 15 cents of its normal value as far as food-purchasing value is concerned," declared Meyer London, Socialist congressman from New York City's East Side at the end of February, 1917.

Government orders to dilute wheat flour with cornmeal added fuel to the fire of discontent. Food riots flared. The lead story on the front page of the *New York Times* of February 21, 1917 began:

> Two thousand women on the East Side—some estimates ran as high as 10,000—fought like mad people to get into the Forward Hall, down on East Broadway last night, where a meeting had been called to protest against the high prices of food. The thousand that got into the hall fought for elbow room to shout denunciations of "capitaliam" which they blamed for having so little to eat in the greatest, richest city in the world. There were a few men in the shrieking, yelling crowd.

The meeting climaxed a day of tremendous demonstrations. A report in the *Literary Digest* went:

> Almost as if by premeditated signal, the women of various tenement districts of New York and Brooklyn began a campaign of riotous protest against the high price of food in the local markets. They upset the push-carts and barrows of the food-peddlers, and in some cases threw kerosene on the stock. They improvised boycotts and drove away intending purchasers. Hundreds of women of the East Side marched to the City Hall, shouting, "Give us food, Mr. Mayor!" "Our children are starving!" "Feed our children!" And later a mass-meeting adopted resolutions calling upon the Government for relief.

The resolutions, in the form of an appeal to President Wilson, were drawn up by a women's committee of members of the ILGWU and housewives. They read:

> We, housewives of the city of New York, working women, mothers and wives of workmen, desire to call your attention, Mr. President, to the fact that in the midst of plenty, we and our families are facing starvation.
>
> The rise in the cost of living has been so great and uncalled for that even now we are compelled to deny ourselves and our children the necessities of life.
>
> We pay for our needs out of our wages and out of the wages of our husbands and the American standard of living cannot be maintained when potatoes are 7 cents a pound, bread 6 cents, cabbage 20 cents, onions 18 cents, and so forth.
>
> We call on you, Mr. President, in this crisis that we are facing to recommend to Congress or other authority measures for relief.[40]

In Philadelphia, on February 21, troops were called out to break up a march of the female relatives of the strikers at the Franklin Sugar Refining Company, who were out for higher wages in the face of rising prices. "As they marched through the street," wrote a reporter, "the women cried that they were starving. The women were led to the refinery by Mrs. Florence Shadle, 32 years old, who carried a baby in her arms, as she shouted encouragement to her followers."[41] "Most of the women in the riot were of foreign birth," commented the *New York Times*, as though that excused calling out the troops. But women born in the United States joined them, and together they attacked provision stores and pushcart peddlers. On February 22 all food stores were barricaded and put under police guard, and martial law was declared in the Philadelphia food shopping district. One woman was killed and nine others wounded before the troops succeeded in breaking the women's occupation of the city's marketplace.[42]

DEVELOPMENTS IN SEATTLE

On the West Coast, too, workingwomen were on the march, and in Seattle, they received a good deal of encouragement and assistance from the *Union Record*, official organ of the Central Labor Council. Unfortunately, the newspaper did not always take an enlightened attitude toward workingwomen. In 1909, for example, it showed its ignorance of the history of women workers and a racist attitude towards Orientals when, in the course of urging enactment of an eight-hour law, it said:

> Twenty years ago, the mothers of the following generation were seldom employed in the stores and factories, wearing out their strength and losing the vitality which should be given in nourishing the unborn; they did not have to stand twelve or fourteen hours a day in a laundry feeding a machine which is continually calling for "more," "more"; they did not have to stand behind a counter trying to wear a smile and have a pleasant word for those who are "just looking around"; they did not have to chase from table to table all day long, taking orders from men in all conditions, drunk or sober, and then being insulted because the orders were not promptly forthcoming or were shy in some particular; they did not have to go into the canning factories and rub elbows with all classes of degenerates from foreign lands, especially the Jap and the Chinaman. No, our mothers and grandmothers had none of these things to contend with, and it was not necessary to grant them a few hours for rest and recreation. Not until the influx of the foreigner to our shores, with their old world traditions of women as beasts of burden, and the greed for gold ever dominant in the heart of men, was woman so degraded that it became necessary for her to seek employment to aid in the maintenance of the family.

The *Union Record* then voiced a typical AFL attitude: "Women at the mouth of the mine cheapened the miners" wages; women in all vocations of life have tended to bring down the wages received, and hence the lower the wages the more necessary it became for women to toil, for the burden became too heavy for men." In short, woman was "the new Chinaman of the working class," threatening the wage standards of men by her presence.[43]

Later, however, the *Union Record* came to understand that nothing could be gained by calling for the exclusion of women from the trades and industries, as well as from the labor unions.* On the contrary, it berated those AFL unions that excluded women. On December 16, 1916, it reprinted the following advertisement from the official organ of the Texas Federation of Labor:

> Refused a Union Shop Card on account of being a woman.
> I am union in principle, want to work as a union barber, and want to do work for union people, but am denied the privilege because—on account of my sex—I cannot get a Union Shop Card.
> All the work in my shop necessary to the installation of fixtures was done by union labor. I respectfully solicit a share of your patronage, assuring your courteous treatment and first-class service.

After criticizing the Texas Federation for being willing to accept the advertisement (but unwilling to criticize the union for its exclusionary policy toward women), the *Union Record* editorialized:

> Pressure of some kind ought to be brought to bear on an international which discriminates so narrowly and will not allow the various locals affiliated to receive efficient members into their union because of their sex. Women are in the industrial field to stay, and just as other exclusive large unions reasoned long ago—"It is better to have a strong force with us than to array them against us." If the women are not permitted to cooperate with the men of their craft, they will be compelled to operate against them.[44]

The *Union Record* did not leave it at that. It launched a campaign to convince Seattle's male workers that women worked because of necessity and that it would be a waste of time and energy to attempt to eliminate them from American industrial life. "Women Must Work Not by Choice But Compulsion," was the heading of a column that appeared regularly in the publication in 1916 and early in 1917. A typical entry went: "Thirty-five percent of the wives and mothers of working men are

---

*When the Seattle Central Labor Council, responding to a suggestion of the local Socialist Party, voted to set aside May 31, 1914, as a Memorial Day for martyrs of the cause of labor, "Mother" Mary Jones, the noted labor organizer and agitator, was invited to head the parade, and deliver the main address at labor's first Memorial Day. (*See* Seattle *Post-Intelligencer*, May 30-June 1, 1914.)

forced to work to keep the wolf from the door."[45] Another regular feature dealt with the contributions made by women to the labor movement.

One entry in the *Union Record* column was headed "Woman Surpasses Man as Militant Striker." The subhead read "Young Waitress Holds Record for Picketing Arrests." The story was about Madge Keith, a member of the Waitresses' Union of St. Louis, who established "the record for the heinous crime of picketing, for she was arrested 12 times in two weeks while doing picket duty in front of Robinson's Restaurant, being discharged each time. She has, altogether, been arrested 22 times for picketing the same restaurant, thereby causing great concern to the police of the city, who seem to be much afraid of the young waitress' picketing activities."[46] The *Union Record* pointed out that there were "Miss Keiths" in their own city, for during the shingle weavers' strike,* it was the women who were the most active, militant pickets and the ones most often arrested. "The women have the men beat two to one doing picket duty. They succeed in getting the men out as fast as the scab herders bring them in."[47]

Prodded by the *Union Record,* Seattle's Central Labor Council established a female auxiliary called the "Union Card and Label League of Seattle," headed by Mrs. George T. McNamara, wife of the editor of the *Union Record.* Among its duties were "to secure equal pay for equal work regardless of sex, and political equality for women" and to assist in the unionizing of women workers. The league established a number of women's auxiliaries of Seattle unions and "assisted many unions in their strikes for better conditions and wages." It also popularized the union label, especially for unions with women members, and was credited with being "an effective factor in the settlement of many labor troubles."[48]

On June 10, 1916, a step was taken in Seattle for the establishment of the second citywide federation of women workers in American history.** Five organizations were represented at the founding conference. Carpenters' Auxiliary, Federal Labor Union, Seattle Union Card and Labor League, United Garment Workers, and Waitress' Local 240. A committee was appointed to call on every union in Seattle that had women in its ranks to inform the leadership about the purpose of the proposed federation and to secure representation from its ranks. The literature distributed by the committee explained that the new organization aimed:

*Shingle weavers were mill workers who manned the saw cutting the lumber into shingles.
**In June, 1835 the working women of Philadelphia formed the Female Improvement Society for the City and County of Philadelphia—the first citywide federation of workingwomen that embraced women from several trades. Committees were chosen from each trade to draw up wage scales. (*See* Philip S. Foner, *Women and the American Labor Movement: From Colonial Times to the Eve of World War I,* New York, 1979, pp. 44-45.)

to do for women of Seattle what the Central Labor Council of Seattle and Vicinity and the Washington State Federation of Labor have done for the men's organizations. Realizing that the spread of unionism among women must come from themselves, we have banded ourselves together for the purpose of strengthening the various organizations already in existence, organizing the unorganized women workers and the wives of union men who have not affiliated with the auxiliaries of the crafts of which their husbands are members. We propose also to take up civic and legislative work that pertains to the further advantage of union women.[49]

The response was gratifying, and in October, 1916, the Federation of Union Women and Auxiliaries was established. It was to be composed of delegates from any of the "trades union women's organizations, women's auxiliaries affiliated with trades unions, and the Seattle Union Card and Label League."

> The object of the organization shall be to increase the membership of all trades union organizations or trades union auxiliaries.
>
> To devise ways and means to organize the unorganized women workers into craft unions of their own, or assist them to affiliate with those already established.
>
> To promote the welfare of union women, financially or physically as the occasion may arise.[50]

FOR A NATIONAL EIGHT-HOUR DAY

One of the federation's first activities was to link up with the movement of women in the East for a national eight-hour day. At the Middle Atlantic State Eight-Hour Conference of the National Women's Trade Union League, held in December, 1916, resolutions demanding legislative action on an interstate basis to secure an eight-hour day provoked intense discussion. "Trade union women forgot their usual timidity and unaccustomedness to public expression," wrote an observer, "and argued the issue so warmly the chairman had to resort to rigorous restrictions to keep the debate from extending beyond the hour marked for adjournment." Delegates were instructed to urge their organizations to introduce a bill for an eight-hour day into their respective state legislatures "so as to prevent interstate competition, and to urge the women not already organized to organize themselves into trade unions for the purpose of demanding an eight-hour day through collective bargaining as well as through legislation."[51]

The Seattle Federation of Union Women and Auxiliaries joined the crusade for the shorter working day, but it proposed that the ultimate objective should be a four-hour day. The proposal was picked up by Melinda Scott, president of the New York Women's Trade Union League, who recommended that "the league work to secure a reduction of the workday hours from ten to eight, then to six, and then to four hours. Working only four hours would give every one a chance for employment."[52]

Thus, on the eve of America's entrance into the First World War, women workers were involved in militant struggles and organizational activities—activities that foreshadowed the many battles women were to wage during the war years and in the postwar wave of industrial unrest.

CHAPTER 12

Black Workers on the Eve of America's Entrance into World War I

In 1914 Black labor was overwhelmingly concentrated in agriculture and personal and domestic service. According to the census of 1910, more than half of the 5,192,535 Negroes listed as gainfully employed—2,881,454—were engaged in agricultural pursuits. Another fourth—1,357,598—were employed in domestic and personal services. No other group in the American population showed such a vast preponderance of its workers in the two lowest paid occupations. While over 53 percent of all women earned their living as laborers on the land or in the home, a much larger percentage held true for black women. Of 2,013,981 black women workers in 1910, 1,904,494 earned their livelihood in these occupations. Black women comprised only 16,835 of the 1,366,959 women in manufacturing and mechanical industries.[1]*

STATUS OF BLACK LABOR IN 1914

The vast majority of the Black people still lived in the South and were still the chief cultivators of the South's staple crops. Enmeshed in a farm tenantry and sharecropping system that consigned them to a life of tilling the soil under conditions almost as restrictive and pernicious as chattel slavery, they lived in rural isolation and a state of perpetual indebtedness. The lien laws required the tenant or sharecropper to liquidate his debts before he could escape from his share-tenant arrangement, hence he was bound to the soil and denied any opportunity for industrial training.[2]

When the Industrial Revolution swept through the South after 1880,

*The majority of this group labored as unskilled or semi-skilled workers in tobacco and cigar-making plants.

jobs in the new textile, iron, and steel factories fell to the poor whites. The black man's share of the South's industrial development was limited to the dirty, disagreeable tasks of unskilled labor. Of course there were black miners, especially in Alabama, where 46.2 percent of the coal miners in 1889 were Afro-Americans; but many of them worked under the contract lease system. In January, 1888, the State of Alabama gave an exclusive contract to the Tennessee Coal, Iron and Railroad Company, the chief coal operator in the state, on condition that the company use all convicts who were able to work. Blacks were arrested for trivial reasons or for no reason at all and sentenced to work out their penalty in the mines. The contract gave the company cheap labor—it compensated the state at a rate ranging from $9.00 to $18.00 a month per convict, depending on his classification—and at the same time saved the state money. In other Southern states, especially Georgia, the convict-lease system supplied cheap black labor to companies building railroads or cutting timber.[3]

The blacks who gravitated in increasing numbers to Southern cities moved into personal and domestic service, traditionally regarded as the province of the Afro-American. They found employment in urban districts throughout the South as waiters, saloonkeepers, bartenders, janitors, bellhops, barbers, laundresses, and housekeepers. The few who ventured North also found domestic work to be one of the few occupations open to the Afro-American, although there the black worker had to compete with foreign immigrants even for menial positions.[4]

A small but growing segment of the black working force broke out of the traditional pattern of agricultural and domestic employment and gained entrance to manufacturing, mechanical, trade, transportation, and other industrial pursuits. From 1890 to 1910 there was a sizable increase of black workers in trade and transportation occupations. In 1890 the number of blacks engaged in those two fields was 145,717; by 1910 the total had more than doubled.[5]

Almost one-third of the black workers in trade and transportation were railroad workers. The large increase in black railroad workers resulted from the expanding network of railroad construction in the South. Companies engaged in these operations, always in need of a large labor force, looked upon the Afro-American as an important source for cheap labor for rough, heavy work. Only 4.1 percent of the blacks in railroad work were classified as skilled employees; the vast majority were used in repairing and maintaining the road beds. Blacks who held skilled or responsible jobs on the railroads in the South were found primarily in such positions as locomotive engineers, firemen, brakemen, switchmen, and yard foremen. Most blacks in railroad jobs in the North held positions in the Pullman Service as waiters or porters. As we have seen in a previous volume, the rise of the Railroad Brotherhoods, with their bitter animosity toward the Afro-American, caused a decrease in the number of blacks in skilled jobs after 1890.* The determined assault of the Brotherhoods against the skilled black worker had by the outbreak of World War I resulted in his exclusion from almost all responsible positions on the railroads.[6]

The second largest group in trade and transportation were the black teamsters, draymen, hackmen, and chauffeurs, who more than doubled in number between 1890 and 1910. In the South nearly 100,000 blacks were employed in these positions, indicative of the region's custom of acknowledging certain low-level jobs as "Negro work." The scattered black workmen who held jobs of this nature in the North and West were able to obtain employment primarily because whites in those sections of the country preferred the more remunerative factory work.

The remainder of the Afro-Americans in trade and transportation held a wide variety of subordinate positions, such as porters, helpers, longshoremen, hostlers, clerks, copyists, and small merchants. The number of Afro-Americans in trade or business was negligible. Race prejudice on the part of white employer and workers alike restricted all but the most gifted and fortunate black salesmen, bookkeepers, typists and clerks to the black business world.

Some Afro-Americans managed to gain clerical positions in federal and state governments by passing competitive examinations. But the pattern of segregation on the state level limited the number, and during the first year of Woodrow Wilson's administration, with the institution of segregated toilets, lunchroom facilities, and working areas in a number of federal departments, federal employment also became constricted for blacks.[7]

The growing number of blacks in manufacturing and mechanical jobs between 1890 and 1910 indicated an industrial advance of the black worker. In 1910 there were more than 500,000 blacks in skilled and unskilled industrial jobs throughout the nation, a 165.1 percent increase in black industrial workers over the preceding twenty-year period.

The heaviest concentration of blacks in industry was in Southern lumber and mining establishments. In lumber manufacturing alone, rapid expansion saw the number of black workers increase fivefold from 1890 to 1910. The 122,216 Afro-Americans at work in lumbering in 1910 represented almost one-fifth of all black workers in industry. Black

*See Philip S. Foner, *History of the Labor Movement in the United States*, vol. 3, New York, 1964, pp. 238–40; and Philip S. Foner, *Organized Labor and the Black Worker, 1619–1981*, New York, 1982, pp. 102–08.

miners were to be found predominantly in the Deep South, and the central Appalachian coal fields of West Virginia, Kentucky, and Virginia, but a growing number gained employment around the turn of the century in such Northern states as Ohio, Indiana, Illinois, and Iowa. Although he first gained admittance to the Northern mines as a strike-breaker, the Afro-American was soon an established quantity in the industry. Lumbering and mining involved hard, distasteful, and dangerous work at long hours, and low wages, a fact that no doubt contributed to the Afro-American's substantial employment in these industries.[8]

Black workers in the iron and steel industry grew from 8,371 in 1890 to 36,646 in 1910, an increase of 325 percent. Nearly all of the increase took place in the iron and steel mills of the South, where the black workman was a common sight, toiling at rugged, low-paying, unskilled tasks. North of the Mason–Dixon line, few blacks were found in iron and steel work. Blacks first entered the Pittsburgh steel mills during a puddler's strike in 1875. In 1910 they numbered 820 workers and comprised only 2.2 percent of all steel workers.[9] Joseph Frazier Wall notes in his definitive biography of Andrew Carnegie that the iron and steel multimillionaire "made generous contributions to Hampton and Tuskegee Institutes," and "never entirely lost interest in the Blacks." However, there were few blacks in Carnegie's plants—as few as a dozen in the Carnegie steel works in Duquesne prior to 1916[10]—because, Wall explains, "almost none came North to work in his steel mills or mines." Yet prior to World War I the Carnegie Company regularly sent agents to recruit immigrants in Europe for work in its mills. It dispatched no recruiters South for black workers to work in the Carnegie mills. The contradiction between Carnegie's interest in industrial education for blacks and his preference for foreign labor in his mills puzzled the *Christian Recorder,* official organ of the African Methodist Episcoplal Church, which could only surmise that Carnegie, "himself a foreigner, was in natural sympathy with that element and gave them preference."[11]

The preference for white immigrant labor in unskilled and semi-skilled capacities extended throughout Northern industry. Most immigrants from Southeastern Europe arrived as unskilled peasants, so it could hardly be argued that they were more experienced as industrial workers than Afro-Americans. But they obtained work when blacks could not. Ironically, a few light-skinned Negroes did manage to get work in the basic industries by posing as foreigners and affecting an Italian or Slavic accent.[12]

Only Cyrus McCormick's harvester plant in Chicago was willing to integrate blacks into its labor force. Robert Ozanne points out in his study of International Harvester's labor policies, however, that its black workers "were carefully selected so that the first Negroes working in any department were "superior both in qualifications and personality" to the white workers in the department."[13] And this was hailed as equality for black workers!

Virtually the only means by which blacks could challenge the monopoly of foreign immigrants in the developing mass-production industries, even as unskilled workers, was by strikebreaking. Some were able to enter the iron and steel and meat-packing industries by this route.

Blacks registered few gains in such important light manufacturing pursuits as the garment, tobacco and textile industries. They did not obtain widespread employment in the textile mills despite the fact that textile manufacturing in the South was undergoing its greatest advances. For one thing, white mill employees flatly refused to work alongside Negroes. A strike at the Fulton Bag and Cotton Mill in Atlanta in 1897 was described by the Atlanta *Constitution* as a "spontaneous protest against the employment of twenty Negro women spinners, who were to work along with white women." The 1,400 strikers returned to work only after the manager agreed to the "discharge of all Negroes employed by the company except janitors and scrubbers." Another barrier was the mythology that black workers did not measure up to conditions in the textile mills. "A notion is abroad in the South," wrote James Dowd in the *Forum* of June, 1898, "that the Negro could not work in a cotton mill, because the hum of the looms would put him to sleep." However, a Southern industrialist gave a more likely explanation: "It is a question of who will do the dirty work. In this country the white man won't. The Negro must." Then again, the legal system of white supremacy extended into the factory. South Carolina laws forbade Negroes and whites to work together in the same room in a textile factory and to use the same pay windows, or the same toilet and drinking facilities, or even "the same door of entrance and exit at the same time . . . or the same stairway or windows at the same time." It was obviously cheaper to operate a textile factory with poor whites, including white child labor, than with blacks and whites on the basis required by Jim Crow legislation. Black workers rebuffed by the cotton mills were somewhat more successful in finding employment in cottonseed-oil plants, fertilizer factories, brick-and-tile-making plants, bakeries, and other small industries in the South.[14]

DECLINE OF THE BLACK ARTISAN IN THE SOUTH

Although the black worker was increasingly employed in the heavy industries between 1890 and 1914, the Afro-American artisan and mechanic class experienced no improvement in employment opportunities. Instead, the skilled black craftsman declined in importance, even in the South. The black poet and novelist James Weldon Johnson, in his autobiography, recalls black artisans in Jacksonville and elsewhere in the South during the 1880's:

> All the more interesting things that came under my observation were being done by colored men. They drove the horse and mule teams, they built the houses, they laid the bricks, they painted the buildings and fences, they loaded and unloaded the ships. When I was a child, I did not know that there existed such a thing as a white carpenter or bricklayer or plasterer or tinner. The thought that the white men might be able to load and unload the heavy drays of the big ships was too far removed from everyday life to enter my mind.[15]

By the mid-1890's, however, the Afro-American's advancement in the trades of the South was already being seriously checked. By 1899 the Virginia Commissioner of Labor reported that there were "fewer skilled Negro laborers in the state than before the Civil War." Substantially the same picture emerged from reports in other Southern states.

New machine processes were making the skills of many black craftsmen superfluous, just as they were the skills of white mechanics. Then too, the black craftsman, often poorly trained, found it difficult to meet the standards of workmanship set by his white competitors even in the new industrial South. Industrial schools like Tuskegee and Hampton did little to improve the efficiency of the black skilled laboring force. In 1910 there were 119 schools in the country offering some type of industrial training for blacks. Dr. W. E. B. DuBois found that, as a general rule, the caliber of industrial training in them was abysmally low. "Negro youths," he protested, "are being taught the technique of a rapidly disappearing age of handicraft." He concluded that the primitive instruction given Afro-Americans in such institutions perpetuated the black's status as an inferior craftsman and left him completely unequipped to gain a solid footing in the industrial life of the country.[16]

The trouble was that even blacks as good as or better than white workers had little chance to earn a living as skilled artisans. The Reverend C. S. Smith, a critic of Booker T. Washington,* wrote in 1899:

> How can the multiplication of Negro mechanics help to solve the so-called race problem, when those who are already skilled cannot obtain employment? In this city, to my personal knowledge, there are a score or more of skilled Negro mechanics who are subject to enforced idleness by reason of the

*For an analysis of the industrial philosophy of Booker T. Washington and a criticism of this viewpoint, by W. E. B. DuBois, see Foner, History of the Labor Movement 2: 347-50, and Foner, Organized Labor and the Black Worker. pp. 79-85.

colorphobia which dominates the trade-unions. Those who are disposed to advance the Negro's best interests can render him invaluable services by demanding, in tones of thunder loud and long, that the trade-unions shall cease to draw the color line, and that fitness and character shall be the only passport to their fellowship. When this barrier shall have been removed, the time for the multiplication of Negro mechanics, on anything like a large scale, will have become opportune, but not until then.[17]

The Reverend Smith's identification of trade-union exclusion of blacks as a key factor in the deteriorating condition of the black artisan was accurate. In the South, trade-union opposition to the black crafts-man was the spearhead of a general drive by white workingmen to oust blacks from skilled positions they had held since slavery. Beginning in the 1890's, white workers steadily eliminated black labor from jobs in the shipping, railroad, and building industries in the older Southern seaboard cities. The jobs of electricians, plumbers, gasfitters and steam-fitters, railroad engineers and firemen, stationary engineers, cranemen, hoistmen, and machinists and hundreds of other skilled and semi-skilled occupations were labeled "for whites only." A severe blow was dealt to the Negro in the building trades. Black electricians, plumbers, pipefit-ters, and carpenters had constituted a fair percentage of those crafts at the turn of the century. A generation later, black building-trades work had become "almost marginal," and by 1950 blacks accounted for 1 percent of the electricians and 3.2 percent of the carpenters. The figures on black participation in apprenticeship programs were even bleaker: 1 percent for plumbers and pipefitters, and 6 percent for carpenters. In Atlanta the proportion of black carpenters decreased from 36.3 percent in 1890 to 2.5 percent in 1920.

By 1898 John Stephens Durham, a black authority on the Negro working class, was describing how, "as a result of the old guild idea of exclusiveness" in many important crafts and industries in the South, the Negro was being restricted to the lowest menial jobs. Writing in 1936, George Sinclair Mitchell observed that "the Southern trade unionism of the last thirty-odd years has been in good measure a protective device for the march of white artisans in places held by Negroes." The white worker and his trade union displaced black labor on street railways, in firemen's jobs on railroads, in the jobs of switchmen and shopworkers, in construction work shipbuilding, and in hotel service and barbering. Mitchell wrote that the "typical city central labor body of Mobile or Savannah or Columbus or New Orleans or Richmond was a delegate meeting of white men drawn from white locals, jealous of every skilled place held by Negroes." Blacks who had spent years acquiring the skill needed for craftsmen's work were denied membership in white unions, which had signed closed-shop or unionshop agreements with employers, and were forced into menial service at low wages.[18]

The few blacks in the cotton mills were excluded from the AFL's United Textile Workers and were left out as well of that organization's limited schemes to advance the interests of workers in the industry. In the tobacco factories of Virginia and North Carolina, where the machine jobs were reserved for white workers and the blacks were confined to the least desirable and most unhealthy jobs, the Tobacco Workers' International Union, affiliated to the AFL, scarely reached the blacks in its feeble efforts to organize the industry. In November, 1903, the Rucker and Witten Tobacco Company of Martinsville, Virginia, eager to obtain the union label, asked the Tobacco Workers' International Union to organize its plant. The offer was rejected on the ground that "nine-tenths of the labor employed is negroes, and this class cannot be successfully organized into a union."[19]

EXCLUSION OF BLACKS FROM NORTHERN INDUSTRY

In his 1898 inquiry, Durham found the effects of the unions' exclusion policy even "more manifest" in the North. His own city, Philadelphia, offered a convincing illustration. By the 1850's blacks had been pushed out of the skilled trades they had once dominated by German immigrants and out of unskilled work by the Irish. During the Civil War, with increased demands for labor, job opportunities for blacks picked up, but they declined again in the postwar years. On July 12, 1888, the *Christian Recorder*, published in Philadelphia, lamented:

> Competency behind a black face, everything else being equal to the best, weighs very little when applying for a position in Wanamaker's store, or Sharpless's or Strawbridge & Clothier's, or on the Philadelphia streetcar lines, or even on the bricklayer's scaffold. Our chances are not equal. Color is too often pitted against color, rather than competency compared with competency.

Ten years later, Durham observed that "today one may safely declare that all the trades . . . are closed against the colored workman," and for this he blamed both the employers and the trade unions.

In his monumental study of the Philadelphia Negro, published in 1899, DuBois summed up the job situation for blacks:

> No matter how well trained a Negro may be, or how fitted for work of any kind, he cannot in the course of competition hope to be much more than a menial servant. . . .
> He cannot become a mechanic except for small transient jobs, and he cannot join a trades union.

A Negro woman has but three careers open to her in this city, domestic service, sewing, or married life.

When the Armstrong Association began in 1908 as a social experiment dedicated to the welfare of the black citizens of Philadelphia, it discovered that the situation described by Du Bois had not changed in the slightest. Blacks were still fixed in domestic service and as common laborers in trade and transportation. They were still unable to enter factory work in any numbers. They still could not join the city's unions. The Philadelphia *Public Ledger* of April 13, 1913, reported:

The negroes in this section are practically shut out from all the skilled industries. The department stores may draw attention to the underpaid shop girl, but the few colored women who find employment in them receive less pay than the sales people. The colored waitress receives a child's pay. The other opportunities open to negroes in big stores are limited to portering and operating elevators. The great railway sytems, too, discriminate against the negro, and here he is limited, no matter how high a degree of efficiency he may attain, to the menial and poorly paid tasks. Our street railways, with their thousands of workmen in the semi-skilled trades, completely bar the colored man. He is excluded from practically all the great industrial plants. This exclusion is especially striking in one great shop that at this minute employs more than 19,000 mendaily, but carefully avoids the negro. In brief, the negro is denied the opoortunity to earn an honest living in most of the big industries and commercial enterprises of this city.[20]

What was true of Philadelphia was true of much of the State of Pennsylvania. In the entire state, a study revealed in 1911, fewer than 200 blacks boasted skilled union status. And what was true of Pennsylvania was true of the entire North and West. Studies made of the Afro-American in St. Louis, Chicago, New York, Cleveland, San Francisco, and Portland, Oregon, reveal the futility of efforts to breach the barrier of employer and trade-union hostility.[21] Black workers were generally excluded from the trades and played no active part in the industrial life of those cities. "Manufacturers were not reconciled to hiring them; white workers were not reconciled to working with them," a study of the status of the black workers in Ohio concluded. There were few black members of the unions that dominated the trades of that state on the eve of World War. I.

The restrictive membership policy of the trade unions in the North adversely affected immigrant and woman workers as well as Afro-Americans, but they hit the black artisan the hardest because he had to combat racism as well as the union's practice of trying to limit the number of workers in the trades. In some Northern industrial districts unions were less restrictive to foreign-born whites, but the pattern of union discrimination against blacks was followed in every city. Little wonder that the annual earnings of black workers in 1910 were just about one-third the earnings of white workers. Or that W.E.B. Du Bois could write sadly in 1913: "The net result of all this has been to convince the American Negro that his greatest enemy is not the employer who robs him, but his fellow white workingman."[22]

IMPACT OF RACISM

On the eve of the outbreak of World War I in 1914 the black wage-earner had still to claim a place in America's developing industrial society. The millions of workers who toiled in the mines, packing houses, steel works, manufacturing plants, and transportation industries represented a bewildering variety of races and nationalities from the far corners of the globe. But it was rare to see among them one of those whose ancestors first arrived in Virginia in 1619. Rarer still was a black face in the ranks of the nation's working elite, the trade unionists. The total black membership in the AFL at that time is impossible to determine accurately, but a generous estimate would put it at about 55,000, only 3.6 percent of the 1,526,000 members of the federation.

Racism was still the main reason for the Afro-American's economic stagnation. Black leaders insisted that fifty years of freedom had brought scant improvement in the black man's lot, and they despaired of the future. William L. Bulkley, one of the founders of the National Urban League, declared that "there seems to be a purpose to restrict the Negroes within the limits of unskilled labor, to reduce them to a state which, while not nineteenth-century slavery, many be twentieth-century peonage." A black minister stated forlornly: "The young colored men and girls who are graduating from the high schools, the normal schools, and the colleges don't want to be waiting maids and porters or elevator operators, and yet this is about the highest they can hope for in this country."[23]

In July, 1911, Ida Wells-Barnett, a militant black woman, wrote that the key problem facing the black worker, skilled and unskilled, was "the problem of unemployment. To him, especially, it comes with crushing force, for whatever obstacles handicap other working classes, no others of them suffer from the barrier of color. With all the others the question when seeking work is, What and how much work can you do? With him the primary question is, Have you Negro blood in your veins?" She continued:

> The black man who has a trade at his fingers' ends finds all forces combined to prevent him from making a living thereby. First, the employer tells him that he has no prejudice against color, but that his employees will

object and make his business suffer. If per chance the Negro gets by, is given a chance to make good, the employees in the office, factory and workshop combine to injure his work and to make his life miserable for him. The unskilled laborer, who has little of such competition is a shade better off, because his work is usually done alone, but even there he finds that the neighbors of his employer have white servants and that neighbors and white servants look askance at a man who prefers Negro help.[24]

Just when the future seemed to hold out little hope of improvement in the status of the black worker, an important milestone occurred in Afro-American industrial history. The great migration got under way in 1915, and blacks began to leave the South by the hundreds of thousands for the job opportunities and freer life available in the North and West.

CAUSES OF THE "GREAT MIGRATION"

As we have seen, when the European war erupted in the summer of 1914, the flow of immigrants to the United States was greatly curtailed, depriving American industries of their traditional supply of new laborers. Northern railroad and manufacturing firms then turned to the blacks of the South as potential workers to fill the unskilled jobs so necessary to their continued growth and their enormous profits arising from the sales of manufactured goods to the warring nations.

Just prior to America's entry into World War I a series of economic hardships and natural disasters struck much of the South's cotton-growing regions adversely affecting the black population living there. In July, 1916, floods wiped away crops throughout the Black Belt counties of Georgia, Florida, Alabama, Mississippi and Louisiana. With their crops destroyed, many black sharecroppers had no way of repaying their debts for food and provisions advanced to them during the previous winter. Consequently, mules and other items of personal property were claimed for rents and debts at local stores, and many blacks were evicted from their land. Moreover, the boll weevil, which initially crossed the Mexican border into the United States in 1892, infested the Black Belt beginning in 1914, ravaging cotton crops and causing even more black workers to move away from the soil.[25]

To this deteriorating economic condition of the Southern Negro one must add the lack of political rights, social subordination, poor educational facilties, intimidation, and segregation as factors contributing to the "Great Migration." Beginning with the Mississippi Plan to disfranchise black voters in 1890, other Southern states soon followed with their own statutes restricting black political activity: South Carolina in 1895, Louisiana in 1898, North Carolina in 1900, Alabama in 1901, and Virginia in 1902. Approving the "separate but equal doctrine" in its decision of 1896, *Plessy vs. Ferguson,* the Supreme Court gave federal sanction to a whole series of racially discriminatory laws and segregation practices. All of the state legislatures of the South and most Southern communities soon enacted an extensive list of Jim Crow laws requiring complete separation of the races, except where blacks were subservient to whites. These legal sanctions were accompanied by increasing violence against blacks. Beatings, petty abuse, and insults were commonplace, lynchings were all too frequent, and harassment by law enforcement officials was extensive. Everything from a mere charge of rape of a white woman to a breach of racial customs could invite a white mob to lynch the accused member of the black community.

Thus industrial opportunity in the urban North now beckoned to blacks in the South who had longed to escape economic peonage, social degradation, and second class citizenship enforced by Jim Crow laws, and increasing violence against them by Southern whites. Although some blacks actively resisted racial oppression, the vast majority expressed their opposition by leaving the South. Black tenants and sharecroppers responded quickly and eagerly to new employment opportunities in the North. When the Pennsylvania, Erie, and New York Central railroads, the iron and steel manufacturers and others sent recruiting agents into the South offering several dollars a day in wages to people who were working for a dollar or less, they found many blacks willing to leave.

The "Great Migration" that got under way in late 1915 was not the first migration of blacks out of the South. On several occasions since the end of the Civil War, blacks desiring to improve their plight and escape racial discrimination left the South and migrated to the North and West.* But what had had been a trickle before now became a flood. The Pennsylvania Railroad began recruiting blacks in Jacksonville, Florida in early 1916. The New York Central hired 500 men out of the city about June of that year, and a total of 1,500 during the next several months. But the *Indianapolis Freeman,* a black weekly, reported that over 10,000 black Floridians had departed the state for Northern points between September and November, 1916.[26]

*The late 1860's and early 1870's witnessed the departure of thousands of black sharecroppers and laborers from the Black Belts of South Carolina, Georgia, Alabama and Mississippi for the rich "cotton bottom" counties of Arkansas, Louisiana, and Texas. But in the spring of 1879, an agricultural depression and the loss of political and civil rights, sent a large contingent of blacks from Louisiana and Mississippi to Kansas. *See* Carter G. Woodson, *A Century of Negro Migration,* New York, 1918. The most recent study is Nell I. Painter's *Exodusters: Black Migration to Kansas After Reconstruction,* New York, 1977. Some blacks considered settlement in Africa as a means of escaping economic poverty and repression in the South. *See* Edwin S. Redkey, *Black Exodus,* New Haven, 1969.

RECRUITING SOUTHERN BLACKS FOR NORTHERN INDUSTRY

Labor agents played an active role in the economic life of the South during the late nineteenth and early twentieth centuries. They operated quietly, sometimes secretly, urging black laborers to move from one Southern state to another or from one part of the state to another part. But they met with bitter opposition from planters and industrialists who depended on black laborers for the success of their operations. State governments passed emigrant-agent laws, which imposed prohibitive taxes on agents who transported laborers out of a state. When the United States Supreme Court on December 10, 1900 upheld the constitutionality of the Georgia law imposing prohibitive taxes on agents, it placed "a major obstacle in the path of agents who tried to lure laborers away." Anti-agent laws came on top of enticement statutes which made it a crime to employ a laborer under a contract to another person and vagrancy laws which gave police the authority to round up unemployed blacks and put them to work on chain gangs. These laws virtually legalized peonage and forced blacks to remain in the South.[27] Of course, even if they had come North they would have found it impossible to get work except in domestic and personal occupations.

However, with the nation's usual labor force enormously depleted by the drying up of immigrant labor during the war in Europe, Northern industrialists eagerly turned to the Southern blacks, women as well as men, the major untapped source of common labor remaining in the country. An intensive campaign was launched to recruit Southern blacks. American firms had employed labor recruiters for work among European peasants for decades, but this was the first time agents went South to bring black peasants to the North. The agents, sent by railroad and steel companies, initiated the migration by promising high wages, offering transportation subsides, and distributing leaflets like the following, scattered throughout Alabama:

Are you happy with your pay envelope? Would you like to go North where the laboring man shares the profits with the Boss? Are you satisfied with your condition here? Has your family all the comforts they should have during these prosperous times or are you just making "Both Ends Meet" while the other fellow is growing rich on your labor? . . . Let's Go Back North. Where no trouble of labor exists, no strikes, no lock outs, large coal, good wages, fair treatment, two weeks pay, good houses. If you haven't got all these things you had better see us. Will send you where you can have all these things. All colored ministers can go free. Will advance you money if necessary. Go now. While you have the chance.[28]

In addition to the cost of transporting the worker, this particular agency offered to pay the fare for his family, the freight charges on his household goods, and a "reasonable amount" of what he owned in his present town.

Northern industries also asked the National Urban League's assistance in enlisting black labor as a replacement for the dwindling number of immigrant workers. The league helped to recruit blacks for Northern industry and aided them in their adjustment to life in the North.[29]

The black press (more than 400 periodicals) also stimulated the trek of blacks northward. When Florida-born James Weldon Johnson, editor of the *New York Age,* was asked whether he thought blacks stood to benefit "financially, morally and religiously" as well as in "manhood, citizenship, etc." by migrating Northward, he indicated his approval. Migration, Johnson insisted, was good for all, and if the South desired to keep the blacks it should provide fair treatment and impartial execution of the laws.[30] The *Chicago Defender,* the most influential voice favoring migration, insisted, however, that such fair treatment could never be achieved in the South. It reached thousands of Southern Negroes with blistering attacks on life in the South and glowing reports of the high wages and better social conditions in the "Negro Heaven" north of the Mason–Dixon line. Letters from blacks who had already moved North were especially influential. In some states the demand for labor had sent wages for the unskilled as high as thirty-six cents an hour, and even the eighteen to twenty cents hourly wage for unskilled workers on some railroads was considerably above what blacks commanded in the South. In Chicago, Saint Louis, East Saint Louis, Detroit, and Milwaukee, a black worker could make more money in a week than he could for a month's hard toil in the South, where farm laborers averaged fifty to eighty cents a day. Those who worked on cottonseed-oil mills, sawmills, and turpentine refineries received only slightly more.

The ravages of floods, the boll weevil, and crop failures had left thousands of agricultural laborers and sharecroppers without the means of subsistence. As landlords by the hundreds dismissed their tenants and laborers, the lure of a living wage in the North became irresistible. As long as the price of cotton was low, the landlords were not too concerned by the exodus. But with the improving economic situation in the summer of 1916,* they began to fear that the mass departure of blacks would deplete their usual labor supply. "If the Negroes go," asked the

*The price of cotton declined from 12.4 cents in June, July, and August, 1914 to 6.3 cents in November, 1914. It remained low in 1915 and did not rise to 12 cents until June, 1916. (U.S. Department of Commerce, Bureau of the Census, *Historical Statistics of the United States, Colonial Times to 1957,* Washington, D.C., 1958, p. 301.)

Montgomery *Advertiser* in September, 1916, "where shall we get labor to take their places?"[31] New legislation was enacted on local and state levels to protect the cheap labor supply. Recruiters were charged prohibitive license fees subjected to strict regulations, with heavy fines and imprisonment imposed for violators. To stop the migration. Du Bois notes, the South "mobilized all the machinery of modern oppression: taxes, city ordinances, licenses, state laws, municipal regulations, wholesale arrests, and, of course, the peculiar Southern method of the mob and lyncher."[32]

But such efforts now came too late and were too easily circumvented to stem the northward tide of the blacks. Ray Stannard Baker wrote: "Trains were backed into Southern cities and hundreds of Negroes were gathered up in a day, loaded into cars and whirled away to the North. Instances are given showing that Negro teamsters left their horses standing in the streets or deserted their jobs and went to the trains without notifying their employers or even going home."[33]

EMERGENCE OF THE BLACK INDUSTRIAL WORKING CLASS

Once in the North, black migrants entered a variety of industrial occupations, primarily in iron and steel, auto manufacturing, shipbuilding, and railroad labor. They worked in mines of West Virginia and the industries of New Jersey, Pennsylvania,* New York, Ohio, and Illinois. The labor-recruiting efforts of Chicago's packing houses and the Illinois Central Railroad, together with the appeals of the Chicago *Defender*, made that city a magnet for penniless sharecroppers in the South. Some moved along to Detroit, where the pressure of wartime needs forced open the automobile plants to Afro-Americans. In 1914, less than 1,000 black auto workers were employed in area plants. As a result of the migration, however, 12,000 to 18,000 blacks gained employment in the Detroit auto industry between 1916 and 1918.

The stockyards, packing houses, and iron and steel mills of Chicago provided employment opportunities for the city's 50,000 black newcomers, between 1916 and 1918. During the same period, the Pennsylvania, the Reading and the Baltimore and Ohio Railroads, as well as Midvale Steel and several munitions and shipbuilding firms in Philadelphia, hired the majority of their 40,000 employable black migrants.[34]

Between 1910 and 1920, largely because of the wartime migration in the second half of the decade, a net increase of 322,000 occurred in the

---

*For an interesting discussion of the migration to the steel mills of Pittsburgh, see Peter Gottlieb, "Making Their Own Way: Southern Blacks' Migration to Pittsburgh, 1916-30," unpublished Ph.D. dissertation, University of Pittsburgh, 1977.

number of Southern-born blacks living in the North, exceeding the aggregate increase of the preceding forty years. Although the increase is less than the general estimate made at the height of the migration, it is still an impressive figure. Even more impressive is the fact that the booming wartime labor demands of rail lines, factories, foundries, mines, and packing houses, at a time when the normal supply of cheap labor was shut off, opened these industries for the first time to the black worker.[35]

Thus, on the eve of America's entrance into World War I, the first black industrial working class in the United States came into existence.*

*Manning Marble makes this point well when he writes:

"The making of the black industrial working class is a relatively recent historical phenomenon, spanning only three generations. . . . The actual beginnings of the black industrial working class are to be found with the massive migration of black humanity from the Deep South to the North after 1915. The collapse of the common market and the epidemic of black-owned bank failures in the autumn of 1914, combined with the curse of the boll weevil were powerful incentives for blacks to depart Dixie. . . . Most of these rural farmers and sharecroppers settled in crowded yet bustling ghettos, like Cleveland's Hough district and Chicago's Southside. This was the first generation of black workers who earned a living primarily from manufacturing, industrial and commercial labor. . . ." (Manning Mable, "The Crisis of the Black Working Class: An Economic and Historical Analysis," *Science & Society* 46 [Summer, 1982]: 134-35)

CHAPTER 13

The Election of 1916

As the year 1916 opened, relations between the Wilson Administration and the American Federation of Labor were characterized by complete harmony and good-will. In January, Wilson wrote to Gompers: "I think you know how genuinely I am interested in the fortunes of the Federation and how earnest and sincere a hope I entertain that its labors will be crowned with the best sort of success in the promotion of the best interests of the working men of the country."[1]

RELATIONS BETWEEN AFL AND WILSON ADMINISTRATION

In February, 1916, after the appointment of Louis. D. Brandeis to the Supreme Court, an action by President Wilson which greatly pleased the AFL, Secretary of Labor William B. Wilson made the relations even closer by inaugurating a series of luncheons which were to be attended by all members of the President's Cabinet and the members of the AFL Executive Council. Gompers was besides himself with joy. "This event," he wrote James Duncan, AFL Vice-President, "is of such great importance for what what it may mean for the future, or I may say of paramount importance."[2] As for the Administration, its purpose was stated by Secretary Wilson. "I sincerely trust," he wrote to Gompers after the first luncheon, "that it may be the beginning of closer relations and better understanding between the officials of the great labor movement and the administrative officials of our Government."[3]

Wilson himself showed his friendship for the AFL when he broke his self-imposed ban on making any public appearances to deliver the main address at the dedication of the new AFL headquarters, July 4, 1916.* A month later, the President appointed Gompers to the Advisory Committee of the newly created Council of National Defense. Since the Council itself was made up of heads of the departments of the federal government, the appointment practically made the AFL president an ex-officio member of the Wilson Administration.[4]

In the late summer of 1916, Gompers summed up the results of the Wilson-AFL relationship in a letter to a British Columbia labor official:

> September 1916 finds the organized labor movement stronger than ever before. During the past twelve months it has forced a wider recognition of its purpose and of its power. . . . During the past year it has been more generally recognized that the trade union movement is the only organization that distinctly represents the human element and represents human rights and justice in all the various relations of organized society. The achievements have been many, but the greatest thing that the labor movement has accomplished during the last year was to gain more general understanding and appreciation for the ideals of labor.[5]

AFL SUPPORTS WILSON FOR RE-ELECTION

In 1916 it was not difficult for the AFL to decide whether to support Charles Evans Hughes, nominated as the Republican candidate for president, or Woodrow Wilson, re-nominated for the second term by the Democratic Party. To be sure, on the surface, the AFL maintained its traditional non-partisan approach to political action, but this did not prevent the Federation from effectively supporting Wilson. A labor legislative record of the Wilson Administration was prepared by the Federation's legislative committee, along with a tabulation of the judicial decisions adverse to labor in which Hughes had participated. The Wilson Administration, the AFL emphasized, had given labor its "Magna Carta" in the Clayton Anti-Trust Act,** while Hughes, on the other hand, had participated in the decision of the Supreme Court adverse to labor in the Danbury Hatters' case.*** "Mr. Hughes has taken an une-

---

*Wilson had resolved to stick to his desk, following the policy adopted by Lincoln when confronted by the Civil War emergency. But when Gompers invited him to speak at the opening of the AFL headquarters, Wilson replied: "So far as I can see, I shall be free to do this. I need not add that I will do it with a great deal of pleasure." (Wilson To Gompers, June 19, 1916, Woodrow Wilson Papers, Library of Congress.)

**The reference is to Section 6 of the Act which read: "The labor of a human being is not a commodity or article of commerce." Gompers called this "the industrial Magna Carta upon which the working people will rear the structure of industrial freedom." (*See* Foner, *History of Labor Movement* 5 : 137-38.)

***For the Danbury Hatters' case, *see* Foner, *History of the Labor Movement* 3: 309-14, 341-42.

quivocal position," Gompers wrote in July. "He endorsed the abuse of the writ of injunction against which wage earners have vigorously protested."[6] One of Gompers' letters (ten pages in all) supporting the Wilson Administration and attacking Hughes, was printed in pamphlet form and widely distributed.[7*]

DEMOCRATIC PARTY PLATFORM

The platform adopted by the St. Louis convention which renominated Woodrow Wilson had a great deal to say about labor, and was carefully calculated to attract Progressive and independent voters friendly to organized labor as well as the labor movement itself. In the section of the platform entitled "Record of Achievement," the boast was made that the Democratic Party had "lifted human labor from the category of commodities," that it had secured to the working man "the right to voluntary association for his protection and welfare," that the rights of the laborers had been protected against the unauthorized issuance of writs of injunction, and the worker had been guaranteed the right of trial by jury in cases of alleged contempt committed outside the court. As to the promise for the future, the platform declared that the Federal government should set the example to employers by providing a living wage, an eight-hour work day, with one day of rest in seven, safe and sanitary conditions of labor, compensation for accidents, retirement schemes, uniform standards wherever minors were employed, and provisions relative to the employment of women such "as should be accorded to the mothers of the race."

The platform declared faith in the Seamen's Act, commonly known as the LaFollette Bill, and promised concurrence in its enforcement. The platform favored the "speedy enactment" of an effective federal child labor law, as well as the regulation of the shipment of convict-made goods. It recommended the creation of a Bureau of Labor Safety, as well as legislation "to prevent the maiming and killing of human beings." It favored the extension of the field of usefulness of the Bureau of Mines,

*Addressed to H.O. McClurg, Secretary of Labor's Voluntary Cooperative Citizenship and Educational Committee, Birmingham, Alabama, the letter was first published in the *Birmingham Labor Advocate* of September 9, 1916. In addition to the usual praise for Wilson, Gompers gave the President credit for the prohibition of "the Taylor System, stop-watch and speeding-up methods in the United States Navy Yards, manufacturies, and torpedo stations," the prohibition of piecework in the Post Office Department, and for the special Congressional investigations of strikes in the West Virginia and Colorado coal fields, and the Michigan copper region, "wherein all of the complaints and charges made by the men of labor against the mining companies, and the alliance of these companies with the political and military powers of the states were officially verified and demonstrated." (*Birmingham Labor Advocate*, Sept. 9, 1916.)

endorsed the system of employment exchanges inaugurated during the first Wilson administration, and commended the Department of Labor for its record in settling strikes by personal advice and conciliating agents. Under the heading of Public Health, the platform favored the establishment by the government of tuberculosis sanitoriums for needy patients. Another paragraph proposed a scheme of prison reform for federal prisoners.

During the presidential campaign, the Socialist Party, which nominated Allan L. Benson and George R. Kirkpatrick as its presidential and vice-presidential candidates,* conceded that the "Record of Achievement," as outlined in the Democratic Platform, had benefitted labor to a certain extent, "improved the situation with regard to injunctions and contempt of court," and that organized labor, through the AFL, "had long demanded these reforms." But it charged that in a number of cases, there was more verbiage than substance to the reforms. "The LaFollette law," for instance, "has been in many important respects nullified by the administration which it has received at the hands of Mr. Wilson's Secretary of Commerce, Mr. Redfield. . . . At any rate, it was poor tactics for the St. Louis convention to promise to continue to enforce the LaFollette law, for labor perfectly well knows that management to date has been bad, and capital knows that thorough performance in the future would be dangerous to their interests." While the Democratic labor record was judged to be better than that of the Republican administration, and a second Wilson administration held out better hopes for labor than a Hughes regime, it was naive, the Socialist Party insisted, for organized labor to expect that a second Wilson term would be anything but "fully as worthless and fully as treacherous as could be expected under the circumstances."[8]

WILSON'S ACCEPTANCE SPEECH

The AFL, however, had no misgivings, and its enthusiasm for Wilson mounted on September 2, when the President formally accepted the Democratic nomination and stated the reasons for his belief that "the people of the United States will wish the Democratic party to continue in control of the Government." In his speech, Wilson mainly reviewed the legislation passed by Congress during his administration, and defended

*For purposes of economy, the Socialist Party convention of 1916 had been dispensed with, and nomination of S. P. presidental candidates was made by referendum. Eugene V. Debs having declined, Allan L. Benson of Minnesota was nominated as the presidential candidate and George R. Kirkpatrick for vice president. The role of the Socialist Party in the presidential campaign, which dealt mainly with the preparedness issue, will be discussed in the next volume.

the policy pursued with respect to the war in Europe and toward Mexico.* On the issue of labor, he contrasted his administration's accomplishments with the "oblivious or indifferent" attitude of Republican administrations which had preceded his, and declared:

> The Workingmen of America have been given a veritable emancipation by the legal recognition of a man's labor as part of his life, and not a mere marketable commodity,** by exempting labor organizations from processes of the courts, which treated their members like factional parts of mobs and not accessible and responsible individuals;*** by releasing our seamen from involuntary servitude,**** by making adequate provision for compensation for industrial accidents, by providing suitable machinery for mediation and conciliation in industrial disputes and by putting the Federal Department of Labor at the disposal of the workingman in search of work.

Wilson also called attention to the law to keep children out of factories, the equalization of taxation by means of an income tax, and declared, "we have in four years' time come very near to carrying out the platform of the Progressive party, as well as our own."***** And all this in spite of stubborn resistance at every step by the interests which the Republican party had catered to and fostered."[9]

Since the Adamson Act providing for an eight-hour day for workers on the operating divisions of the railroads was not a law, Wilson did not cite it in his acceptance speech. But it was this legislation which became a leading issue in the presidential campaign.

HUGHES MAKES ADAMSON ACT AN ISSUE

In the late summer months the Republican party was having difficulty in getting its presidential campaign off the ground. Hughes was not proving to be the campaigner some of the G.O.P. leaders had expected. "Poor Hughes! He has made a wonderful failure in his speeches out West," historian James Ford Rhodes wrote on August 26, 1916.[10]

---

*These policies will be discussed in the next volume, Volume 7 of the *History of the Labor Movement in the United States.*

**The reference is to the Clayton Anti-Trust Act.

***The reference is to the prohibition of injunctions in labor disputes. Wilson, however, did not mention that the Clayton Anti-Trust Act, in which the prohibition was placed, also included the provision that injunctions could be issued "if irreparable damage" would occur, and as we have pointed out in a previous volume, this effectively wiped out much of the value of the anti-injunction provision. (*See* Foner, *History of the Labor Movement 5*: 139-41.)

****The reference is to the LaFollette Seamen's Act. *See ibid.*, pp. 127-28.

*****For the Progressive Party and its platform in the 1912 campaign, *see* Foner, History of Labor Movement 5: 107-11.

Good popular issues, too, were difficult to advance, The 1914 depression with its accompanying widespread unemployment had given way to prosperity under the impact of orders from war-torn Europe. Since the Republicans, the leading party of imperialism, would not make an issue of Wilson's Mexican policy, the Democratic Party cornered the foreign policy issue with the slogan "He kept us out of war." The Republicans tried to raise doubts about the effectiveness of the preparedness campaign the administration was supporting, but they found it impossible to oppose peace.[11]

This left the administration's domestic reform program as the major area in which the Republicans believed the Democrats were vulnerable. The Adamson Act appeared to be the one reform which could be made the center of an attack on the President. Big business and many small business groups had bitterly opposed the Act, and most of the commercial press had sharply attacked Wilson for "selling out" to the Railroad Brotherhoods in particular, and organized labor in general, for political gain.[12]*

On September 8, 1916, the *New York Times* editorialized: "Mr. Hughes and the Republicans having failed in the first two months of the campaign to discover any issue to which the country would pay attention, have eagerly seized upon the issue of the threatened railroad strike and they are using it to the best of their knowledge and ability." The day before in a speech at Hampton Beach, four days after Wilson signed the Adamson Act, Hughes "vigorously assailed the Democratic methods of disposing of the railroad controversy." Later that month, he went beyond merely attacking the procedure, charging "The Adamson bill is a force bill," and on October 9, in New Jersey, Hughes cried:

> The administration threw up its hands, abandoned the principle of arbitration, of fair inquiry before legislative action, and in a panic of fear rushed to Congress to get this bill passed as the price of peace. The Administration bill thus came to embody the terms of a humiliating surrender.[13]

The *Wall Street Journal* hailed Hughes' attacks on the Adamson Act as doing more "to advance his candidature" than all he had said since his nomination. The conservative New York *Evening Post*, which had voiced disappointment with all of Hughes's campaign speeches, now

---

*This charge especially angered the President. "The statement that the eight-hour law was simply adopted for political effect is a gross falsehood," he wrote. "I have myself enlisted to do all I can for the recognition of the eight-hour day throughout our industries as the right basis of labor." (Woodrow Wilson to S. W. Pickens, November 4, 1916, Woodrow Wilson Papers, Library of Congress.)

declared that his criticism of the Adamson Act was an "unquestionable reminder of what the country has always known Hughes to be."[14]

Leading Democrats, too, spoke out, and they advised Wilson that Hughes was attracting a large section of the middle-class vote by attacking the Adamson Act. Unless the President hit back, he would lose many votes.[15]

Wilson therefore decided to change his campaign strategy. Up to this point, he had refrained from any extensive speech-making. The ineffectiveness of Hughes' early campaign, he informed Bernard Baruch, had convinced him to follow the advice of a certain friend who "has always followed the rule never to murder a man who is committing suicide, and clearly this misdirected gentleman [Hughes] is committing suicide slowly but surely."[16] But now Wilson decided that he had to take the offensive, and he began a strong defense of his actions in the railroad controversy and the adoption of the Adamson Act.[17]

ORGANIZED LABOR INTENSIFIES SUPPORT FOR WILSON

The AFL and the Railroad Brotherhoods, too, intensified their political campaign in support of the Wilson administration. By the middle of October, the AFL had completely abandoned any pretense of non-partisanship, and came out directly for Wilson's re-election. In a political circular from its Washington headquarters, addressed to all officers of the labor movement, Gompers indicated clearly that the future of organized labor was with President Wilson and his administration. In order that the rank-and-file member understand this clearly, the circular urged that special meetings be held by all trade unions, national, state, and local, at which the significance of re-electing Wilson would be demonstrated.[18] The President was aware of, and fully appreciated this activity by the AFL in his behalf. On October 30, Wilson wrote "in haste" to Gompers to express his "warm appreciation of the generous support you are giving the administration."[19]

For their part, the Railroad Brotherhoods made what one brotherhood official called the first effort the railroad unions had ever made "to show our strength" in an election.[20] Working both among their own memberships and those of other unions, brotherhood officials circulated petitions in support of Wilson's re-election, carried on word-of-mouth campaigns for the Democratic candidate, and held public meetings in key cities. "This matter," one brotherhood official wrote a member of the Wilson administration, "is now assuming definite form in every part of the country. The railroad men are a unit for Mr. Wilson." The brotherhood officials were convinced that "all other union men" would be with them on election day.[21]

Union members were certainly indicating this confidence was justified. Whenever Hughes spoke in October, unionists interrupted his speech, and asked if he would repeal the Adamson Act if he were elected. Hughes replied that "a surrender could not be repealed," but went on to denounce the Act and assure his audience that he would do little to persuade the railroads to abide by it. An outburst of heckling usually interrupted the speech as trade unionists in the audience voiced their displeasure.[22]

On the eve of the election, the AFL appealed:

> It is up to the workers, the masses, of our liberty-loving citizenship, to decide whether President Wilson, with his clear vision and courageous heart and mind, shall be supplanted by the reactionary candidate of predatory wealth—Mr. Hughes. President Woodrow Wilson had advocated, urged and signed legislation protecting human rights and promoting the welfare of the workers and all of the masses of the people. Mr. Hughes had declared that if elected president he will insist upon the repeal of the legislation. It lies with the working people—the masses—on Election Day to determine by their votes whether the policy of progress, justice, freedom and humanity shall prevail in the re-election of Mr. Wilson to the presidency of the United States or whether the pendulum shall swing backward and the policy of reaction shall be enthroned.[23]

WILSON NARROWLY RE-ELECTED

Wilson was re-elected by a narrow margin. The electoral vote was 277 for Wilson, and 254 for Hughes, while the popular vote was 9,129,606 for Wilson and 8,538,221 for Hughes. "If there was a mandate for Wilson's progressive reform in the election of 1916," writes one student of the campaign, "It was not an overwhelming one."[24] Nevertheless, it was widely asserted that the labor vote was an important factor in the narrow victory Wilson scored.* After the passage of the Adamson Act in early September, 1916, the *Baltimore News* declared that "it rests with the labor element in this country to decide the turn the

---

*Wilson also won the support of many Progressive Party members who refused to follow Theodore Roosevelt's advice that they should support the Republican candidate (*Literary Digest*, Nov. 25, 1916, p. 1392). For a picture of how the Progressive Party was used by Roosevelt in the interests of monopoly capital, see Amos R. E. Pinchot, *History of the Progressive Party, 1912-1916*, edited with a biographical introduction by Helene Maxwell Hooker, (New York, 1953.)

The Socialist Party vote in 1916 declined to 585,000 as against 900,000 in 1912. The Socialist campaign in 1916, mainly directed against intervention in Mexico and the European war, will be studied in the next volume.

[presidential] campaign should take."[25] This "labor element" did come through, and it played a major role in the outcome of the election.[26*]

To this "element" must be added the fact that the slogan "He kept us out of war," won Wilson the votes of radicals, progressives, and independents.[**] Although Hughes won support among some progressive women by coming out boldly for the woman suffrage amendment, while Wilson refused at first to endorse a federal amendment and insisted on suffrage for women on a state-by-state process, the Republican candidate lost much of this advantage, for Wilson began to retreat from this position as the campaign advanced.[***]

The fact that Wilson had championed a number of social justice measures, especially the Adamson eight-hour law, the Keating-Owen Child Labor Act, and a federal workman's compensation act, as well as the exemption of labor from injunction provisions of the anti-trust act (even if only temporarily), influenced many workers, former Bull

---

*Arthur Link and William Leary conclude that the labor vote was decisive in Wilson's victories in Washington, Idaho, and New Mexico, and very helpful in California, Ohio, and New Hampshire. (Arthur S. Link and William M. Leary, Jr., "Election of 1916," in Arthur M. Schlesinger, Fred L. Israel, and William P. Hansen, eds., *The Coming to Power: Critical Presidential Elections in American History* [New York, 1972], pp. 313-15). *See also* William Thomas White, "A History of Railroad Workers in the Pacific Northwest, 1883-1934," unpublished Ph.D. dissertation, University of Washington, 1981, p. 151.

**Usually this slogan referred to the war in Europe, but at a workingmen's meeting in New York City on July 4, 1916, Frank P. Walsh, chairman of the Industrial Relations Commission, urged labor to support Wilson for re-election for having refused to go to war with Mexico. "Thank God," Walsh cried, "for the sublime patience of President Wilson, who has kept us out of war with Mexico." (*New York Times*, July 5, 1916.) Evidently the dispatch of the U. S. Army under General John J, Pershing into Mexico constituted for Walsh an act of "peace."

***The National Woman's Party supported Hughes, sponsored the "Hughes special," and campaigned actively for the Republican candidate, especially in the West. But Wilson's shift from opposing to supporting a federal woman suffrage amendment brought him support among members of the National Woman Suffrage Association. (*See* Christine A. Lunardine and Thomas J. Knock, "Woodrow Wilson and Woman Suffrage: A New Look," *Political Science Quarterly* 95 [Winter, 1980-81]: 662-64.)

This was not the only issue on which Wilson shifted his position because of the exigencies of the 1916 election. He had taken a strong stand against child labor legislation, arguing that such legislation "affords a striking example of a tendency to carry Congressional power over interstate commerce beyond the utmost boundaries of reasonable and honest interference." But Wilson shifted his position during the 1916 campaign, not only embracing the child labor measure but assuming a position of leadership in the campaign for reform. While the Republicans also came out for enactment of a child labor law, it was Wilson, by virtue of his refusal to accept formal renomination until the Keating-Owen Act passed, who received credit for its enactment. On September 1, Wilson signed the Keating-Owen Act, and in accepting renomination the next day, pointed to a record which included "the emancipation of the children of the nation by releasing them from hurtful labor." (*New York Times*, Sept. 3, 1916.)

Moose Progressives and even Socialists to support the president for re-election. But it was the war in Europe that weighed most heavily on the minds of Americans as they went to the polls on November 7, 1916. With the popular campaign slogan, "He kept us out of war!" Wilson emerged triumphant.[27]

Little did these voters dream that just a few months later, the President who "kept us out of war" would be addressing a Joint Session of Congress calling for a declaration of war by the United States against Germany and her allies.

REFERENCE NOTES

CHAPTER 1

1. *New York Times*, Jan 6, 1914.
2. Stephen Meyer, "Adapting the Immigrant to the Line: Americanization in the Ford Factory, 1914-1921," *Journal of Social History 14* (1980): 69.
3. *Ibid.*
4. Keith Sward, *The Legend of Henry Ford*, New York, 1948, p. 126.
5. Melvyn Dubofsky, *We Shall Be All: A History of the Industrial Workers of the World*, Chicago, 1969, pp. 214–16; Allan Nevins (with the collaboration of Frank Ernest Hill), *Ford, The Times, The Man, The Company*, New York, 1954, p. 537; Sward, op. cit., pp. 126–27.
6. Philip S. Foner, *History of the Labor Movement in the United States*, New York, 1965, vol. 4, pp. 385–88.
7. Sward, *op. cit.*, pp. 128–30; Nevins, *Ford*, op. cit., pp. 379–80.
8. Nevins, *Ford, op. cit.*, pp. 393–94.
9. *Ibid.*, pp. 410–11.
10. Robert W. Dunn, *Labor and Automobiles*, New York, 1928, pp. 14, 18, 20, 27, 117.
11. John A. Fitch, "Ford of Detroit and His Ten Million Dollar Profit Sharing Plan," *Survey* 31 (Feb. 7, 1915): 545–550.
12. Sward, *op. cit.*, p. 372.
13. Nevins, *Ford*, op. cit., p. 542.
14. *Solidarity*, Feb. 14, 1914.
15. Upton Sinclair, *The Flivver King*, New York, 1928, pp. 242–43.
16. Meyer, op. cit., pp. 69–70.
17. Quoted in Sward, *op. cit.*, pp. 372–73.
18. Nevins, *Ford, op. cit.*, pp. 413.
19. Antonio Gramsci, "America and Fordism," in *Letters From Prison*, New York, 1962, pp. 121–35.
20. Ford Motor Company, *Helpful Hints and Advice to Employes to Help Them Grasp the Opportunities which Are Presented To Them by the Ford Profit Sharing Plan*, Detroit, 1915; *A Brief Account of the Educational Work of the Ford Motor Company*, Detroit, 1916; Fitch, *op. cit.*, pp. 545–50; Stephen Meyer, "Mass Production and Human Efficiency: The Ford Motor Company," unpublished Ph.D. dissertation, Rutgers University, 1977, pp. 156–86, and published under the title, Stephen Meyer III, *The Five Dollar Day: Labor Management and Social Control in the Ford Motor Company, 1908-1921* (Albany, New York, 1981).
21. Meyer, "Mass Production and Human Efficiency," pp. 187–216.
22. Gramsci, *op. cit.*, p. 132.
23. *Helpful Hints and Advice*, pp. 15–17.
24. Nevins, *Ford, op. cit.*, pp. 502–03.
25. Daniel Nelson, *Frederick W. Taylor and the Rise of Scientific Management*, Madison, Wisconsin, 1980, pp. 212–15.
26. Sward, *op. cit.*, pp. 422–23.
27. *New York Times*, Dec. 12, 1915; *Industrial World*, Jan. 14, 1916.
28. David Montgomery, "Labor and the Republic in Industrial America: 1860-1920," *Mouvement Social* (France) 111 (1980): 211.

CHAPTER 2

1. "A Strike Without Disorder," *New Republic*, Jan. 22, 1916, p. 304.
2. "The Arizona Copper Miners," *Outlook*, Feb. 2, 1916, p. 250.
3. *New Republic*, Jan. 22, 1916, p. 304.
4. Mike Casillas, "Mexican Labor Militancy in the U.S.: 1896-1915," *Southwest Economy & Society* 4 (Fall, 1978): 34.
5. Victor S. Clark, "Mexican Labor in the United States, *Bulletin of the Bureau of Labor* 8 (September, 1908): 498.
6. *Engineering and Mining Journal*, April 4, 1908, p. 702; Nov. 5, 1910, p. 914.
7. Quoted in John A. Fitch, "Arizona's Em-

bargo on Strike-Breakers," *Survey*, May 6, 1916, pp. 143-44.
8. *Ibid.*
9. *Ibid.*
10. *Outlook*, Feb. 2, 1916, p. 250.
11. *New Republic*, Jan. 22, 1916, p. 304.
12. *Arizona Daily Star*, Sept. 16, 1915.
13. *Outlook*, Feb. 2, 1916, p. 250.
14. *Arizona Daily Star*, Sept. 23, 1915; Fitch, *op. cit.*, p. 144
15. *Arizona Daily Star*, Sept. 25, 1915.
16. *Ibid.*, Oct. 3, 1915; *New York Times*, Oct. 4, 1915.
17. Alan V. Johnson, "Governor G. W. P. Hunt and Organized Labor," unpublished M.A. thesis, University of Arizona, 1964, pp. 3-47; G. W. P. Hunt. "The Autobiography of George Wiley Paul Hunt, "*Arizona Historical Review*, January, 1933, pp 253-63.
18. *Arizona Daily Star*, Sept. 1, 1915; January, 1933, pp. 253-63.
19. Letter of Governor Hunt to the *Outlook*, Feb. 2, 1916, p. 251.
20. Fitch, *op. cit.*, p. 144.; *Arizona Daily Star*, Sept. 17-21, 1915.
21. *Ibid.*, Sept. 20, 1915.
22. Johnson, op. cit., pp. 31-32; *New Republic*, Jan. 22, 1916, p. 304.
23. *The Survey*, May 6, 1916, p. 146.
24. *Bisbee Review*, Oct. 5-8, 1915; *Arizona Daily Star*, Oct. 5-8, 1915.
25. *New Republic*, Jan. 22, 1916, p. 304.
26. *Arizona Daily Star*, Oct. 22-24, 1915.
27. Johnson, *op. cit.*, pp. 66-67.
28. *Arizona Daily Star*, Nov. 2, 1915; Johnson, *op. cit.*, p. 67.
29. Fitch, *op. cit.*, p. 144.
30. *Outlook*, Feb. 2, 1916, p. 250.
31. *Arizona Daily Star*, Jan. 8-10,. 1916; *Bisbee Review*, Jan. 8-10, 1916; *Survey*, May 6, 1916, p. 145.
32. *Outlook*, Feb. 2, 1916, p. 251.
33. *New Republic*, March 18, 1916.
34. Johnson, *op. cit.*, pp. 60-61.
35. Dale Featherling, *Mother Jones, The Miners' Angel*, Carbondale, 1974, p. 143.
36. *Outlook*, Feb. 2, 1916, p. 251.
37. *Ibid.*

CHAPTER 3

1. *New York Times*, Dec. 30, 1915.
2. New York *Call*, Jan. 2, 3, 1916.
3. *Ibid.*, Jan. 14, 1916.
4. David Brody, *Steelworkers in America: The Non Union Era*, Cambridge, Mass., 1966, pp. 30-38; J. A. Garraty, "The United States Steel Corporation Versus Labor," *Labor History* 1 (Winter, 1966): 24-26.
5. U.S. Congress, Senate, *Report on the Strike of the Bethlehem Steel Workers* (Senate Document No. 521, Washington, D.C., 1910), p. 9, Robert Hessen, "The Bethlehem Steel Strike of 1910," *Labor History* 15 (Winter, 1974): 3-8; Charles Hill, "Fighting the Twelve-Hour Day in the American Steel Industry," *Labor History* 15 (Winter, 1974): 19-35.
6. *Ibid.*, p. 34: John Fitch, *The Steelworkers*, Pittsburgh, 1911, p. 102.
7. Quoted in Brody, *op cit.*, p. 171.
8. *Ibid.*, pp. 174-75, Steven C. Levi, "The battle for the eight hour day in San Francisco," *California History* 57 (1978): 349.
9. *Ibid.*, p. 179.
10. Philip S. Foner, *History of the Labor Movement in the United States* (New York, 1964) 3: 266.
11. *New York Times*, Jan. 9., 1916.
12. *Survey*, January 22, 1916, p. 479.
13. New York *Call*, Jan. 14, 1916.
14. *New Republic*, Jan. 29, 1916, pp. 330-31.
15. *Survey*, Jan. 22, 1916, p. 479.
16. *Ibid.*, p. 477; New Republic, Jan. 29, 1916, p. 331.
17. New York *Call*, Jan. 14, 1916.
18. Quoted in Brody, *op. cit.*, p. 181.
19. George P. West in *New Republic*, Jan. 29, 1916, p. 331.
20. Youngstown *Vindicator*, Dec. 20, 1915.
21. *Ibid.*, Dec. 26-29, 1915.
22. *Ibid.*, Jan. 2, 3, 1916.
23. *Ibid.*, Jan. 3, 1916.
24. *Ibid.*, Jan. 7, 1916.
25. *Ibid.*, Jan. 8, 1916.
26. *Ibid.*
27. *Outlook*, Jan. 19, 1916, p. 122.
28. *Ibid.*
29. *Survey*, Jan. 22, 1916, p. 428.
30. New York *Tribune*, Jan. 9-10, 1916; New York *Call*, Jan. 10, 1916.
31. New York *Call*, Jan. 9, 1916.
32. *Ibid.*, Jan. 12, 1916.
33. *New York Times*, Jan. 12, 1916.
34. George P. West, "Youngstown," *New Republic*, Jan. 29, 1916, p. 330; New York *Call*, March 9, 1916.
35. *Survey*, Jan. 22, 1916, p. 480
36. Youngstown *Vindicator*, Jan. 12, 13, 1916.
37. *Ibid.*, Jan. 13, 14, 1916.
38. *Survey*, Jan. 22, 1916, p. 479.
39. Brody, *op cit.*, pp. 181-83.
40. Youngstown *Vindicator*, March 9, 1916; *New York Times*, March 9, 1916.
41. *Ibid.*

42. *Ibid.*
43. *New York Times*, March 20, 1916.
44. *Ibid.*, March 19, 1916.
45. New York *Call*, March 12, 1916.
46. *Ibid.*, March 9, 1916.
47. *New York Times*, March 29, 1916; Youngstown *Vindicator*, March 29, 1916.
48. New York *Call*, March 12, 1916.
49. *The American Labor Year Book*, New York, 1916, p. 53.

CHAPTER 4

1. Herbert Gutman, *Work, Culture, and Society in Industrializing America*, New York, 1977, p. 236.
2. *Ibid.*, p. 245.
3. *Ibid.*, pp. 273-74.
4. Ronald Prezioso, "The Oil Industry in Bayonne: Its Rise and Decline," unpublished manuscript in Bayonne Municipal Library; Minutes of the Board of Councilmen of the City of Bayonne, 1879-1880, p. 22.
5. Minutes of the Board of Councilmen of the City of Bayonne, 1881-1882, p. 43.
6. Ransom Noble, *New Jersey Progressivism Before Wilson*, Princeton, N.J. 1946, p. 3.
7. *Bayonne Herald*, August, 1915.
8. T. Gladys Sinclair, *Bayonne Old and New*, New York, 1940, pp. 57-58; Prezioso, *op. cit.*, pp. 1-2; Otey S. Jones, in collaboration with Tim Zibro, "A Short History of Bayonne, New Jersey," unpublished manuscript in Bayonne Municipal Library.
9. Federal Writers' Project of the W.P.A., *New Jersey—A Guide to the Present and the Past*, New York, 1939, p. 282; George Gibb and Evelyn Knowlton, *The Resurgent Years 1911-1927, History of the Standard Oil Company of New Jersey*, New York, 1956, vol. 2, pp. 138-39.
10. Edward Levinson, *I Break Strikes: The Technique of Pearl L. Bergoff*, New York 1935, pp. 57-59; Gladys Sinclair, *Bayonne Old and New*, New York, 1940, p. 34.
11. *Bayonne Evening Review*, May 2, 10, 15, 18, 22, 23, 1913.
12. Bureau of Statistics of Labor and Industries, *Annual Report of the New Jersey Bureau of Statistics of Labor and Industries*, Trenton, N.J., 1914, pp. 76-78.
13. Gibb and Knowlton, *op. cit.*, p. 140, Prezioso, *op. cit.*, p. 11.
14. "The Bayonne Strike," *New Republic*, Aug. 14, 1915, p. 38.
15. *Survey* 34 (July 31, 1915), 387.
16. *Jersey Journal*, July 20, 1915; New Republic,

Aug. 14, 1915, p. 38; Giff and Knowlton, *op. cit.*, p. 142.
17. *Survey* 34 (July 31, 1915), 387; *New Republic*, Aug. 14, 1915, pp. 38-39; Gibb and Knowlton, *op. cit.*, p. 142.
18. *Jersey Journal*, July 12-13, 1915.
19. *Ibid.*, July 20-21, 1915.
20. New York *World*, New York *Sun*, and New York *Tribune*, reprinted in *Literary Digest* Jan. 30, 1915, pp. 181-82.
21. Newark *Evening Star*, June 2, 1915; *New York Times*, June 3, 1915, Chester M. Wright in *American Labor Year Book* New York, 1916, pp. 47-48.
22. *Annual Report of the New Jersey Bureau of Statistics of Labor and Industries*, Trenton, 1916, p. 211.
23. *Jersey Journal*, July 22, 1915; *New York Times*, July 22, 1915; *New York Times*, July 22, 1915.
24. *New Republic*, August 14, 1915, p. 38.
25. *Bayonne Evening Review*, July 21, 1915; *New York Times*, July 21, 1915.
26. New York *Call*, July 23, 1915.
27. *New York Times*, July 21, 23, 1915.
28. New York *Call*, July 26, 1915.
29. *Jersey Journal*, July 22, 1915.
30. *New York Times*, July 21, 1915.
31. *Ibid.*, July 20, 1915.
32. *Jersey Journal*, July 23, 1915.
33. John Fitch, "The Explosion in Bayonne," *Survey* 37 (October 21, 1916): 61-62.
34. New York *Sun*, reprinted in New York *Call*, Aug. 11, 1915.
35. *New York Times*, July 26, 1915.
36. *Ibid.*, July 25, 1915.
37. New York *Call*, July 25, 1915; *Annual Report of the Bureau of Statistics of Labor and Industries of New Jersey*, 1916, p. 222.
38. *New York Times*, July 25, 1915.
39. "Sheriff Kinkhead's Busy Day," *Literary Digest*, 51 (August 7, 1915): 256-61.
40. New York *Call*, July 21, 1915; and New York *Mail* reprinted in *Ibid.*, July 30, 1915.
41. Prezioso, *op. cit.*, p. 47; *New York Times*, July 27, 1915.
42. John Fitch, "When a Sheriff Breaks a Strike," *Survey* 34 (July 31, 1915): 416.
43. New York *Call*, July 30, 1915.
44. *New York Times*, July 27, 1915.
45. *Jersey Journal*, July 27, 1915.
46. Fitch in *Survey* 34 (July 31, 1915): 414-16; *New York Times*, July 27, 1915.
47. Prezioso, *op. cit.*, p. 49; Fitch, *Survey* 34 (July 31, 1915): 414.
48. New York *Call*, July 30, 1915; *Jersey Journal*, Sept. 10, 1915.
49. Bayonne *Evening Review*, Oct. 4-6, 1916.

50. *Ibid.*, Oct. 6-7, 1916.
51. *Ibid.*, Oct. 7, 1916.
52. *Ibid.*
53. *Ibid.*, Oct. 9, 1916.
54. *Ibid.*, Oct. 10, 1916.
55. *New Republic*, Oct. 21, 1916, pp. 283-85.
56. Bayonne *Evening Review*, Oct. 10, 1916; *Jersey Journal*, Oct. 13, 1916.
57. *Survey* 35 (October, 1916): 314.
58. *New York Times*, Oct. 13, 1916.
59. New York *Evening Telegram*, Oct. 14, 15, 1916.
60. *Ibid.*, Oct. 16, 1916.
61. Bayonne *Evening Review*, Oct. 18, 1916.
62. New York *Globe*, Oct. 11, 1916.
63. New York *Evening Post*, Oct. 13, 1916.
64. *Jersey Journal*, Oct. 13, 1916.
65. New York *Call*, Oct. 13, 1916.
66. *Ibid.*, Oct. 15, 1916.
67. *Jersey Journal*, Oct. 14-16, 1916.
68. Bayonne *Evening Review*, Oct. 17, 1916.
69. "The End of the Strike," *The Independent* 88 (Oct. 30, 1916): 166; *New York Times*, Oct. 20, 1916.
70. *See also* Independent 88 (Oct. 30, 1916): 166
71. *Outlook* 114 (Oct. 25, 1916): 199; *Jersey Journal*, Oct. 25, 1916; *Survey* 34 (July 31, 1915: 387.
72. New York *Tribune*, Oct. 30, 1916.
73. Gibb and Knowlton, *op. cit.*, p. 151.
74. Bayonne *Evening Review*, Nov. 25, 1916.
75. New York *Call*, Oct. 12, 1916.

CHAPTER 5

1. Melvyn Dubofsky, *When Workers Organize: New York City in the Progressive Era*, Amherst, Mass., 1968, p. 126.
2. Philip S. Foner, *American Labor Songs of the Nineteenth Century*, Urbana, Illinois, 1975, p. 246.
3. *Brooklyn Daily Eagle*, Jan. 27, 29, Feb. 16, 1895.
4. Philip S. Foner, *History of the Labor Movement in the United States*, New York, 1964 vol. 3: 103-106.
5. *Motorman and Conductor*, May, 1915, p. 36.
6. *New York Times*, Aug. 5, 1916.
7. James Joseph McGinley, *Labor Relations in the New York Rapid Transit Systems 1904-1944*, New York, 1949, pp. 248-51.
8. *Ibid.*, p. 252.
9. New Republic 8 (Aug. 12, 1916): 28-29.
10. New York *Call*, July 29, 1916.
11. *New York Times*, July 26, 1916.
12. New York *Call*, July 28, 1916.
13. McGinley, *op. cit.*, p. 257.

14. Samuel Waitzman, "The New York Transit Strike of 1916," unpublished M.A. thesis, Columbia University, 1952, pp. 29-30; *New York Times*, Aug. 15, 1916.
15. Quoted in Dubofsky, *op. cit.*, p. 127.
16. James Henley, "When the Carmen Quit," New York *Call*, Aug. 20, 1916.
17. Dubofsky, *op. cit.*, pp. 128-30.
18. *New York Times*, Jan. 5, 8, 10, 1913.
19. Waitzman, *op. cit.*, pp. 7-8.
20. *New York Times*, Jan. 5, 1913.
21. *Ibid.*, Jan. 5, 6, 8, 12, 1913.
22. Waitzman, *op. cit.*, p. 12.
23. *New York Times*, July 27, 1916; New York *Call*, July 26-27, 1916.
24. *New York Times*, July 26, 27, 1916; Waitzman, *op. cit.*, p. 14.
25. *New York Times*, July 29, 1916; New York *World*, July 29, 1916; New York *Call*, July 29, 1916.
26. *New York Times*, July 30, 1916.
27. New York *Call*, July 30, 1916.
28. *New York Times*, July 30, 1916; New York *Tribune*, July 30, 1916.
29. *New York Times*, July 30, 1916.
30. *Ibid.*, New York *Call*, July 30, 1916.
31. *New York Times*, Aug. 1-2, 1916; New York *Call*, Aug. 1-2, 1916.
32. *New York Times*, Aug. 3, 1916.
33, *New York Call*, Aug. 5, 1916; New York *World*, Aug. 5, 1916; *New York Times*, Aug. 5, 1916.
34. New York *Call*, Aug. 5, 1916.
35. *New York Times*, Aug. 5-6, 1916.
36. New York *Call*, July 30, Aug. 5, 1916.
37. "When We Aid the Street Car Men" by Arthur Walker, New York *Call*, Aug. 7, 1916.
38. *New York Times*, July 28-29, 1916.
39. *Ibid.*, Aug. 6, 1916.
40. *Ibid.*, Aug. 7, 1916.
41. *New York Times*, July 27, 1916.
42. *Ibid.*, July 28-29, 1916.
43. *Ibid.*, July 30, 1916; Edward Levinson, *I Break Strikes: The Technique of Pearl L. Bergoff*, New York, 1935, p. 175.
44. New York *Call*, July 31, 1916.
45. *See Yonkers Herald*, July 23, 1916; *New York Times*, July 24, 31, Aug. 2, 3, 5, 1916.
46. *New York Times*, Aug. 5, 1916; Waitzman, *op. cit.*, p. 28.
47. New York *Call*, Aug. 4, 1916.
48. *Ibid.*, July 27, 1916.
49. *Ibid.*, July 31, 1916.
50. *Motorman and Conductor*, October, 1917, p. 27.
51. *New York Times*, Aug. 5, 1916.

52. Waitzman, *op. cit.*, p. 34., *New York Times*, Aug. 5, 1916.
53. Dubofsky, *op. cit.*, p. 133.
54. *New York Times*, Aug. 7, 1916.
55. Amalgamated Association of Street and Electric Railway Employees, *Constitution and By-Laws*, Revised, 1907, pp. 22-23.
56. *New York Times*, Aug. 8, 1916.
57. New York *Call*, Aug. 7, 8, 1916; Dubofsky, *op. cit.*, p. 135.
58. *Ibid.*, Aug. 20, 1916.
59. *Ibid.*, Aug. 22, 1916.

CHAPTER 6

1. *New York Times*, Aug. 4, 1916.
2. *Ibid.*, Aug. 5, 1916.
3. *Ibid.*, Aug. 8, 1916.
4. *Ibid.*, Aug. 16, 1916.
5. New York *Call*, Aug. 10, 15, 1916.
6. *Ibid.*, Aug. 16, 1916.
7. New York *Call*, Aug. 22, 1916; Dubofsky, *op. cit.*, p. 137.
8. Dubofsky, *op. cit.*, p. 137.
9. *New York Times*, Aug. 15, 31, 1916.
10. New York *Call*, Aug. 25, Sept. 2, 1916.
11. *New York Times*, Sept. 2, 1916; New York *Call*, Sept. 2, 1916.
12. New York *Call*, Sept. 6, 1916.
13. *New York Times*, Sept. 2, 1916.
14. Waitzman, *op. cit.*, p. 47.
15. *New York Times*, Sept. 4-5, 1916.
16. *New York Times*, Sept. 7, 1916; New York *Call*, Sept. 7, 1916.
17. *New York Times*, Sept. 7, 1916.
18. New York *Call*, Sept. 8, 1916.
19. *International Socialist Review* 16 (November, 1916): 289-90.
20. *Ibid.*
21. *New York Times*, Sept. 11, 1916; New York *Tribune*, Sept. 12, 1916.
22. New York *Call*, Sept. 7, 1916.
23. Minute Book, Central Committee, Local New York, Socialist Party Sept. 3, 1916, p. 280, Tamiment Institute Library, New York University.
24. New York *Call*, Sept. 21, 1916.
25. *Report of the Public Service Commission for the First District of the State of New York for the Year Ending December 31, 1916*, Albany, 1917, pp. 383-87.
26. *New York Times*, Sept. 14, 1916.
27. New York *Call*, Sept. 14, 1916.
28. *Report of the Public Service Commission, op. cit.*, pp. 387-89.
29. New York *Call*, Sept. 15, 1916; *New York Times*, Sept. 15, 1916.
30. *New York Times*, Sept. 15, 1916.
31. *Ibid.*, Sept. 11, 1916.
32. *Ibid.*, Sept. 9, 1916.
33. *Ibid.*, New York *Call*, Sept. 9, 1916.
34. *New York Times*, Sept. 12, 1916.
35. *Ibid.*
36. John R. Commons and Associates, *History of Labor in the United States*, New York, 1935, vol. 3, p. 349.
37. New York *Call*, Sept. 17, 1916. The report was drawn up by Dante Barton, a member of the Committee, who investigated the strike.
38. *New York Times*, Sept. 16, 18, 19, 1916; New York *Call*, Sept. 16-20, 1916.
39. New York Times, Sept. 21-22, 1916.
40. *Ibid.*, Sept. 22, 1916.
41. Waitzman, *op. cit.*, p. 67.
42. *New York Times*, Sept. 23-24, 1916.
43. *Ibid.*, Sept. 22, 1916.
44. *Ibid.*, Sept. 23, 1916; New York *Call*, Sept. 23, 1916.
45. New York *Call*, Sept. 23, 1916.
46. *Ibid.*
47. *Ibid.*, Sept. 24, 1916.
48. *Ibid.*, Sept. 28, 1916.
49. Waitzman, *op. cit.*, pp. 69-70.
50. *New York Times*, Sept. 28-Oct. 1, 1916; New York *Call*, Sept. 29-Oct. 1, 1916.
51. New York *Call*, Oct. 3, 1916.
52. *Ibid.*, Oct. 4, 1916.
53. *The Headgear Worker* 1 (October-November, 1916): 5.
54. Quoted in "The New York Strike Failure," *Literary Digest*, Oct. 14, 1916, p. 939.
55. *Typographical Journal*, January, 1917, pp. 132-40.
56. *New York Times*, Jan. 22, 1917.
57. *Weekly People*, Jan. 27, 1917.
58. New York *Call*, Sept. 15, 1916.
59. *Ibid.*, Oct. 5-7, 1916; *New York Times*, Oct. 6-7, 1917.
60. New York *Call*, Oct. 31, 1916; *New York Times*, Oct. 31, 1916; Waitzman, *op. cit.*, pp. 71-72.
61. New York *Call*, Dec. 17, 1916.
62. *Motorman and Conductor*, October, 1917, p. 91.
63. Quoted in *And Then Came TWU*, New York, 1950, p. 21, For James Connolly's role in the United States, *see* Carl Reeve and Ann Barton Reeve, *James Connolly and the United States: The Road to the 1916 Irish Rebellion*, Atlantic Highlands, 1978.
64. *Weekly People*, Sept. 16, 1916.
65. *New York Times*, Oct. 16, 1916.
66. *Ibid.*, Sept. 18, 1916; Waitzman, *op. cit.*, p. 72.
67. *And Then Came TWU*, p. 22.

CHAPTER 7

1. James Dyche, *The Strike of the Ladies' Waist Makers of New York*, New York, 1910, p. 191.

2. *Ladies' Garment Worker* 3 (February, 1912): 11; Hyman Berman, "Era of the Protocol: A Chapter of the History of the International Ladies' Garment Workers' Union, 1910-1916, "unpublished Ph.D. dissertation, Columbia University, 1956, pp. 287-88; Jack Hardy, The Clothing Worker, New York, 1935, pp. 30-39.

3. Carolyn Daniel McCreesh, "On the Picket Lines: Militant Women Campaign to Organize Garment Workers, 1882-1917," unpublished Ph.D. dissertation, University of Maryland, 1975, p. 246.

4. *Ladies' Garment Worker* 5 (April, 1914): 16-17; June, 1914, p. 25.

5. *Ibid.*, August, 1914, pp. 22-23.

6. Philip S. Foner, *History of the Labor Movement in the United States*, New York, 1980, vol. 5, pp. 260-264; Charles Elbert Zaretz, *The Amalgamated Clothing Workers of America*, New York, 1954, pp. 73-96; Earl D. Strong, *The Amalgamated Clothing Workers of America*, Grinnell, Ia. 1940, pp. 2-10.

7. *Documentary History of the Amalgamated Clothing Workers of America*, 1914-1916, New York, 1922, pp. 4-25.

8. Zaretz, *op. cit.*, pp. 96-98.

9. Matthew Josephson, *Sidney Hillman, Statesman of American Labor*, New York, 1952 pp. 95-99; McCreesh, *op. cit.*, pp. 250-51; *Garment Worker* 14 (Oct. 23, 1914: 1; October 30, 1914, pp. 1,4; Joel Seidman, *The Needle Trades*, New York, 1942, pp. 115-25; Warren R. Van Tine, *The Making of a Labor Bureaucrat*, Amherst, Mass. 1973, p. 157.

10. Bernard Mandel, *Samuel Gompers: A Biography*, Yellow Springs, Ohio, 1963, p. 166; Zaretz, *op. cit.*, pp. 102-05; *Documentary History*, pp. 74-75.

11. Philip S. Foner, *Women and the American Labor Movement: From Colonial Times to the Eve of World War 1*, New York, 1979, pp. 378-79.

12. McCreesh, *op. cit.*, p. 251; Bessie Abramowitz to Sidney Hillman, November 20, 1914, April 13, 1915, Amalgamated Clothing Workers' files, Amalgamated Clothing Workers Headquarters, New York City.

13. McCreesh, *op. cit.*, p. 251; Selma Goldblatt to Joseph Schlossberg, November 30, 1915; Schlossberg to Goldblatt, February 10, 1915, Amalgamated Clothing Workers files.

14. McCreesh, *op. cit.*, pp. 251-52; Dorothy Jacobs, "Baltimore Women Workers Were Leaders in Building up a Strong Organization," *Advance* 1 (July, 1917): 6; "Biography of Dorothy Jacobs," Amalgamated Clothing Workers files; Herbert Gutman, "Dorothy Jacobs Bellanca," in Edward T. James, Janet Wilson James, and Paul S. Boyer, editors, *Notable American Women, 1607-1950*, Cambridge, Mass., 1971, 1: 124.

15. *Documentary History*, p. 181; *Garment Worker* 15 (March 26, 1915): 1-2; Barbara Wertheimer, *We Were There: The Story of Working Women in America*, New York, 1977, p. 329.

16. *Garment Worker* 14 (May 28, 1915): 1-2.

17. *Proceedings*, A. F. of L. Convention, 1915, pp. 144-46, 360-61; *Garment Worker* 14 August 27, 1915): 1, 4.

18. Abraham Cahan to Benjamin Schlesinger, November 23, 1916, Samuel Gompers Papers., State Historical Society of Wisconsin, cited in Melvyn Dubofsky, "New York City Labor in the Progressive Era: A Study of Organized Labor in an Era of Reform,": unpublished Ph.D. dissertation, University of Rochester, 1960, pp. 302-03.

19. Josephson, *op. cit.*, pp. 116-18.

20. *Ibid.*, pp. 121-23; McCreesh, *op. cit.*, p. 274; Leo Wolman et al., *The Clothing Workers of Chicago*, Chicago, 1922, pp. 95-98.

21. Josephson, *op. cit.*, pp. 125-26; *Proceedings of the Second Biennial Convention of the Amalgamated Clothing Workers of America, Rochester, New York*, 1916, pp. 150-51.

22. Josephson, *op. cit.*, pp. 124-25; Leo Wolman, et al., *The Clothing Workers of Chicago*, pp. 99-100; McCreesh, *op. cit.*, pp. 274-75.

23. Mary "Mother" Jones to Secretary W. B. Wilson, October 18, 1915; Wilson to Jones, October, 1915, Conciliation Service, file 313121, National Archives. Washington, D. C.; Sidney Hillman to Joseph Schlossberg, October 22, 24, 1915, Amalgamated Clothing Workers files; Mandel, *Samuel Gompers*, p. 308; McCreesh, *op. cit.*, pp. 275-76; Josephson, *op. cit.*, pp. 126-28; Melech Epstein, *Jewish Labor in the U.S.: An Industrial, Political and Cultural History of the Jewish Labor Movement*, New York, 1950-1953, 2: 252.

24. *New Republic*, Jan. 1, 1916, p. 218; Feb. 19, 1916, pp. 73-74; March 4, 1916, p. 130; Ellen Gates Starr to Gompers, January 8, 1916; Gompers to Starr, February 10, 1916, Amalgamated Clothing Workers files; Benjamin Larger to Gompers, January

31. October 4, 1916, A.F. of L. Correspondence, Wahington, D.C.
25. Josephson, op. cit., pp. 144-45; Epstein, Jewish Labor, 2:51; McCreesh, op. cit., p. 270.
26. Jacobs, "Baltimore Women Workers," p. 6; McCreesh, op. cit., pp. 276-77.
27. Dorothy Jacobs to Joseph Schlossberg, Sept. 10, 1916, Amalgamated Clothing Workers files; McCreesh, op. cit., p. 278.
28. Proceedings of the Second Biennial Convention of the Amalgamated Clothing Workers, 1916, p. 193.
29. Dorothy Jacobs to Joseph Schlossberg, September 10, 1916, Amalgamated Clothing Workers files; McCreesh, op. cit., p. 278.
30. General Executive Board to Joint Boards, District Councils, and Local Unions, Oct. 30, 1916, Amalgamated Clothing Workers files; McCreesh, op. cit., p. 279.
31. Dorothy Jacobs to Joseph Schlossberg, July 20, 27, August 13, 20, Sept. 10, 17, November 5, 8, 1916, Amalgamated Clothing Workers files; McCreesh op. cit. pp. 279-80.
32. Advance 1 (March 9, 1917): 1.
33. McCreesh, op. cit., p. 280.
34. Rose Schneiderman, with Lucy Goldwaithe, All for One, New York 1967 pp. 110-12; Emily Barrows, "Trade Union Organization Among Women of Chicago," unpublished M.A. thesis, University of Chicago, 1927, pp. 61-69; Agnes Nestor, Woman's Labor Leader: An Autobiography of Agnes Nestor, Rockford, Ill., 1954, p. 163; Wilford Carsel, A History of the Chicago Ladies' Garment Workers' Union, Chicago, 1940, pp. 88-91; McCreesh, op. cit., pp. 280-82.
35. Pauline Newman, interview in Columbia Oral History Collection, Socialist Movement Project, vol. 8, pp. 7-8.
36. Schneiderman, All for One, pp. 113-17; McCreesh, op. cit., pp. 282, 284.
37. Proceedings of the Thirteenth I.L.G.W.U. Convention, Philadelphia, 1916, pp. 27, 48-50.
38. Ladies' Garment Worker 7 (March, 1916): 20; April 1916, pp. 1-3; June, 1916, pp. 12-13; New York Times, May 3, 1916; Berman, "Era of the Protocol," pp. 411-15.
39. Ladies' Garment Worker 7 (July, 1916): 10-11; August, 1916, p. 18; September, 1916, pp. 18-20; New York Times, May 26,29, June 11,15,28, July 19, 1916.
40. New York Times, May 27,29, June 3, 1916; Berman, "Era of the Protocol," pp. 415-16.
41. New York Times, Aug. 4, 1916; Ladies' Garment Cutter 4 (August 5, 1916): 1-2.
42. Proceedings of the Thirteenth I.L.G.W.U. Convention, p. 12.
43. Ladies' Garment Worker 6 (November, 1916): 4; Fannia M. Cohn, "Our Educational Work—A Survey," New York, 1916, pp. 10-11.
44. Proceedings of the Thirteenth I.L.G.W.U. Convention, p. 27.
45. Philip S. Foner, The Fur and Leather Workers Union, Newark, N.J., 1950, p. 35.
46. Ibid., pp. 58-60.
47. Newark (N.J.) Times, April 13-21, 1915; Foner, Fur and Leather Workers Union, p. 56.
48. Fur Worker, March 13,20, April 17, 1917.
49. Jacob N. Budish and George Soule, The New Unionism in the Clothing Industry, New York, 1920, pp. 13-65; John H. M. Laslett, Labor and the Left, New York, 1958, pp. 121-25.
50. "Using 'Gangs' in Labor's Wars," Literary Digest, May 29, 1915, p. 1260.
51. Dr. Louis L. Harris to A.W. Miller, July 26, 1917, International Fur Workers Union Archives; Dr. Louis L. Harris, "A Clinical and Sanitary Study of the Fur and Hatters' Fur Trade," Monthly Bulletin of the Department of Health New York City, October, 1915; Foner, Fur and Leather Workers Union, pp. 64-65.
52. Foner, Fur and Leather Workers Union, p. 65; Jack Hardy, The Clothing Workers New York, 1935, p. 117.
53. Foner, Fur and Leather Workers Union, pp. 62-70. For similar trends in other AFL unions, see Foner, History of Labor Movement, 3: pp. 136-60.

CHAPTER 8

1. Philip S. Foner, Women and the American Labor Movement: From Colonial Times to the Eve of World War I, New York, 1979, p. 470.
2. Ibid., pp. 470-71.
3. New York, Department of Labor, Statistics of Trade Unions in 1914, Bulletin No. 74, September 1915, p. 21; Labor Organizations in 1915, Bulletin No. 69, April, 1914, p. 109.
4. Samuel Gompers, "Working Women Organize," American Federationist 21 (March, 1914):232.
5. New York Factory Investigating Commission, Third Report, 1914, pp. 111, 144; Fourth Report, 1915, 2:144-56, 165, 224-25, 232, 237, 243, 267-69, 304-12, 337-57,416.
6. Sue Ainsley Clark to Margaret Dreier

Robins, April, 1912, National Women's Trade Union League Papers, Arthur and Elizabeth Schlesinger Library on the History of Women, Radcliffe College, hereinafter cited as NWTUL Papers.

7. Philip S. Foner, *History of the Labor Movement in the United States*, vol IV, *The I.W.W., 1905-1917*, New York, 1965, pp. 339-40; Mary K. O'Sullivan, "The Labor War at Lawrence," *Survey* 28 (April 1912): 72; Mary Kenney O'Sullivan, n.d., Schlesinger Library, Radcliffe College.

8. Elizabeth Glendower Evans to Margaret Dreier Robins, March 25, 1912, Margaret Dreier Robins Papers, University of Florida, Gainesville, Florida. Hereinafter cited as Robins Papers.

9. Sue Ainsley Clark to Margaret Dreier Robins, April 1912, NWTUL Papers.

10. Minutes of the National Executive Board of the NWTUL, Apr. 17-19, 1912, pp. 2,15, NWTUL Papers.

11. Mary E. McDowell to Mr. Leard (1912); McDowell to Homer D. Call, (1912), and May 28, 1912, Mary E. McDowell Papers, Chicago Historical Society.

12. Margaret Dreier Robins to Leonora O'Reilly, July 19, 1911, Leonora O'Reilly Papers, Schlesinger Library, Radcliffe College, hereinafter cited as O'Reilly Papers. *See also Proceedings of the National Women's Trade Union League Convention, 1911*, p. 4.

13. Homer D. Call to Mary E. McDowell, May 27, June 10, 1912, McDowell Papers; Minutes of the National Executive Board of the NWTUL, Apr. 17-19, 1912, NWTUL Papers.

14. Minutes of the National Executive Board of the NWTUL, Apr. 17-19, 1912, NWTUL Papers; Carolyn Daniel McCreesh, "On the Picket Lines: Militant Women Campaign to Organize Garment Workers, 1882-1917, "unpublished Ph.D. dissertation, University of Maryland, 1975, p. 212.

15. Mary Dreier Robins to Gompers, May 3, 1913, NWTUL Papers.

16. Helen Marot to Margaret Dreier Robins, March 28, 1912, NWTUL Papers; Secretary's Report, Women's Trade Union League of New York, Nov. 27, 1912, Women's Trade Union League of New York Papers, New York State Library of New York, New York City. Hereinafter cited as WTUL of N.Y. Papers. *See also* Homer D. Call to Mary E. McDowell, June 10, 1912, McDowell Papers.

17. McCreesh, "Picket Lines," pp. 238-39.

18. *Ibid.*, p. 243.

19. "Training Women in Union Leadership," *Survey*, Dec. 16, 1916, p. 312.

20. Violet Pike, *New World Lessons for Old World People*, New York, 1912, "Lesson Four: A Trade Without a Union" and Lesson Five: A Trade With a Union." *See also* Ruth Austin, "Teaching English to our Foreign Friends," *Life and Labor* 1 (Sept 1911): 260.

21. Mildred Rankin to Margaret Dreier Robins, May (N.D.), Robins Papers.

22. Secretary's Report, *Proceedings of the Fourth Biennial Convention of the National Women's Trade Union League of America*, St. Louis, 1913; Josephine Pacheco, "NWTUL, A.F. of L., I.W.W.: A Study in Labor and Violence," paper in possession of present writer, p. 5.

23. *Proceedings of the Sixth Biennial Convention of the NWTUL, 1915*, pp. 188-90; Gompers to Margaret Dreier Robins, July 31, 1915, NWTUL Papers.

24. Elizabeth Brandeis, "Labor Legislation" in John R. Commons and Associates, *History of Labor in the United States, 1896-1932* (New York, 1935) 3: 501-39; James T. Patterson, "Mary Dewson and the American Minimum Wage Movement," *Labor History* 5 (Spring, 1964): 134-52; Thomas J. Kerr, IV, "The New York Factory Investigating Commission and the Minimum-Wage Movement, *Ibid* 12 (Summer, 1971): 373-91.

25. *Proceedings of the Eighteenth National Convention of the National Association of Manufacturers*, New York, 1913, pp. 71-74; *Twentieth National Convention* New York, 1915, pp. 126-29.

26. *Proceedings of the A.F. of L. Convention, 1912*, p. 231; *1913*, pp. 59-64, 299-300; Samuel Gompers, "The American Labor Movement," *American Federationist* 21 (July, 1914): 543-44; "Women's Work, Rights and Progress," *ibid* 22 (July, 1915): 517-19; Samuel Gompers to Abraham L. Elkus, June 5, 1914, Gompers Letter-Books, Library of Congress.

27. "A Living Wage for Women," *Independent* 74 (April 17, 1913): New York *Call*, June 15, 1915; Nancy Schrom Dye, "The Women's Trade Union League of New York, 1903-1920, "unpublished Ph.D. dissertation, University of Wisconsin, Madison, 1974, pp. 420-22.

28. "Little Sister" to Leonora O'Reilly, April 27, 1908, O'Reilly Papers.

29. Aileen S. Kraditor, *The Ideas of the Woman*

Suffrage Movement, 1890-1920, New York, 1965, Chapter 6; Ida Husted Harper, editor. *History of Woman Suffrage,* vol. 5, 1900-1920, New York, 1972, p. 78; *New York Times,* Dec. 31, 1909.

30. Rose Schneiderman, with Lucy Goldthwaite, *All for One,* New York, 1967, pp. 121-22; Margaret Dreier Robins to Leonora O'Reilly, July 19, 1914, O'Reilly Papers; Robin Miller Jacoby, "The Women's Trade Union League and American Feminism." *Feminist Studies* 3 (Fall, 1975): 130-31.

31. Jacoby, "Women's Trade Union League," pp. 132-34; Dye, "Women's Trade Union League," p. 360; Mary Beard to Leonora O'Reilly, n.d., O'Reilly Papers.

32. Margaret Hinchey to Leonora O'Reilly, n.d., O'Reilly Papers.

33. "Senators vs. Working Women: Miss Rose Schneiderman Replies to New York Senator," in Wage Earners' Suffrage League, New York, O'Reilly Papers; Jacoby, "Women's Trade Union League," p. 133.

34. "Report of the Fifth Biennial Convention," *Life and Labor* 5 (July, 1915):118; *New York Call,* June 2, 1910.

35. Leonora O'Reilly to Electrical Workers, April 19, 1911, O'Reilly Papers.

36. U.S. Commission on Industrial Relations, *Final Report,* Washington, D.C., 1916, pp. 37-38; *New York Times,* May 28, 1915.

37. *New York Times,* May 28, 1915; *American Federationist* 15 (October, 1915): 861-62.

38. *New York Times,* April 12, 1916; Barbara Klaszynska, "Why Women Work: A Comparison of Various Groups—Philadelphia, 1910-1930, *Labor History* 17 (Winter, 1976): 225-27.

39. *American Federationist* 15 (October, 1915): 861-62.

40. Leonora O'Reilly to Mary Dreier Robins, August 31, 1915, O'Reilly Papers; McCreesh "Picket Lines," pp. 382-84.

CHAPTER 9

1. 30 *U.S. Statutes* 424.

2. *U.S.V. Scott,* 148 Fed 431; *U.S. V. Adair* 208 U.S. 161.

3. Richard B. Olney, "Discrimination Against Union Labor—Legal?" American Law Review 42 (March-April, 1908): 164.

4. Harry D. Wolf, *The Railroad Board,* New York, 1943, p. 7; Howard S. Kaltenborn, *Government Adjustment of Labor Disputes,* New York, 1950, pp. 38-39; "Mediation and Arbitration Under Erdman Act, December 1906, June 30, 1913," Records of the Department of Labor, RG/174, National Archives. Hereinafter cited as NA.

5. Wolf, *op. cit.,* p. 8.

6. Dallas L. Jones, "The Wilson Administration and Organized Labor, 1912-1919," unpublished Ph.D. thesis, Cornell University, 1956, pp. 241-42.

7. Edward Berman, *Labor Disputes and the Presidency,* New Haven, 1951, pp. 73-74.

8. William B. Wilson to Ralph M. Easley, March 12, 1913; Seth Low to William C. Redfield, June 1, 1913, Records of the Department of Labor, Erdman Act, NA.

9. Seth Low to William C. Redfield, June 11, 1913; Seth Low to William B. Wilson, June 28, 1913; Ralph M. Easley to William B. Wilson, July 3, 1913, Rec. Dept. of Labor, Erdman Act, NA.

10. *New York Times,* July 15,16, 1913; Allen La Verne Shepherd, "Federal Railway Labor Policy, 1913-1926," unpublished Ph.D. thesis, University of Nebraska, 1971, pp. 22-25.

11. Jones, *op. cit.,* pp. 250-51; Shepherd, *op. cit.,* p. 27.

12. W. L. Chambers to Woodrow Wilson, July 26, 1904, Woodrow Wilson Papers, Library of Congress. Hereinafter cited as Woodrow Wilson Papers.

13. *New York Times,* Aug. 1, 1914.

14. Woodrow Wilson to A.W. Trenholm, August 2, 1914, Woodrow Wilson Papers.

15. A.W. Trenholm to Woodrow Wilson, August 3, 1914, Woodrow Wilson Papers.

16. *New York Times,* Aug. 5, 1914.

17. Berman, *op. cit.,* pp. 103-04; Jones, *op. cit.,* pp. 253-54.

18. Jones, op. cit., p. 254.

19. Shepherd, *op. cit.,* p. 28, *Railway Age Gazette,* 53 (November 29, 1912): 1022, 1038-44.

20. *Locomotive Firemen & Enginemen Magazine* 54 (March, 1913): 278-79.

21. "The Railroad Man's Right to a Shorter Day," *Railroad Trainman* 33 (April, 1916): 349-50; W. S. Carter, "Why the Eight-Hour Day is Right," Woodrow Wilson Papers; Shepherd, *op. cit.,* pp. 77-78.

22. *The Railroad Trainman* 33 (January, 1916): 3-5; Edwin C. Robbins, "The Trainmen's Eight-Hour Day—1," *Political Science Quarterly* 31 (Dec, 1916): 545-46.

23. *New York Times,* December 16-17, 1915; Berman, *op. cit.,* p. 106.

24. New York *Sun,* reprinted in *Literary Digest,* Feb. 5, 1916, p. 275; Robbins, *op. cit.,* pp. 547-48; Perlman & Taft, *op. cit.,* p. 381.

25. Reprinted in New York *Call*, July 4, 1916.
26. *Railway Conductor*, 33 (March, 1916): 205-09.
27. Reprinted in New York *Call*, July 4, 1916. See also *Literary Digest*, June 4, 1910, pp. 1109-10, and *New York Times*, July 7, 1916.
28. Reprinted in New York *Call*, July 9, 1916.
29. "The Eight Hour Day and Safety First," *Railroad Trainmen* 33 (April, 1916) 349-50.
30. Railway Conductor 33 (March, 1916); 205-09; Perlman and Taft. *op. cit.*, p. 381; Robbins, *op cit.*, pp. 347-51.
31. Reprinted in New York *Call*, Aug. 9, 1916.
32. *Ibid.*
33. *Railroad Trainman* 33 (April, 1916): 354-55.
34. Reprinted in *Literary Digest*, Feb. 5, 1916, p. 275.
35. Reprinted in *ibid.*, p. 276.
36. Reprinted in *ibid.*
37. *New York Times*, June 2, 16, 17, 1916; Robbins *op. cit.*, pp. 551-58; Jones, *op. cit.*, pp. 251-52; Shepherd, *op. cit.*, 78-79; *Railroad Trainman*, 33 (July, 1916): 634; *Railway Conductor* 33 (July, 1916): 530-31.
38. New York *Sun*, reprinted in *Literary Digest*, Aug. 8, 1916; *New York Times*, Aug. 9, 1916.
39. New York *Call* reprinted in *Literary Digest*, Aug. 9, 1916. p. 392.
40. *Railway Age Gazette*, reprinted in *ibid.*
41. New York *World*, Aug. 9, 1916.
42. *New York Times*, Aug. 10-13, 1916.
43. Judge William Chambers to Representative H. M. Towner, July 26, 1916, Records of the U.S. Board of Mediation & Conciliation, Recorded Group No. 13, NA. *See also* William B. Wilson to Martin A. Knapp, March 9, 1916, and Knapp to Wilson, March 11, 1916, *ibid.*
44. *New York Times*, Aug. 11-12, 1916.
45. Chambers to Wilson, August 13, 1916, Woodrow Wilson Papers.
46. Woodrow Wilson to W. G. Lee, W. S. Carter, W. S. Stone, A. S. Garretson, and Elisha Lee, August 13,1916; Woodrow Wilson Papers; *New York Times*, Aug. 14, 1916; Shepherd, *op. cit.*, pp. 82-83.
47. New York *Call*, Aug. 14, 1916.
48. Shepherd, *op. cit.*, pp. 83-84; Jones, *op. cit.*, pp. 244-45.
49. *New York Times*, Aug. 3, 1916; Edwin C. Robbins, "The Trainmen's Eight-Hour Law, II," *Political Science Quarterly* 22 (September, 1917): 426.
50. *See* New York *Herald*, Aug. 23, 1916.
51. Reprinted in New York *Call*, Aug. 14, 1916.

52. Reprinted in *New York Times*, Aug. 3-5, 1916.
53. *See* Henry Ford to Wilson, Sept. 1, 1916; William G. McAdoo to Wilson, July 28, 1916; James Reed to Wilson, Aug. 9, 1916; C. S. Hamlin to Wilson, August 30, 1916, Woodrow Wilson Papers; Ben Tillman to William Chambers, Aug. 16, 1916, RG/131, NA; Shepherd, *op. cit.*, pp. 86-88.
54. *Providence Journal*, Aug. 8, 1916; *New York Times*, Aug. 27, 28, 1916.
55. St. Paul *Dispatch*, Aug. 26, 1916.
56. *Springfield Republican*, Aug. 31, 1916; New York *Evening Post*, Aug. 18, 1916.
57. New York *Call*, July 4, 1916.
58. New York *Call*, Aug. 7, 1916.
59. Philadelphia *North American*, Nov. 17, 1914; Deseret *Evening News*, Nov. 17, 1914; *Proceedings*, A.F. of L. Convention, 1914, pp. 112-15.
60. Jones, *op. cit.*, pp. 261-62.
61. New York *Call*, Aug. 14, 1916.
62. Memorandum, unorganized railroad workers to Woodrow Wilson, August, 1916. Woodrow Wilson Papers, *New York Times*, Aug. 9, 1916; Shepherd, *op. cit.*, p. 94.
63. Samuel Gompers to E. L. Marcellus, August 30, 1916, Gompers Letter Book, Library of Congress, Manuscripts Division. Hereinafter cited as GLB.

CHAPTER 10

1. Woodrow Wilson to Senator William J. Stone, February 22, 1916, Woodrow Wilson Papers.
2. Woodrow Wilson to W. C. Adamson, April 7, 1916, *ibid.*
3. James Reed to Woodrow Wilson, April 10, 1916; William G. McAdoo, to Woodrow Wilson, April 15, 1916; Richard B. Olney to Woodrow Wilson, April 16, 1916; Benjamin F. Tillman to Woodrow Wilson, April 18, 1916, all in Woodrow Wilson Papers.
4. Woodrow Wilson to William G. McAdoo, July 27, 1916, *ibid.*
5. Joseph Tumulty to Woodrow Wilson, July 18, 1916; William G. McAdoo to Woodrow Wilson, July 31, 1916, Records of the Board of Mediation & Conciliation, NA.
6. *New York Times*, Aug. 3, 1916.
7. William B. Wilson to Woodrow Wilson, August 5, 1916, Woodrow Wilson Papers.
8. *Ibid.*
9. Woodrow Wilson to William B. Wilson, August 9, 1916, Woodrow Wilson Papers.

10. Charles F. Weed to Woodrow Wilson, August 9, 1916, and Henry F. Wheeler to Charles F. Weed, August 11, 1916, Woodrow Wilson Papers.
11. *New York Times*, Aug. 4, 9, 1916.
12. Philip S. Foner, *History of the Labor Movement in the United States*, New York, 1980, vol. V, pp. 112-15.
13. Charles Smith, "Woodrow Wilson and Organized Labor," unpublished Ph.D., Catholic University of America, 1963, pp. 485-86.
14. Woodrow Wilson to John A. Wilson, August 22, 1916, Woodrow Wilson Papers.
15. Woodrow Wilson to Adamson, March 22, 1916; Woodrow Wilson to H. E. Niles, *et. al.*, National Legislative and Information Bureau (Conductors, Trainmen, Locomotive Engineers, Firemen, and Enginemen) to Woodrow Wilson, June 1, 1916, Woodrow Wilson Papers. *See also* "The President as Arbiter," *Christian Science Monitor*, Aug. 5, 1916.
16. Arthur S. Link, *Wilson: Campaigns for Progressivism and Peace, 1916-1917*, New York 1965, p. 84; Shepherd, *op. cit.*, pp. 84-85; *New York Times*, Aug. 25, 1916.
17. *New York Times*, Aug. 15, 1916; Link, *op. cit.*, p. 84
18. Woodrow Wilson to Senator Newlands, August 19, 1916, RG/13 NA.
19. Shepherd, *op. cit.*, pp. 85-86.
20. Jones, *op. cit.*, p. 253.
21. *New York Times*, Aug. 18, 1916.
22. *Ibid.*, Aug. 16-17, 1916.
23. *Literary Digest*, Sept. 2, 1916, p. 544.
24. *Ibid.*
25. *New York Times*, Aug. 19, 20, 1916.
26. Los Angeles *Times*, Aug. 20, 1916.
27. *New York Times*, Aug. 20, 1916.
28. *Ibid.*, Aug. 21, 1916.
29. *See*, for example, petition of what was said to be thousands of workers on the Union Line, dated August 17, 1916, in Woodrow Wilson Papers.
30. George Pope to Woodrow Wilson, August 18, 1916, *ibid.*
31. Woodrow Wilson to George Pope, August 20, 1916, *ibid.*
32. George Pope to Woodrow Wilson, August 23, 1916; *ibid.*; *Literary Digest*, Sept. 2, 1916, p. 544.
33. *New York Times*, Aug. 23, 26, 1916; Jones, *op. cit.*, pp. 244-45; Shepherd, *op. cit;* p. 87
34. Representatives of the Brotherhoods (Garretson, Stone, Lee, Carter) to Woodrow Wilson, August 29, 1916, Woodrow Wilson Papers.
35. Representatives of the Brotherhoods (Garretson, Stone, Lee, Carter) to Woodrow Wilson, August 27, 1916, *ibid.*; Note of Garretson attached to letter of August 29, 1916 to Wilson, *ibid.*; *New York Times*, Aug. 29, 1916.
36. Jones, *op. cit.*, p. 247.
37. New York *Call*, Aug. 31, 1916.
38. Reprinted in *Literary Digest*, Sept. 2, 1916, p. 544.
39. New York *Call*, Aug. 27, 1916.
40. Memorandum of Conversation between White House and Representatives of the Railway Executives, August 28, 1916; Memorandum of Conversation between White House and A. B. Garretson, August 28, 1916, Woodrow Wilson Papers; *New York Times*, Aug. 28, 1916; Jones, *op. cit.*, p. 249.
41. New York *Call*, Aug. 28, 30, 1916.
42. Woodrow Wilson to Norman Hapgood, August 30, 1916, Woodrow Wilson Papers; *New York Times*, Aug. 31, 1916.
43. Berman, *op. cit.*, pp. 122-23; Jones, *op. cit.*, p. 250.
44. New York *Sun*, Aug. 31, 1916.
45. New York *Call*, Sept. 2, 1916.
46. Woodrow Wilson, "Address to Congress, August 29, 1916," in Ray Stannard Baker, *The Public and Private Papers of Woodrow Wilson*, New York 1928, vol. II, pp. 267-72; *Congressional Record*, 64th Congress, 1st Session, pp. 1336-63; *New York Times*, Aug. 30, 1916.
47. New York *Call*, Aug. 30, Sept. 1, 1916.
48. Jones, *op. cit.*, pp. 252-53; Shepherd, *op. cit.*, pp. 89-90.
49. New York *Call*, Aug. 27, 1916.
50. U.S. Congress, *Committee on Interstate Commerce, Hearings on the Threatened Strike of Railway Employees*, 64th Congress, 1st Session, pp. 41-42; *New York Call*, Sept. 27, 1916.
51. New York *Call*, Sept. 27, 1916.
52. William C. Adamson to Ray Stannard Baker, February 9, 1927, in Ray Stannard Baker Papers, Library of Congress; *New York Times*, Aug. 30-Sept. 1, 1916
53. *New York Times*, Sept. 1-4, 1916. Samuel Gompers to William B. Wilson, September 1, 1916, and R. Guard for Samuel Gompers to Grant Gamilton, GLB; New York *Call*, Sept. 2, 1916.
54. *New York Times*, Sept. 3, 1916.
55. R. Guard for Samuel Gompers to Grant Hamilton, Sept. 2, 1916, GLB.
56. Gompers to L. W. Quick, Secretary and Treasurer of the Order of Railroad Telegraphers, Sept. 18, 1916, GLB.

57. Shepherd, *op. cit.*, p. 91; Jones, *op. cit.*, p. 258; W. E. Giles to Woodrow Wilson, August 31, 1916, Woodrow Wilson Papers.
58. Shepherd, *op. cit.*, pp. 91-92. Shepherd bases much of his conclusion on the discussion in Arthur S. Link, *Woodrow Wilson and the Progressive Era, 1900-1917*, New York, 1954, pp. 223-29
59. *Congressional Record*, 64th Congress, 1st Sessions, pp. 13655, 13608.
60. *New York Times*, Sept. 20, 1916; Jones, *op. cit.*, p. 262.
61. *New York Call*, Sept. 3, 1916.
62. Robbins, *op. cit.*, II. pp. 421-22; Jones, *op. cit.*, p. 264.
63. *New York Times*, Oct. 2, 1916.
64. *Literary Digest*, Dec. 2, 1916, p. 1447.
65. *Ibid.*
66. *New York Times*, Dec. 12, 1916; Gompers, *Seventy Years of Life and Labor 2*: 143-45.
67. *Ibid.*, Oct. 6, 1916.
68. *Report of the Eight-Hour Commission*, Washington, D.C. 1918, pp. 7-23.
69. *New York Times*, March 15-18, 1917.
70. Woodrow Wilson to Elisha Lee, and Woodrow Wilson to the chiefs of the four Brotherhoods, March 16, 1917, Woodrow Wilson Papers.
71. *New York Times*, March 17, 1917.
72. Shepherd, *op. cit.*, p. 99.
73. *New York Times*, March 19, 20, 1917.
74. *New York Times*, March 20, 1917; Wilson v. New, 243, U.S. 32; "A Statesmanlike Decision," *"New Republic* 10 (March 24, 1917): 2; 7-18.
75. W. J. Adams to C. C. Simons (1917) in Woodrow Wilson Papers.

CHAPTER 11

1. *New York Call*, June 15, 1915.
2. *Proceedings*, A.F. of L. Convention, 1913, p. 409.
3. John Graham Brooks, "The Challenge of Unemployment," *The Independent* 81 (March 15, 1915): 383-85.
4. McCreesh, op. cit., pp. 235-36.
5. New York, Department of Labor, *Bulletin No. 69*, March, 1915; p. 6; N.Y. Department of Labor, *Bulletin No. 73*, August, 1915, p. 2; *Massachusetts Industrial Review*, no. 7 (March, 1922).
6. Philip S. Foner, *History of the Labor Movement in the United States*, vol. IV, *The I.W.W.*, 1905-1917, New York, 1965, pp. 435-61.
7. J. Edward Morgan, "The Unemployed in San Francisco," *New Review*, April, 1914, pp. 193-99.
8. *Solidarity*, Jan. 24, 1915.
9. Carolyn Ashbaugh, *Lucy Parsons: American Revolutionary*, Chicago, 1970, pp. 238-39.
10. *Chicago Tribune*, Jan. 18, 1915; Ralph Chaplin, "A Hunger 'Riot' in Chicago," *International Socialist Review* 15 (March, 1915); 517-20; Ashbaugh, *Lucy Parsons* pp. 237-44.
11. Foner, *History of Labor Movement 5*: 458-61.
12. McCreesh, *op. cit.*, pp. 235-36.
13. U.S. Bureau of Immigration, *Annual Report of the Commissioner-General of Immigration*, 1913-1919.
14. U.S. Department of Labor, Women's Bureau, "Variations in Employment Trends of Women and Men," Bulletin No. 73, 1931, pp. vii, 2; Maurine Weiner Greenwald, *Women, War, and Work: The Impact of World War I on Women Workers in the United States*, Westport, Conn., 1980, p. 12.
15. Women's Bureau, *Bulletin No. 73*, pp. 3-5.
16. *Ibid.*, pp. 34, 37, 55-56, 68, 78.
17. "Women Favored in Making of War Munitions," Cincinnati *Times Star*, May 23, 1917; "Where Women Supplement Men Because of the War," *New York Times*, Dec. 30, 1917; The speaker quoted in the Cincinnati *Times Star* was Arthur L. Humphrey of Wilmerding, Pennsylvania.
18. Amy Hewes, "Women as Munition Makers,: *Survey* 37 (January 6, 1917): 381: *New York Times*, Jan. 5, 1917.
19. Hewes, *op. cit.*, pp. 382-83.
20. Florence Peterson, "Strikes in the United States, 1880-1936," U.S. Department of Labor, *Bulletin No. 651*, Washington, D.C., p. 21.
21. *Bridgeport Post*, July 22, 23, Aug. 10, 1915; New York *Call*, July 23, 1915; David Montgomery, *Workers' Control in America*, New York, 1980, p. 127.
22. *New York Times*, July 31, 1915.
23. *Ibid.*, July 19, 1915.
24. *Bridgeport Post*, July 21, 26, Aug. 3, 5, 10, 1915.
25. *Ibid.*, Sept. 10, 15, 1915.
26. New York *World* reprinted in *Literary Digest*, Nov. 6, 1915, p. 996.
27. *Ibid.*; Peterson, *op. cit.*, p. 21.
28. *Justice*. (Pittsburgh), Jan. 31, Feb. 7, 1914.
29. *Pittsburgh Daily Dispatch*, April 22, 1916; *Pittsburgh Post*, April 23, 1916.
30. Pittsburgh *Daily Dispatch*, April 24, 1916.
31. *Pittsburgh Leader*, April 24, 1916.
32. *Pittsburgh Gazette-Times*, April 25, 1916; *Pittsburgh Daily* April 25, 1916.
33. Dianne Kanitra, "The Westinghouse Strike

of 1916," unpublished M.A. thesis, University of Pittsburgh, 1917, p. 15.
33. *Pittsburgh Post,* April 30, 1916.
34. *Pittsburgh Daily Dispatch,* May 2, 1916.
35. *Ibid.,* May 3, 4, 1916; *Pittsburgh Gazette-Times,* May 3, 1916.
36. *Kanitra, op. cit.,* pp. 67-68.
37. *New York Call,* Feb. 27, 1917.
38. *Literary Digest,* March 3, 1917, p. 533.
39. *New York Call,* Aug. 11, 1916.
40. *New York Times,* Feb. 21, 1917; Leslie Marcy, "Food Riots in America,: *International Socialist Review* 17 (April, 1917): 585.
41. *Philadelphia Press,* Feb. 22, 1917; *New York Times,* Feb. 22, 1917.
42. *New York Times,* Feb. 22, 1917; *Philadelphia North American,* Feb. 21-23, 1917.
43. *Seattle Union Record,* Feb. 27, 1909.
44. *Ibid.,* Dec. 16, 1916.
45. *Ibid.,* Feb. 17, May 26, 1917.
46. *Ibid.,* March 17, 1917.
47. *Ibid.,* July 22, 1916.
48. *Ibid.,* Sept. 2, 1916.
49. *Ibid.,* June 27, 1916.
50. *Ibid.,* Oct. 21, 1916.
51. *Ibid.,* Dec. 16, 1916.
52. *Ibid.,* Dec. 23, 1916.

CHAPTER 12

1. Maurine Weiner Greenwald, "Women, War, and Work: The Impact of World War I on Women Workers in the United States," unpublished Ph.D. dissertation, Brown University, 1977, p. 14.
2. Thomas J. Woofter and Associates, *Landlord and Tenant on the Cotton Plantation.* Washington, D.C., 1936, pp. 12-23; Ira De A. Reid and Arthur Franklin Raper, *Sharecroppers All,* Chapel Hill, N.C., 1941, pp. 25-140;
3. Ray Stannard Baker, *Following the Color Line,* New York, 1964, Chapter IV.
4. Lorenzo J. Greene and Carter J. Woodson, *The Negro Wage Earner,* New York, 1930, pp. 30, 76-77.
5. United States Bureau of the Census, *Negro Population 1790-1915,* Washington, D.C., 1915, p. 526.
6. *Ibid.;* Greene and Woodson, *op. cit.,* p. 115.
7. Philip S. Foner, *Organized Labor and the Black Worker, 1619-1981,* New York, 1982, pp. 121-22.
8. United States Bureau of the Census, *Negro Population,* pp. 25, 526-27; Charles H. Wesley, *Negro Labor in the United States, 1850-1925: A Study in American Economic History,* New York, 1927, p. 250; Greene

and Woodson; *op. cit.,* pp. 59-60, 115, 133; Robert D. Ward and William W. Rogers, *Labor Revolt in Alabama: The Strike of 1894,* University of Alabama Press, 1965, pp. 21-22, 44-47.
9. Helen A. Tucker, "The Negroes of Pittsburgh," in *Wage Earning Pittsburgh, The Pittsburgh Survey,* New York, 1914, p. 106.
10. Joseph Frazier Wall, *Andrew Carnegie,* New York and London, 1970, pp. 147, 167, 972-77; Tucker, *op. cit.,* p. 106.
11. *Christian Recorder,* March 24, 1893.
12. Foner, *Organized Labor and the Black Worker,* p. 122.
13. Robert Ozanne, *A. Century of Labor-Management Relations at McCormick and International Harvester,* Madison, 1967, pp. 188-89.
14. Broadus Mitchell, *Rise of the Cotton Mills of the South,* Baltimore, 1921, pp. 220-21; Jerome Dowd, "Textile War Between the North and the South," *The Forum,* June, 1898, pp. 442-43; *Atlanta Constitution,* Aug. 5-8, 1897; and Claude H. Nolen, *The Negro's Image in the South: The Anatomy of White Supremacy,* Lexington, Ky., 1967, p. 190.
15. James Weldon Johnson, *Along This Way,* New York, 1933, p. 31.
16. W.E.B. Du Bois, *The Negro Artisan,* Atlanta, 1902, pp. 180-85.
17. Philip S. Foner, editor, *The Voice of Black America: Major Speeches of Negroes in the United States, 1797-1972,* New York, 1972, p. 608.
18. John Stephen Durham, "The Labor Unions and the Negro," *Atlantic Monthly,* February, 1898, pp. 222-23; George Sinclair Mitchell, "The Negro in Southern Trade Unionism," *Southern Economic Journal* 2 (January 1936): 27-38.
19. Foner, *History of the Labor Movement* 3: 39-41; *Richmond Planet,* Oct. 21, 1899.
20. W.E.B. Du Bois, *The Philadelphia Negro: A Social Study,* Philadelphia, 1899, p. 323; Richard E. Wright, Jr., *The Negro in Pennsylvania: A Study in Economic History,* Philadelphia, 1911, pp. 94-99; Philip S. Foner and Ronald L. Lewis, editors, *The Black Workers: A Documentary History from Colonial Times to the Present,* volume V: *The Black Worker from 1900 to 1919,* New York, 1980, pp. 19-55.
21. W. A. Crosslands, *Negroes in St. Louis,* Saint Louis, 1910, p. 82; Lillian Brandt, "The Negroes of St. Louis," *American Statistical Association* 8 (March, 1903): 233-40; Seth M. Scheiner, *Negro Mecca: A History of the*

Negro in New York City, 1865-1920. New York, 1965, 45-85. John Gilmer Speed, "The Negro in New York," *Harper's Weekly* 44 (December 22, 1900): 1249-50; Mary White Ovington, "Negroes in the Trade Unions of New York," *Annals of the American Academy of Political and Social Science* 28 (May, 1906): 89-96; Leslie Fischel, Jr., "The Negro's Welcome to the Western Reserve," *Midwest Journal* 2 (Winter, 1959): 49-53.

22. *New Review*, January 1, 1949; 50-63.
23. Foner, editor, *Voice of Black Americans*, pp. 692-931, 745-47.
24. Ida Wells Barnett, "The Negro's Quest for Work," Chicago *Daily News*, reprinted in New York *Call.*
25. R. H. Lovell, et al., *Negro Migration in 1916-1917*, Washington, D.C., 1919, pp. 59-61.
26. Jerrell H. Shofner, "Florida and the Black Migration." *Florida Historical Quarterly* 57 (1979): 268-69.
27. William F. Homes, "Labor Agents and the Georgia Exodus, 1899-1900, *South Atlantic Quarterly*, June 1980, pp. 438-48; Oscar Zeichner, "The Legal Status of the Agricultural Laborer in the South," *Political Science Quarterly* 55 (September, 1940): 412-28.
28. Handbills of Jones-Maddox Labor Agency, Bessemer, Alabama, Record Group 174, Files of the Secretary of Labor, National Archives; also quoted in John D. Finney, Jr., "A Study of Negro Labor During and After World War I," unpublished Ph.D. dissertation, Georgetown University, 1957, p. 81.
29. Nancy J. Weiss, *The National Urban League, 1910-1940*, New York, 1974, pp. 109-10.
30. *New York Age*, Aug. 24, 1916; Eugene Levy, James Weldon Johnson: *Black Leader, Black Voice*, Chicago, 1973, p. 192.
31. *Montgomery Advertiser* reprinted in *Literary Digest*, October 7, 1916.
32. W.E.B. Du Bois, *Darkwater*, New York, 1919, p. 43.
33. Ray Stannard Baker, "The Negro Goes North," *World's Work* 34 (July, 1917): 325.
34. George E. Haynes, *Negro Newcomers in Detroit*, New York, 1918, p. 14; Allan Spear, *Black Chicago*, Chicago, 1967, pp. 141, 152; Sadie Tanner Mossell, "The Standard of Living Among One Hundred Negro Migrant Families in Philadelphia," *Annals of the American Academy of Political and Social Science*, November, 1921, p. 175.

35. Greene and Woodson, *The Negro Wage Earner*, pp. 342, 344.

CHAPTER 13

1. Woodrow Wilson to Gompers, January 7, 1916, Woodrow Wilson Papers.
2. Gompers to James Duncan, February 19, 1916, GLB.
3. William B. Wilson to Gompers, March 4, 1916, copy in GLB.
4. Smith, *op. cit.*, p. 193.
5. Gompers to R.P. Pettipiece, August 8, 1916, GLB.
6. Gompers to Thomas H. Nichols, July 31, 1916, GLB.
7. Gompers to H.O. McClurg, August 19, 1916, GLB.
8. *American Labor Year Book*, 1916 (New York, 1916), pp. 332-35.
9. *New York Times*, Sept. 3, 1916; *Literary Digest*, Sept. 16, 1916, p.654.
10. *New York Times*, Sept. 8, 1916; James Ford Rhodes to George Myers, August 26, 1916, in John A. Garraty, *The Barber and the Historian, New York, 1968, p. 52.*
11. *New York Times*, Sept. 8, 1916.
12. *Ibid.*, Sept. 10, 1916.
13. Providence (R.I.) *Journal*, Sept. 8, 1916; New York *Evening Post*, Sept. 9, 1916; Smith, *op. cit.*, pp. 188-191.
14. Reprinted in *Literary Digest*, Sept. 16, 1916, p. 651.
15. Wilbur Marsh, Democratic National Committee, to Woodrow Wilson, Sept. 29, 1916; Woodrow Wilson Papers; Springfield *Republican*, Sept. 25, 1916; Philadelphia *Press*, Sept. 27, 1916.
16. Woodrow Wilson to Bernard Baruch, August 9, 1916, Woodrow Wilson Papers.
17. *New York Times*, Sept. 28, Oct. 1, 1916.
18. Gompers to the Officers of Organized Labor, October 14, 1916, GLB.
19. Wilson to Gompers, October 30, 1916, copy in GLB.
20. J.B. Hendricks to G.S. Jacoby, October 13, 1916; in Woodrow Wilson Papers.
21. John T. Pew to A.M. Palmer, October 14, 1916, Woodrow Wilson Papers; Smith, *op. cit.*, pp. 197-98.
22. *New York Times*, Oct. 18, 20, 1916.
23. *American Federationist* 33 (November, 1916): 1068.
24. Smith, *op. cit.*, pp. 198-99.
25. Reprinted in *Literary Digest*, Sept. 16, 1916, p.652.
26. *New York Times*, Nov. 7, 1916.
27. Smith, *op. cit.*, p. 198.

INDEX